10/01

D0396763

Dances
with Luigi

Dances with Luigi

A Grandson's Determined Quest
to Comprehend Italy and the Italians

Paul Paolicelli

St. Martin's Press
New York

THOMAS DUNNE BOOKS.
An imprint of St. Martin's Press.

Frontispiece at top (the photo of the man and the woman): My paternal grandparents, Francesco Paolo Paolicelli and Caterina (Buono) Paolicelli, in their official "American" portrait, taken a few years before Francesco's untimely death in a Pittsburgh steel mill.

Frontispiece at foot (the photo of the man with two children): Pietro DePasquale, my maternal grandfather and the American dream come true, with me and my cousin, Donna Jean, on the steps of his house on the hill.

Library of Congress Cataloging-in-Publication Data

Paolicelli, Paul
    Dances with Luigi : a grandson's determined quest to comprehend Italy and the Italians / Paul Paolicelli.
        p.   cm.
    ISBN 0-312-25188-2
    1. National characteristics, Italian. 2. Italy—Civilization—1945-
3. Paolicelli, Paul E.—Journeys—Italy. I. Title.

DG442.P28   2000
945.092—dc21   99-098196

10   9   8   7   6   5   4   3

For Dad.
And for Cara.
And, of course,
for Luigi.
All of them.

CONTENTS

Author's Note ix

Prologue 1

1. Rome . . . 14

2. In Search of La Famiglia 35

3. Amendolara and Alessandria . . . 67

4. Rome, Ancora 91

5. Gamberale . . . 103

6. The Road Widens 136

7. Andata e Ritorno (Round-trip) 161

8. La Bella Italia 176

9. Holy Water, Heartbreak, and Blue Jeans 211

10. Gamberale, Ancora 222

11. Onoranze Funebri 238

12. Gamberale: La Festa 250

CONTENTS

13. The Last Waltz   280

14. Matera . . .   287

15. Epilogue   301

Sources and Reading Materials   302

AUTHOR'S NOTE

Houston, May 1999

The character of Luigi in this book represents both my neighbor in Rome and the contemporary Italian. For the sake of continuity, I have Luigi in some situations where other friends actually accompanied me, but it was the contemporary Italian view I have attempted to record and, for me, Luigi represented it best.

Luigi and his generation, born during and after the Second World War, are a fascinating group; they could, like Walt Whitman, claim—"I am large, I contain multitudes." I found them to be both contemporary and traditional in outlook; proud of present-day Italy and extremely critical of it; loving of Americans yet somewhat resentful toward them; preening and boastful with women, yet, at the same time, more compassionate and romantic than any of their other European brothers.

Members of Luigi's generation work too hard and too much on the upward track, yet family remains as the core of their existence and their principal form of relaxation. Luigi lives among the ruins of empires lost and pines for modern architecture. His streets can be littered with trash, yet his home and person are always immaculate. He drives like a maniac, yet is the most polite person on earth when he is not driving his automobile.

His life is an elaborate ebb and flow—a Felliniesque montage of past, future, and present. In all, he is constantly on the move in a vaguely organized ballet and makes for a fascinating dancer.

I learned many things from my study of this dance. I have gained a profound respect and love for those people in my family whom I knew only as old, and Old World, in my youth.

I have learned that love is primarily holy—a sacred bond that bridges time and language and even death. I have learned that my people were capable of love and constructed their lives for the lives of others. They did so in that mystical and elusive binding of blood called *family*.

And it was Luigi, and many other contemporary Italians, who helped lead me to these insights into the past and present.

It was an amazing journey. An experience that has forever altered my vision and given me heroes.

Map of Italy

Predappio

Foligno

Lanciano
Gamberale

★ Roma

Adriatic Sea

Bari

Napoli
Pompeii
Salerno
Potenza · Matera
Miglionico
Taranto

N

Amendolara
Gulf of Taranto

Tyrrhenian Sea

Ionian Sea

© 2000 Jeffrey L. Ward

0   Miles   100

0   Kilometers   200

Dances
with *Luigi*

Prologue

I arose early in the small Italian provincial town of Rocarasso, downed a quick cappuccino and breakfast roll, then sped off into the nearby mountains to visit, for the first time, the birthplace of my mother's father.

I was a man on a mission.

I had spent nearly the entire previous year trying to learn the Italian language and poring over contemporary and ancient Italian and Roman history. I had polled every living member of my family for their recollections, papers—anything and everything they considered relevant to who and where our family might be and be from.

Here I was in the middle of the Apennines, nearly due east of Rome and straight up—a place I only vaguely learned about in very distant history and geography classes—tracking down family mysteries. Not exactly the most logical route for an American television journalist supposedly in mid-career. I was also a third-generation Italian-American who, until just a few years before that chilly morning in Abruzzo, wasn't much concerned about the hyphened heritage.

But, by that sunny, cold day, the search for the past had all but taken over my life and was drawing me to a personal and, ultimately, spiritual quest in search of the past. I was trying to learn whatever I could about the history of the generation that went to America, many of whose members couldn't write and left very few records. And some of those from that same time who were literate had kept silent about key issues.

By now I had framed the questions, it was time for answers. I would visit many more villages, meet dozens more people, and spend another two years in Southern Italy before I was through.

Here I was in the middle of my life and career trying to sort things out from another generation's past. Why was I willing to take nearly three years and go off in search of family mysteries? What was driving my sometimes quixotic adventures?

I suppose it all started in San Francisco in the early eighties. I was working as an executive producer at the NBC affiliate in town when the Italian consulate published a booklet designed to inform the offspring of Italian immigrants about modern-day Italy. The press release and booklet was being supplied to all the major news outlets throughout California.

I found myself surprised by much of the information. According to the booklet, Italy was the fifth-wealthiest nation in the world. Richer than England! A major exporter of fashion, clothing, shoes, wine, cinema, and, of course, food. Modern Italy was a fashion statement. That wasn't the Italy my grandparents left. That wasn't the Old Country they only occasionally mentioned. I filed the subject somewhere in the back of my mind and moved on.

Then, in San Francisco again, I went to see the 1989 baseball World Series. I wound up surviving a catastrophic earthquake. And, the Series aside, I was also at this point the news director for the NBC television affiliate in Houston. I was the only local TV representative from my station or my city in San Francisco that evening. I assigned myself the role of reporter—something I hadn't done in years. I got on the phone and made a live report for the ten P.M. broadcast.

The day after the quake we made arrangements to feed through a regional satellite truck. I appeared on the air in Houston for the first time in my new role. The staff enjoyed giving me a detailed critique of my on-camera performance. The CEO of our parent company also saw one of the reports and sent my boss a humorous note saying, in part, "that new *Italian* reporter ain't bad." My boss sent the note along to me.

There it was: all of my life, in school, in the army, in the television news business, the first descriptive term of me and that of my family was always "Italian."

I didn't so much mind, it was just that I didn't know much about *being* Italian. My family was as American as you could get; I was raised in the suburbs, had been a Cub and Boy Scout, had played in Little League, was the beneficiary of excellent dental care and public schools, and was a veteran of the U.S. Army. *Italian,* especially at this time of my life, just wasn't a ready or often-used adjective when I was describing myself.

During the next and very hot summer of 1990, the G-7 Economic Summit met in Houston. The heads of state for West Germany, Italy, France, Great Britain, Japan, and Canada all came to explore economic interests in the high humidity of George Bush's adopted hometown. The meetings were especially focused on Europe that year, given the recent and sweeping changes in Eastern Europe, and particularly in East Germany.

I was invited to a reception for the Italian premier, Giulio Andreotti. It was to be hosted by the Houston Italian-American Cultural Society. I hadn't known there was such an organization. The woman from the organization made a point of saying they were trying to invite all the "prominent Italians" from the Houston area.

"But I'm American," I said.

"Your parents are not Italian?"

"American," I said.

"Your name is not Italian?"

"My grandparents came here from Italy," I replied.

"That's what I mean," she said, sounding somewhat exasperated. "It's the same thing."

Is it? I wondered.

Despite the fact I was still being described as such, the only information I had about my heritage were the old, nonspecific stories of my family told to me as a child.

I became determined to learn more. I signed up for an Italian-language class at the Cultural Society to see if there was, hopefully, anything familiar about the language no one had ever really spoken to me. There wasn't. The only thing it reminded me of was how much I had dreaded Latin classes in high school.

For years I had been making a pilgrimage back to Pittsburgh for the holidays. I was always saddened at how many fewer people there were back home. Our tribe was shrinking. My knowledge of them, and theirs of me, was becoming dim.

I had come home from the army in 1969, having been stationed in Germany, for which I was very thankful. It was the height of the Vietnam conflict. I returned unharmed from what could be viewed as an extended visit to Western Europe. I had a long reunion with my maternal grandfather, Pietro De-Pasquale—"Popa" the only grandfather I ever knew and the only member of his generation in our family who had actually returned to Italy after emigrating to America.

Popa asked me about postwar Europe. He had not been back across the Atlantic since before the start of the Second World War. He was, of course, curious about my impressions of Italy.

"Popa," I said, "it was the most beautiful place I've ever seen." I told him the story of waking one morning in the hills above Naples and looking out over the Tyrrhenian Sea. The water was the clearest and deepest green I had ever seen. The mist rising off Capri was spectacular—beyond imagination. "How could anyone leave such a place?" I asked.

"You saw it with a full stomach," he said, dismissing the subject.

Because of comments like that, I had always assumed my grandparents had come to the United States to escape poverty, that the lives of their families in Italy had been deprived and difficult. I never really knew for sure. Now, in the 1990s, there was no one around from the first generation to answer my growing list of questions.

My sister, Marie, had dubbed all of our family movies over to videotape. I found them difficult to watch. I could still feel the strength and solidity of my family in those old and slightly faded Kodacolor films. But a deep sadness would sometimes overwhelm me. *So many people gone.* And I was losing the ability to hear their voices, recall their laughter, remember the very special sense I always felt as part of that once big clan.

I wondered about those rich, dark eyes on the celluloid. They were all from the Old Country. They lived thousands of miles from where their life had started. Most had left parents and relatives behind, never to be seen again. All spoke English with obvious traces of Italy in their pronunciation. I had always assumed they were happy about their circumstance. Now I wondered, was it laughter and humor in their eyes, or merely sadness and resignation—the ironic acceptance of a people who must live in a place where they were not born?

I yearned to know who they were, these people I had called family, and what they had thought about moving to a new "world" where they didn't know the language or the customs and knew there was no going back once the voyage was made.

I pestered my father for any information about his family. His father had been killed in a steel mill accident in Pittsburgh in 1922. Dad was only nine years old. He didn't have any more information than I. He could only recall a few dim memories of a big and loving man, and of continually becoming lost and having been rescued on each occasion by his father in New York's Greenwich Village. It was in the Village, heavily settled by Italian immigrants, where the family first moved and where my father was born—the first child in his family born in the new country.

Because of my father's and his brothers' wanderings, my grandmother insisted that they leave Manhattan and move to the "country." They went to the Pennsylvania mill town of

Clairton, where Grandma's brother, Dad's uncle Charlie, had achieved the remarkable status of foreman at the Carnegie Steel Company. It was a place where the children could be found simply by calling for them. In Grandma's mind, the smoke and pollution of the mill was infinitely better than the confusion and danger on New York's streets. Dad said his father hated the move to Pennsylvania.

Grandma died at age ninety-nine. Throughout her long life, she always lamented that she had been forced to leave her village and family, and was always saddened by the fact she had never seen her mother again. There was considerable evidence she was never completely comfortable in the new country. Her language, fashion, and outlook remained very different from that of her Americanized children—and they remained curiously indifferent to stories about the Old World.

We all knew about my mother's father, Pietro DePasquale. He was the American Dream fulfilled, the poor boy who had left his hillside village in Italy in 1898 and gone on to seek his future and fortune in twentieth-century America. He found both. He had been a role model for his community and family.

Or did we really know about his life?

We knew he returned to Italy at least three times between 1920 and 1940, where he met with Benito Mussolini, apparently at the dictator's invitation. Pietro had been an outspoken supporter of Il Duce. He had hired professional film crews during at least two of his visits to Italy. They filmed extensively in his native Abruzzo, a quasi-documentary on the region. I saw the film only once as a young boy. The movies were on ancient 35mm silver nitrite stock. Those not intentionally destroyed (my mother says Popa went after them with scissors the day after the bombing of Pearl Harbor—apparently eliminating every scene of Mussolini and anything to do with Fascism) eventually disintegrated with age.

Mussolini's declaration of war on the United States also ended all of Pietro's ties with the Old Country. He refused to speak about this period.

No one in my generation had been very interested in the subject of Italy during my grandfather's lifetime. We were all little Americans—baby boomers—and very happy about it. We assumed he was, too. No one ever questioned the fact he'd left his village at the age of fourteen, his wealth on his back, yet somehow came to know a dictator. How could that have happened?

As a grandson, I had never questioned the fact. Now the journalist in me was very curious.

Through my newfound friends at the Italian Cultural Society in Houston, I learned I was eligible for an Italian passport, since my paternal grandfather, Francesco, died prior to becoming an American citizen. A European passport couldn't hurt; the world was getting smaller, and who knew? Maybe an opportunity knocking? All I needed to do was collect the paperwork to prove my grandfather's birth, death, and a few relevant documents in between. Sounded simple.

I was named for this man I had never known—Francesco Paolo Paolicelli. There was only one photograph of him hanging over the mantel in my grandmother's little house in Clairton, Pennsylvania. It was a formal wedding portrait—my grandfather in a suit and tie, his new bride stiffly at his side. He had a mustache, the only clear fact I had about the man. I grew one as soon as I was able because of that photo. It was my only relationship with him, our only known similarity.

Francesco's death haunted my father. When he'd issue his

own children a well-deserved punishment, he'd always question his strictness. "I don't know if I'm doing the right thing," he'd muse. "I never had a father to teach me how to do this." Then he'd do exactly the right thing. But in Dad's mind, if his father had been there, he wouldn't have ever been unsure of himself.

On a visit to Pittsburgh, I asked Dad again for any memory, any recollection he might have about his father. He recalled my grandfather, told of him coming home from his job in the steel mill—a job he hated—and showing his blistered and bleeding hands to his small son. Dad repeated the story of how Francesco had been killed working on a construction gang while operating a crane—a task for which he had no training and no background. Dad had never known the details of the accident until he after he had graduated from high school and was working in New York City. A cousin detailed what had happened.

Apparently, some equipment became entangled. My grandfather tried to straighten things out, slipped and fell, and was run over. The crane, which ran on railroad tracks, severed Francesco's legs from his body. The story had been told to our cousin by a man who knew "Frank" Paolicelli and who had been with him when the accident occurred.

The man said he could clearly remember cradling my grandfather in his arms as he lay puddled in blood. He recalled my grandfather saying over and over, "*povri figli mie', povri figli mie'*"—my poor kids. His dying thoughts were about his children and his responsibility to his family, not his bad luck or his mutilated body.

My father choked up when he repeated the ungrammatical Italian phrase, almost seventy-five years after his father had spoken it.

Now, because of the ancient tragedy of Francesco's early death, I was eligible for a European passport.

Other factors in my life coincided with inevitable change; my company was being put up for sale, and I had the option of cashing in my contract. It was time to move on to something else. I was burning out on television news.

I knew something was clearly missing in my life. I had known it for a long time. I had grown up in a big, noisy family. My parent's best friends were brothers, sisters, and cousins. And so it was with our generation when we were children. My cousins and I were as close as siblings. We had a manner of communication that was special and apart from the outside world, our neighborhood, and school acquaintances. We were family, and that meant intimate familiarity, nonspoken allegiance, blood ties, and love.

We simply accepted the fact, none of us questioned it. We were each other's best friends. We arranged for each other's first dates, went to proms together, sneaked cigarettes, shared jokes, knew each other's most secret secrets. There was always laughter.

My first job in television was at KDKA-TV in Pittsburgh. I had lucked out, stumbled into a job and a career because of a Pittsburgh newspaper strike—the local television news time had expanded to fill the void. They needed writers and reporters. I was fresh out of college, visiting my father, and had news reporting experience from the army. I applied for and was given the job of news writer. Assuming it was temporary, I didn't inform my cousins of the new assignment.

The first time my credit ran on the air was after the six P.M. news one spring evening in 1971. Not ten seconds later, I received a phone call. It was my cousin Donna Jean. She said the name looked great on TV. I wasn't the least surprised by her call.

By the early nineties, I was a vice president of news, and all of that sense of extended family was gone. Long gone. Donna Jean had been killed by a drunk driver just a few years after that first credit had appeared. Many others of the older generation had died as well. Those of us surviving in the younger generation had journeyed into our own typically American lives and had scattered throughout the country. Everything that my youth had been about didn't exist any longer.

I had survived the army, worked my way through college, gone off into my own private world of sound bites and videotape and talent negotiations. I had a career. I had left family behind.

And there were no children in my life, either. I had been saving, probably since my first paycheck, to pay for my kids' education if any ever showed up. While still in my twenties, I had a vision of a little girl sitting on the piano bench and playing "Für Elise" on my fiftieth birthday as I surrounded myself with friends, family, the aroma of an expensive cigar, and basked in a sense of self-satisfaction.

I was now past forty. There was no wife or daughter. "Für Elise" was out of the question. I had quit smoking and, just recently, there had been surgery—a piece of my hip had been "harvested" to replace a collapsed disk in my neck. I came out of the anesthesia and looked around at the stark, sickly lime-green enamel-painted hospital walls. What if it had ended here, I wondered. What if I hadn't come to? Would my brief obituary have recorded the life I would have wanted?

Of course, I knew the answer only too well.

I wanted to get back to something spiritually important.

Something of the heart. I had the money in the bank to educate my nonexistent daughter. Why not educate myself? Why not use the money to fill the void in my life and learn about the thing that had been most important to me? I knew I didn't want to take another television job, move to another city, work in another newsroom. Not just yet.

I was reading, *A Soldier of the Great War,* a novel by Mark Helprin. It had been given to me by a friend during my recuperation from surgery. It was a brilliant story by a young American writer about an Italian veteran of the First World War. When I came to the following passage, the words jumped off the page and landed somewhere deep inside me:

> Though he knew it was not true, he felt that in Rome someone would be waiting for him. Perhaps it was because the magic of cities is that they provide the illusion of love and family even for those with neither. Lights, the business of the streets, the very buildings close together, the interminable variety and depth, serve to draw lonely people in, and no matter what they know, they still feel in their heart of hearts that someone is waiting to embrace them in perfect love and trust.

I decided, then and there, to set up a bank account with the education money and to go to Italy. I'd return to the States and another job when the money was gone, but since I'd been frugal and my needs weren't extravagant, I could anticipate a long stay.

The decision was undoubtedly a great combination of things, but I was convinced it was the correct one to make. After all, there had been all those signs along the way; the invitation to the Italian Center, my father's memories, the Italian classes—

all of which led to more information, more questions, and more reading, until Helprin's passage leaped into my eyes and heart. By now I felt a sense of fate guiding my steps, and while I knew there was no one in Rome waiting for me I was convinced there was *something* in Italy I needed to find.

I thought about my grandfather's dying words, "my poor kids." The phrase hung in my imagination. I wanted to know more about this man for whom I was named—more than just the sad scene at the end of his life. I wanted to know about the beginning. I wanted to *know* this man. I wanted to ease my father's pain.

On the other side of the family, I wondered about Pietro's refusal to talk about the Second World War. What was it he wanted to avoid, was trying to hide? Was it simply the association with the Italian dictator prior to the War? Something didn't add up there. There had to be more to the story.

And then there were the looks on the faces of all those people I'd called family in the fading films. They all guided me to that chilly morning in the middle of the Apennines. I was trying to solve the mysteries of Francesco's dying words, Pietro's break with the Old Country, and those still so poignant home-movie eyes.

Through friends I found an apartment in Rome and, in the late summer of 1991, I began my "dances with Luigi."

1

Rome . . .

The Immersion

Luigi and I were neighbors. We had met after I responded to a notice posted in the window of the guard's shack for our huge apartment complex. The note asked for English speakers to contact "Laura" for English practice.

I needed a translator-interpretor to help me with my papers and an appointment with the Italian State Department. I called the number.

Laura spoke flawless idiomatic English—thanks to her Yankee mom—and said she'd be very interested in helping me; she was studying journalism at Rome's university, *La Sapienza,* and was excited about the prospect of helping an American journalist weave through the bureaucratic process.

One problem, though. Her father, Luigi, had to give his approval. We made arrangements for me to visit their apartment, just a few buildings down the hill from mine, that evening.

Luigi scowled, his goatee pushed forward. "I mean no offense, but I don't know anything about you, other than who you *say* you are. I see what happens on the news every night," he waved toward the television set in the adjoining living room. We sat at a large square table in the dining area, which was the center room of the spacious and well-furnished apartment. "I know what can happen to young women today. Just last week there was a shooting not far from here."

There was no way Luigi was going to allow his attractive nineteen-year-old daughter to go off with a stranger, American or no American.

"No offense taken," I assured him. "I appreciate your concern and will certainly respect your wishes." I had to laugh to myself. This is exactly what my father would have said in the same circumstance regarding one of my sisters. Was this cultural or parental?

It was hard for Luigi to buy my story; a middle-aged man living alone, signing a long-term lease on an apartment in the very un-touristy Portuense section of Rome—going off to Italian classes three days a week like a schoolboy. It didn't add up to him. Luigi considered himself something of an expert on Americans; his ex-wife was from Boston. Luigi was forty-five years old, drove a Fiat, spoke fluent English, and had a broken heart.

"So, what is it you're hoping to find here?" Luigi asked at that first meeting. "It seems like a great distance to travel just to study Italian."

"My family," I replied. "I want to know who they were, where they were born. Why they left."

"They never talked about such things? You never asked?"

"A long time ago," I replied. "Now all the people with the real answers are gone."

"Why do you care? You're an American. Most Americans are happy with America. Why does it matter where your grandparents were born?"

I smiled at him. "I'm here to learn about you," I said.

His eyes widened. I studied his features, his slightly hooked nose, his black hair streaked with gray. He even looked like family.

"I'm hoping," I said, "that learning about you will help me learn about my family. I'm hoping that in modern Italy, I can find the foundations to the old things that made my grandfathers who they were. I'd like your help."

"What do you want me to do?" he asked.

"Just tell me about yourself."

It was during this initial encounter that Luigi solved my first problem in acclimating to my new environs; he decided *he* would accompany me to meet with the Italian officials. He was my guide and self-appointed adviser ever after.

Our dance had begun.

Rome . . .

The very word was synonymous in my mind with *city, gathering place, civilization.* It represented to me a magnetic pole, a place that must be considered. There are only a few cities that have that universal aura. San Francisco, Paris, New York, London. All world-class, all written about, visited, dreamed of—all with millions of adherents.

Rome, like Paris, had always been more of a fantasy to me

than an actual place. It took some time to fully realize where I was.

Rome is more of a noise, more of an atmosphere, a multisensual environment. It is both stimulating and fatiguing. But the first thing that hit me was the din, the constant whirring and beeping and spinning of the place. I had read descriptions of the city during the Renaissance that described it as nearly empty, resting. The city that I found took no rest, was crammed full of old and new life, and, like New York, in perpetual motion.

There was an incredible affluence to the place. The people were well dressed, the children all equipped with the latest electronic gadgetry. Men and women walked along the streets speaking emphatically into cellular phones. They climbed into new and expensive German, French, Swedish, and Italian cars in which they seemed to drive everywhere, notwithstanding the price of five dollars per gallon for gasoline. Apartments were priced like New York, the cost of living one of the highest in the Western world. Yet there seemed to be no lack of luxury for the Romans.

Standing in the ruins of the *Foro Romano,* walking by the Colosseum on a moonlit night, spending an hour or so at the long, empty field that had been the Circus Maximus, the ruins of the Palatine Hill brooding above, my thoughts were lifted far beyond the present. There was something so fundamental about the place.

On my second night in Rome, before Luigi, before any of the huge learning curve that was about to overtake me, I walked along the swiftly moving Tiber. I watched its rapids swirling over ancient rocks with a beguiling power as the river worked its way to the sea. I wanted to go to the river and touch it, to commune with the millennia, to add my atomic salt to the water. It was, in a sense, a part of me, this aquatic source that helped form Rome and had inevitably touched those mysterious ancestors who passed on to me my peculiar compound of blood and bone and brain.

When I walked Rome's streets, listened to the music of its traffic and crowds, the rush of its river, the high-pitched shouts of its children; when I breathed the dust of a thousand ancient forms, I felt a presence that did not exist for me elsewhere. I was not concerned with future, I was absorbed with present and past.

One night there was an incredible, full, bright, white moon. I watched the energetic life of my Portuense neighborhood over an espresso at a sidewalk café. I saw mothers and lovers, the city's ever-roaming stray cats, beggars, children.

I watched as an old man slowly passed by. He wore a faded straw hat and moved with the aid of a cane. His hands were liver-spotted and quaked slightly. In his eyes I saw energy and light.

That night, I could sense the moon on my exposed arms, could feel its strength. I thought about that moon shining on this spot and on the nearby Appian Way. It must have given solace to ancient traders as they moved at night on that same road. It has always been kind to lovers. It now cast a shadow from the ruins of ancient aqueducts onto moonlit fields that have been giving sustenance for aeons.

I truly felt a connection there, felt a part of the mothers and children and old men and even the lovers, though I was alone. Portuense suited me well.

As time went by, I found it equally fascinating to watch

others as they reacted to the city. Americans on their first visits, Germans, Poles, Swedes, anyone from the potential Roman gene pool. There were seldom neutral reactions to Rome; feelings toward the city were strong and immediate, and were either very positive or negative, but never in between.

It was not unusual to meet someone at a café who had been in town all of several hours, raving about Rome's beauty and swearing they would return—even before they had truly begun or completed their current tour. It was as if something had taken over their thoughts, something larger than themselves, and they knew themselves to be a part of it.

I had the same reaction in 1968. I had come to Rome on a brief leave with a couple of other soldiers from Germany. We had only a little time and even less cash. I knew I had to go back to the city one day. I vowed to return for a long vacation and with enough money to dine anywhere I chose.

Others couldn't leave Rome fast enough. They simply hated the place, found no glory or grandeur, and no humor in the chaos. They complained about the climate, prices, Italians; everything. They, too, I believe might have been reacting to some ancient blood code.

It was said that, during the terrible fighting in the mountains northeast of Venice during the First World War, the Austrians overrunning the dispirited Italian lines shouted the ancient chant of the Barbarians: *"Rom, Rom,"* as if on an obsessive drive to sack their ancient foe.

I often wondered about this, about all of us who so viscerally and immediately reacted to this place along the Tiber. Did we hear ancient echoes of ourselves? Was their some psychic calling? Could our DNA have a memory of old blood once circulated in this city? They were large questions, much too large for me, but I was happy to include myself among the many who felt the pull.

Language Class . . .

My first months in Rome were spent in language immersion. My classes were held only in Italian, my lessons from the Cultural Center in Houston held up for about the first three days. Then the real test began.

I found myself surrounded by a group of young European kids, mostly German and Swiss, on vacation and whose idea of a good time was to learn another language beyond the two or three they already knew. There were a few diplomat's spouses in the class, two nuns—one elderly and the other quite young— and a German airline security expert.

Our school was on the Via Vittorio Emanuele, just a short walk from the Tiber and across the river from the Castel Sant' Angelo.

My classmates gave me constant insights into modern Europe. Almost all of them had traveled to the United States, spoke good English, and were adding Italian simply as a diversion. All complained about Americans' lack of language skill. Easy to say for people raised in an area when a long bicycle trip could end where another language is spoken. It was an affluent group, except for the two religious sisters.

The only other American was a demanding and quite vocal lady who refused to comply with the basic rule; she insisted on speaking and asking questions in English, knowing most of these kids understood her completely. She was right, of course, but the others refused to respond except in Italian, playing carefully within the rules. She was quite frustrated before long.

One day our instructor asked the nuns about their background—the basic questions in any language; what country were they from?

Czechoslovakia.

From what city?

A rural farming area in the northeast.

How big was their family? The younger sister, Sister Gertrude, had nine brothers and sisters, her father was a shepherd. *A shepherd.* I didn't know people still had such jobs. No one in my experience had.

Sister Berta had been orphaned. How long had they been nuns? Four years. Thirty years.

Then the instructor asked a one-word question. It took a while for the word to settle in.

"*Klan-des-teen-ah?*" he asked.

I mulled the meaning. It hit me. *Clandestine.* They had practiced their faith and their vocations in secret. They were in Rome at the invitation of the Pope, a statement of appreciation for their obviously deeply held faith. It was the 1990s and I was face-to-face with people who had been forced to secretly practice their religion. Unthinkable in America, still a living part of European culture.

Over time the sisters became the class favorites. They were completely open women who giggled more than laughed and who readily recognized their own naïveté. Any sexual references, marital or otherwise, caused them both to blush brilliantly.

One day our assignment was to tell, in Italian of course, a funny story about something that had happened to us since coming to Rome.

Sister Berta related a tale about herself: the only terms she knew in Italian prior to our class had been: *grazie* (thank you), *prego* (please), and (I'm sorry) *mi dispiace*. But she hadn't fully understood the term. While *mi dispiace* means "I'm sorry," the very similar *mi piace*—without the *dis*—means, "I like it, I'm pleased."

One day Sister Berta was riding on a crowded bus, a trying experience for anyone in Rome. There are few seats and the buses bounce like basketballs over the ancient streets. Sister Berta, attempting to keep hold of the stainless-steel overhead rail, stood above an elderly man calmly reading his newspaper in the seat below. The bus hit a great bump and, before the Sister knew what was happening, she found herself sitting on the man's lap. Mortified, and obviously confused, she repeated over and over, *"mi piace, mi piace*—I like it, I like it."

I can only imagine what the old gent must have thought.

When the two sisters returned to what is now the Czech Republic they gave each classmate a handmade card with a personal message. An orphan and the daughter of a shepherd gone back to a homeland where they could now openly practice their faith.

I still think of them as heroic.

Walks with Luigi . . .

The turning point in my friendship with Luigi might have been the Saturday morning I was to report for my documents. Luigi had warned me that assigned time meant little in Italy; I'd probably spend most of the day waiting around. He packed his Fiat with magazines and newspapers to fill the time. He insisted on driving into the city. He didn't like the Volkswagen I had bought on an overseas delivery program. He felt I had snubbed the Italian automakers.

The State Department Office waiting room was packed with foreign applicants waiting to process visa and other requests. Most of the petitioners were Filipino women who were then flocking to Rome to work as domestic help.

I was called almost immediately. My *"Permesso di Soggiorno"*—my permission to stay in Italy for an extended period of time—was sponsored by NBC News. A letter vouched that I was, indeed, a broadcast journalist and might be called on from time to time to do some freelance work for the network. I wasn't even required to pay for the stamps on the document. *Bolli* for accredited journalists were paid for by the state.

"So, you are somebody important who doesn't need to wait," sniffed Luigi, after I soared through the procedure. I felt guilty knowing I had been placed ahead of several others. "Why didn't you tell me you were reporting for American television?"

"I'm not," I said. "I'm here to learn Italian, look up my family, and maybe do a little consulting work."

"But your papers say American television."

"I was told a letter of recommendation would help the process," I explained. "When I mentioned that to a friend at NBC in New York, he volunteered the letter."

"Humph." Luigi pulled on his beard. He was still suspicious but I could tell he was thawing. At least, I hoped, now he knew I wasn't an ax murderer.

We stopped in a bar for coffee. I was to quickly learn that "bar" in Italy means coffee, not the boozy connotation its American counterpart has taken.

"How can you just quit working and move to Italy? You must be rich."

Luigi ordered mineral water. "I have a bad stomach," he complained, "I can't drink this strong Italian coffee."

I laughed. He was the only Italian I had ever met, and the only one I've ever known since, who didn't crave frequent, small hits of the rich brews.

"I'm not rich. It's just that I started saving for my daughter's education many years ago. It was a mania with me. There was quite a little pile there. I decided to use it now for myself."

"I didn't know you had a daughter."

"I don't. That's the whole point," I explained.

It was the first time I was to get what I came to know as the "Luigi-eye." He stared at me over the bridge of his long nose, his eyes narrowed under a furrowed brow. I'm sure he was trying to decide if I was a complete lunatic or merely eccentric.

"I'd been saving money all these years," I continued. "Ever since my first job. Ever since the army. One morning I woke up and had a little conversation with myself. I don't have children. I'm not even married. So why am I saving for an imaginary child's education? I decided to do something exciting."

That day we began the first of our endless, probing conversations, each of us trying to determine if there were any similarities between us, other than the vowels at the end of our names.

We downed our coffee and mineral water and went for the first of what was to be innumerable walks about the beautiful streets of Rome.

Luigi wanted to know why my parents hadn't taught me Italian. How could my parents have been the children of immigrants, have spoken the language at home when they were young, yet not pass it on to their children?

"I don't understand," he said. "The Chinese don't lose their language when they go to America. The Mexicans and Cubans and Puerto Ricans all keep their Spanish, the Vietnamese keep Vietnamese. Why do the Italians have to be such good Americans?"

"Benito Mussolini," I replied.

"*Beh,*" he said, "how can one man have done this?"

"He declared war on the United States. And there's not many third-generation German-Americans who speak German, either. Think the war might have had something to do with that?"

It would be a theme Luigi and I would return to many times as I probed my own nature to see if there was an "Italian" side to my thinking. I was born on the other side of the Atlantic and on the near side of the great divide called World War Two. Luigi was born during the war, and in the Old Country. It separated us. Part of my quest was to find our common ground. In the process, I came to know Luigi very well.

Over time I learned that, since he was a boy, Luigi had desired the company of women; like most Italian men of his generation, he says it is a part of him, a part of his culture. Yet he had not had many happy encounters with women. His memories mostly made him sad.

More than anyone I'd ever known, Luigi felt the sadness of the world. He said the stereotype of the singing happy-go-lucky Italian is a mask—a clever disguise that covers the true identity of the modern Italian man. His sadness extended to even the most basic of things—in our walks about Rome Luigi would often point out the trash that littered many of the streets.

"Don't make me think about this," he'd say, as we continued on. It was as if the very thought of such wanton pollution crushed him.

Our conversations were wide-ranging. His patience with this curious American seemed endless. Like other European men I've known, Luigi viewed his American contemporaries as naive with a one-sided view of history. We discussed everything from Italian curse words to American film as we walked about the magnificent city, but Luigi never strayed too far from the subject of women.

He was frustrated by the process of dating. He said he was among the first generation of Italian men to have to go through this process as a fully grown man with grown children of his own. It was an unfamiliar world, uncharted for him.

"I suffer from the American disease of divorce," he said, more than once. We shared the illness in common. It seemed more troublesome for Luigi. "But don't make me talk about this," he'd say. "What are they teaching you in this Italian class?"

I'd go over some lessons with Luigi, ask him endless questions about verbs and tenses, all so confusing to my adult, American brain, yet fascinating at the same time.

"So, soon I'll be able to take you to Zanussi's and you will talk like a true Romano?" Luigi joked. Zanussi's was a dance hall in San Giovanni where Luigi went often on weekend evenings to meet friends and exercise his considerable dancing skills.

"I don't know about fluency," I said. "I don't think I'll ever learn this language as well as you speak English, but it is truly teaching me a lot about how the Italians think."

"How do you mean that?" he asked.

I tried to explain. Consider the language, its expressions, verb forms, and idioms—many of which Luigi would teach me. It is not only a tongue but an outlook.

So much has been written by scholars and linguists about the beauty and expressiveness of the Italian language. But even those of us with a simple grasp of basic words could get the idea of how expressive the language truly is.

Just a few examples that jumped to mind; in English we describe something as being so many years old, as in, "The Colosseum is two thousand years old." Its life has ended at a distant point. The person or thing is in a dead, decaying state. It is the absolute worst thing you can be in contemporary American society—old.

But in Italian, *"Il Colosseo ha due mila anni di vita";* literally, it *has* two thousand years of life. It is a living, soulful entity with both a past and present. The verb is active, not passive; *it has life.* In the Italian language it retains a vibrancy and existence. It cannot have such a life in English or German, where action and life are over, its central meaning in the past.

Should it be any surprise that the Italians show such respect for the elderly—who are not older, but have "more years of life"—and for their surroundings, which, in their language, are filled with the spirit of both the living past and active present. If you like someone in Italian, you say they are very *"gentile."* Gentle. A kinder word than simply "nice."

Lovers in Rome call one another *"cara," "carissima," "mio amore."* In London or New York we say "darling"—slightly harsher but still soft and kind—"honey," "sweetie," "babe." In Bonn and Berlin, it's *"liebling," "schatzie," "mein schatz."* In

German you can shoot a gun or call a lover, if you don't pay close attention you might get confused. In Italian you would never confuse the two.

The harshest words I've found in Italian deal with self-deprecation or death; *"ho sbagliato,"* I have made a mistake—a terrible thing and a profoundly apologetic statement. *"Ammazzato,"* he was killed, not a gentle word, the "z" is stressed.

Perhaps nothing demonstrates this more than the simple idiomatic use of the words for love and for lovemaking. Can any word in the English language be as harsh as the word "fuck"? In German, *"zum ficke"*—the same thing. A hard, harsh term to describe what is probably, next to nursing a child, the most tender act in the human repertoire. Yet, we describe the act in English with a word on the edge of violence.

In polite English we "make love," a far more tender and endearing term. Same in Italian; in polite Italian it is *"per fare l'amore,"* to make love. But in the idiom, the people on the street in everyday life say, *"scopare."* The verb literally translates as "to sweep," a vigorous brushing against, an act of cleanliness. And it's not very far away—just two little letters—from the verb *"scoprire,"* to discover.

So, in Italian one doesn't use vulgarity to describe an act of lovemaking—one speaks of sweeping, brushing against, involving oneself in a cleansing act of discovery. It is a word without shame and indicates behavior not shameful, violent, or harsh. It is a moving against; it can be a mere brush, a deep involvement, or a deep cleansing. Most of all, it is not vulgar.

The person on the street does not yell to another, "Go sweep yourself." And, could you imagine if our worst curse in English were to be "Go get discovered"? In that sense, the gentle Italian language speaks for itself.

What is the worst curse, the most damning thing you can call another in Rome? *"Maleducato."* Badly mannered. A public disgrace for not having learned better or having been better taught. Ultimately a reflection on both you, your background, and your parents. A horrible fate, not knowing manners or mores, cutting a *"brutta figura,"* or an ugly figure. Nothing can be worse to the Italian than making a poor showing in public. One who has a *"bella figura"* has style, grace, elegance, charm.

Luigi would stroke his goatee when I'd tell him of my new-found insights. Though he never said so, I could sense he was pleased with my enthusiasm.

"We will go to Zanussi's one night," he said on that first Saturday as we walked past the Presidential Palace on the Aventine Hill. "I will show you what *bella figura* means."

It was a promise he would keep.

Portami a Ballare . . .
Take Me Dancing

Luigi liked to go to the dance hall in San Giovanni at least once a week. Sometimes, when I'd phone him, he'd sound unhappy.

"Come stai?" I'd ask.

"Oh, I'm not so good."

"What's wrong?"

"Oh, the same. I feel a little depressed. I need to go dancing."

This was generally shorthand for the fact he had failed, once again, to find a date for the weekend. Without conversation, contact, or confusion with the opposite sex, Luigi felt out of balance, slightly tilted, and just plain uncomfortable.

"We will go to Zanussi's, but it won't be very good," he said, shortly after our weekend at the passport office.

I was learning his habit of lowering my expectations. I was coming to believe it was a cultural adaptation; if one doesn't expect much it is easier to be satisfied.

"Why go if it won't be good?" I asked, knowing he had an answer waiting.

"It won't be crowded, there won't be many people to meet, but you can see if you want to go back."

"I'd love to go dancing with you," I kidded. "I can't dance a step, but it beats sitting around watching television I can't understand."

The following Saturday evening we arrived at the San Giovanni dance hall just after dark. We paid our ten-dollar admittance fee—ladies were admitted free—and sauntered into the huge open barnlike structure. The band was taking its position on the stand at the opposite end of a large, elevated, wooden dancing surface surrounded by candlelit tables.

Before long, the gigantic floor became crowded with well-dressed and well-trained dancers, all moving gracefully to the various rhythms of a very good band. This was no discotheque—no records were played.

"I thought you said there wouldn't be any people here?" I asked, nodding toward the rapidly filling tables.

"You should see this place when it is truly busy," Luigi said, dismissing my observation.

I focused on the musicians and, as is usual for me with live music, was soon totally caught up in the sound.

Luigi must have seen my entrancement. "Do you like this kind of music?"

"Like? I love it," I replied honestly. "I studied music at college. My happiest days were spent playing in a jazz big band."

"So, you are a musician? A man of many talents."

"I am a journalist. There are a lot more newspapers or television stations than bandstands. I learned, very early, that I enjoy eating well. But in my heart . . ."

"Yes." He smiled, not needing to hear the rest of my sentence. "There is always something in our hearts we cannot do or have."

I sat and listened to the music and watched the busy floor. The band performed waltzes, fox-trots, mambos, and sambas; they knew polkas, ballads, bossa novas and cha-chas. The crowd, including Luigi, actually knew the steps to all the various dance forms. They twirled about the floor with expert precision, wearing smiles to complement their graceful movement. It was the epitome of the *bella figura.*

The hall reminded me of the big Italian weddings of my youth at the San Lorenzo Club in Pittsburgh, only the room was much bigger and held many more people. And, like the gatherings in my childhood, all ages were represented.

I was introduced to an eighty-year-old man who seemed to know everyone in the hall. He said he danced for the exercise. He never lacked a partner or missed a tune, and his completely bald head never so much as glistened with a single bead of sweat.

I watched as young girls laughed and occasionally stumbled in a new step as their mother or father gently guided and directed.

I saw preening young men, dressed in the latest fashions—

hair pomaded and perfectly placed—rove about the tables. They bent courteously before prospective partners and made conspiratorial requests for a *meringa* or *salsa*.

Families sat together at the little tables, the ladies fanning themselves after a fast set. There was a rhythm to all this, both on and off the floor. It was a fascinating show.

The admission ticket entitled everyone to two drinks of any sort at the bar. Most of the people I saw drinking opted for fruit juice or sodas.

"Can you imagine a dance place in America where no one drinks alcohol?" asked Luigi.

I did find it unusual. These Italians were innocent, I thought. Almost childlike. I was enjoying the dance and the show very much, even though my role was only that of alien spectator.

There was a contemporary Italian song, *"Portami a Ballare,"* that I'd heard a lot of since my arrival in Italy. "Typically Italian," one of my American women friends quipped. "Only in Italy would one of the prettiest popular songs be sung by a son to his mother." The band at Zanussi's played an unadorned version of the tune, a straight ballad in a medium-slow tempo.

I found the melody interesting and spent several hours one afternoon listening carefully and translating the tune into English.

"Let me take you dancing," says a son to his mother. A low piano note sustained the bass as the melody developed softly and slowly in the upper piano range. "Let's you and I spend an evening together. Put your hair up like you used to do when you were a girl. Let's go to one of those places where they dance like they used to dance when you were young."

"But tonight," the son continues in rhyme, "it will be just you and me. Let me look at you. Let's talk, let's take our time.

I want you to *parlarmi di te;* tell me about yourself. Tell me your dreams. Tell me what you expected from your life, and what you found."

By this point, a full orchestra, complete with strings, was playing in the background, the vocalist in full voice. "And Mom," he adds, "I want you to know how much you mean to me. And even though I don't see you as often as I'd like, you're always at my side. I want only good things for you . . ."

I had some friends visiting from the States not long after I translated the song. I played the cassette tape and gave my English version as we sped down the Autostrada from Rome toward Naples. As the song concluded the three of us had tears streaming down our faces.

"Great," my friend said, "now we'll have to tell our kids we cried all the way to Pompeii."

I think I found the song so touching because I never had the chance to have that sort of conversation with my mother, or with my grandparents. And I was now at a point in my life where I truly wanted to know about *their* lives. Youth is so preoccupied with itself and my youth had been no different. This entire journey into Italy and the past was about trying to learn who my family had been, what their expectations were, what they found. How much easier it would have been if I had thought to ask those questions when the people who had the answers were still here and could have replied.

My father, of course, had the same questions of his family, having been denied a father to tell him the ancient family stories. His long separations from my grandmother after his father's death—Grandma had returned to Manhattan to earn a living as a seamstress and had left her boys in care of her brother, Dad's uncle Charlie in Pennsylvania—had interrupted her story. Uncle Charlie had a secret life to hide—a secret that would be uncovered by me—and no desire to discuss the past.

Over the years I knew her, my grandmother conveyed only a sense of loss and shame. Like her brother, she never seemed interested in visiting the past. My mother believed Grandma felt guilty for Francesco's death. It was Grandma who had forced Francesco to move to Pittsburgh. Work in the steel mill was the only work available for him in the smaller city and it cost him his life. It was obvious to us that Grandma felt defeated by her early widowhood and the extremely hard experience her life had been.

How I would have loved to be able to turn back the clock and take my adult sensibilities into the past and have a conversation with all of my family. I would have cleared up all the questions about my maternal grandfather, Pietro DePasquale; known his true thoughts and the real reasons for the complete break with Italy. On the other side of the family, I would have tried to find the way to open my grandmother's heart, to help ease her sense of loss and frustration. Did she miss the Old Country? Did she ever want to go back?

My goal now was to try and learn the answers to my questions without primary sources, increasing the degree of difficulty for any journalist. And even more difficult since my story lay in an emotional and spiritual landscape where even direct answers, and in first person, are hard to verify.

And, posing a still more formidable challenge, could I find any linkage between my family and me and this modern Italian society now dancing before me at Zanussi's in San Giovanni, in Rome, in the middle years of my life?

I was starting to fully comprehend the enormity of my self-made mission.

2

In Search of La Famiglia

"When I was a *guy*," said Luigi, "the families in Italy were very big. There was never enough of anything to go around. Now, there's too much and no one is having babies."

What Luigi meant to say was, "when I was a boy," or "when I was young," but for some reason he had confused "guy" with "boy." I found the term endearing and chuckled each time he said it. I never corrected him.

Billboards were posted throughout Rome urging Italians to have children. *"Forza Italia,"* they read—a football cheer—"go Italy." The boards had pictures of darling babies doing darling-baby sorts of things; one dumping a bowl of food—spaghetti, of course—on her own head; another of two little cuties exchanging a kiss. The most Catholic country in the world now had the distinction of also having the lowest birth rate. It was just one of the constant contradictions I was to learn about modern Italy.

"When there was no wealth here, the family was our wealth. Now we have money and no one wants kids," Luigi lamented, as we sipped coffee and mineral water on his small balcony overlooking part of our complex's parking lot.

"Actually," Laura piped up from inside the apartment, where she and a friend had been doing homework, "there are studies which show exactly that. Poorer countries always have more children. Children of the poor empower the family—there's always a chance one of the children will grow up, get rich, and take the family with him. The more children, the better the chance."

Luigi pulled on his goatee as he studied his daughter through the screen door. "What if *she* gets rich?" he asked.

Laura giggled.

"So," Luigi returned his gaze to me, "what can you want to learn about your family in Italy? Don't you already really know everything you need to know?"

"I think I know why they left . . . no one likes poverty. I want to find out more about where they lived. What their life had been like. What it's like today for the people who stayed. That sort of thing."

"What *do* you know?"

I told him about my mother's family, my grandfather Pietro's association with Mussolini, and the success my grandfather had enjoyed in America. "What troubles me," I explained, "is how this might have happened. How could Mussolini, or anyone in the Italian government back in the 1930s, have known about my grandfather?"

"Nothing politicians do surprises me," Luigi said as he studied the parking lot. "And your father's family?"

"I have one document—a marriage certificate which has the

date my grandparents, Francesco and Caterine, were married and the names of the town and church where the ceremony occurred. My father said the family was from Potenza, but the church is in a village miles away. That's all I have."

"Southerners," said Luigi, pronouncing the word almost like a curse. "All of the people with any skill left the south."

It was a theme I had heard much about since arriving in Italy—an enormous rift between the upper and lower peninsula. A political party was forming in the rich, industrial North with the stated intention of breaking completely with the poorer, agricultural South, forming two separate nations. Everyone defined my family as "Southerners." I was starting to get a complex.

"I guess they were from the South, if Potenza is in the South."

"You didn't know your family was Southern?" Luigi seemed surprised.

"It was never an issue."

By anyone's standards, we had been the typical American family, living happily in post–World War Two suburbia. We didn't think of our heritage as historical or Old World. History began for our generation in phrases like, "after the war your father and I . . ." or, "back in the Depression . . ." We never had to ask which war or what depression. We knew.

Our society was American and that society began when our grandparents or great-grandparents had arrived in the United States. *Our* history began at the same place and at the same time. This, despite the fact that my grandparents and a goodly portion of my friend's grandparents, especially in our hometown of Pittsburgh, spoke with richly accented speech and many dressed with a peculiar and individual sense of fashion.

Our parents used the Italian language only when they needed to communicate something we weren't meant to hear. They'd utter a phrase to one another, then laugh uproariously. We'd fruitlessly beg to be let in on the joke. The Italian language, for our generation, became the language of suggestive jokes or to be used only with some greenhorn fresh off the boat. Americans spoke English.

And for my father, at least, I suspect the language was a source of shame. His family spoke a dialect that even other Italians couldn't understand or thought uneducated. He recalled his mother referring to other countrymen as snobs. *"Alti Italiani,"* she called them; people on high looking down. Now that I had learned the family was Southern, I realized she was probably referring to the Northerners.

I wondered how much this had affected my father, who showed up at school his first day surprised that the other kids spoke another language. It didn't seem to have hurt him. He obviously learned English very quickly—he was promoted by the public school in Clairton, Pennsylvania, to the third grade without having to attend the second.

Dad had no real interest in going to Italy. He had heard stories from friends who had been there, they pleased him, but he never stated any desire to go or to see the place where his parents had been born.

Would my travels and questions uncover something uncomfortable? Would I find ghosts? Would I stumble across something my grandparents didn't want to remember or were happy to leave in the past? Did my father's sense of shame over his Southern dialect run deeper than self-consciousness of grammatical structure and pronunciation?

I prayed I would find nothing to harm or embarrass him, and hoped to eliminate his Italian sense of inferiority.

"So, what's your plan?" Luigi demanded.

"To go to the South and visit the villages I have references for, once I feel comfortable in this language. To ask stupid questions in bad Italian and hope to find some answers."

Luigi sipped his water.

"What particular answers do you need to know?"

"Anything I can learn about Francesco, Dad's dad. Anything at all. Where he was born, why he left, what kind of family he had. I'm curious. And why Pietro, Mom's dad, wouldn't talk about the war. How did he hook up with Mussolini? What was that all about? There's more to the story than I know."

"Maybe he didn't want you to know. Most old and unknown family stories are best left to the past," Luigi said, ominously.

"Perhaps," I said. "We'll see. But what about *your* family? Is your family's history better left in the past?"

"We are from Umbria," he said. "My town is Foligno. My mother and sister are still there. I came to Rome in my military service and stayed."

"Your father?"

"My father was a barber. He was made a *Cavaliere* by the government. He died young. That means I will, too."

Laura came through the door with a tiny pot of fresh espresso that she poured in my small cup. "Ugh, Foligno," she said, wrinkling her nose. "Papa, stop talking about dying." She disappeared back into the shaded apartment.

"She hates my town," said Luigi. "It is too provincial for a university woman of Rome whose mother is from Boston."

"Why was he made a *Cavaliere?*"

"Because he survived the war. He kept his business. He wasn't political. Only the survivors get medals. In the end, only the nonpolitical are trusted by the politicians."

"And his family? Your mother's family?"

"I never learned very much. I never really thought much about it. We've been from Umbria forever. Maybe we're Etruscan? I can't say. What does it matter?"

"Aren't you curious about your ancestors? Don't you want to know more than just the region where you were born?"

"You Americans have such a short-term sense of history. You want to know everything in your own lifetime."

"The Italians don't?"

"I think we have a much longer view of things. It seems to me that the Americans think you have to accomplish everything for yourself during your own lifetime. Here it's different—if we can't get to it during our lives, we believe our children will continue on. We don't need to know everything about the past. We are more content to let the future take care of itself."

He sipped his water. "It doesn't matter at all to me about a hundred or two hundred or a thousand years ago. It matters to Americans because you have such a new country."

I thought about what he said. What happened a hundred years ago *did* matter to me. I didn't know if that was American or not, but I believed it was important.

"Well, let's just say then, I want to see if what they say about the South is true," I replied.

He shot me the Luigi-eye.

Ferie di Augusto
Southerners and the First Trip South

In August, in Rome, it is not unusual for the shops and restaurants to close for the entire month. Since ancient times the Romans have fled the city in droves during the hottest month of the year. In antiquity, there were very good health reasons for this urban flight; the city was surrounded by swampy marshland that bred mosquitoes. Disease could be rampant.

As we'd drive through the outskirts of Rome, Luigi would point out that the land had remained swampy until Mussolini had engineers figure out a way to drain the place. Luigi considered that a great accomplishment. He reminded me that the ancient Romans, along with their households full of relatives, clients, and slaves, went to the sea in the summer. The remains of grand villas are scattered along the Italian shores. They are still in ruins and jut through the sand on countless modern beaches.

Today's Romans, the majority of whom, like Luigi, aren't from Rome in the first place, also flee during *le Ferie* in August. They don't take slaves and clients, but they can be seen with refrigerators tied on the roofs of cars, their little Fiats bulging with the necessary food supplies and luxuries for a month at the beach.

All Italian systems come to a near halt during this period. Neighborhoods are eerily quiet. The little shops are shuttered tight. Only an occasional grocery store or fruit stand remains open for irregular hours. The restaurants that do remain open serve a brisk outdoor sidewalk business. Few diners venture inside, and even fewer dine before nightfall. It is just too hot to do otherwise.

Not many public buildings are air-conditioned. The Italians

have strict beliefs about the use of cooled air and conventional fans . . . believing fans cause drafts and drafts cause stiff necks and joints. And, air-conditioning the indoors, beside stiffening the joints, requires electricity. For a country with no natural fuel deposits and no nuclear power plants, one doesn't waste electricity on luxuries. Air-conditioning is only for the tourists, mostly Americans. For Italians, the month of August—named for the first Roman emperor—is spent avoiding the heat and using only nature's resources.

Luigi had a friend, a University of Rome professor who was returning to the South during the August holidays for his hometown's yearly festival. Luigi and I were invited along. Since I had the largest car, I was appointed driver.

The professor, Sebastiano, was a curious young man in his early thirties. He wanted to know all of my impressions of Italy and Rome. He seemed fascinated by my story.

"Of course you know," he said, as we sped along the speed-limitless Autostrada, "you have an old Roman name?"

"My father says his family was from Potenza."

"Ah, we will be driving right by Potenza," he said. The comment surprised me. We were on our way to Calabria—Italy's "toe." Potenza is about midpoint in the arch of the Italian "boot." My knowledge of the geography was incomplete; Sebastiano explained we were going to the easternmost part of Calabria, through the province of Potenza, the adjoining region of Basilicata, and would pass what was theoretically my family's original area.

"No," said Sebastiano. "You may have family in this region, but they aren't from there, that is for certain. Your name is originally Roman." He said it with authority.

"How can you possibly know that?" I asked.

"I'm a classics professor, it's my job."

He then launched into an explanation of the name. According to Sebastiano, the name goes back to at least post-Roman, and probably Roman times. The name breaks down into two components; *Paolo*—or Paul, and *celli*—a diminutive suffix. It literally means the "little Pauls," the adherents or followers of Paul.

I was amazed a complete stranger could possibly be so glib regarding my surname. "It's not a mystery," he said. "We've been keeping surnames here for a long time. In fact, we invented them."

"Of course, in America, you were probably thought of as a criminal," mused Luigi.

"Not really," I said. "There are always the jokes about Italian surnames, but nothing I've ever taken offense at."

"Many Americans were prejudiced against Italians. We all heard the stories. Sacco and Vanzetti. We all learned in school how the American Congress wrote laws in the 1920s restricting the immigration of Southern Europeans. We knew that meant us and the Greeks. Surely you felt that prejudice, too?"

"No, not really," I replied. "My grandfather said 'they threw apples at us when we first arrived.' But he never said who 'they' were, and he used the story as proof of how far the Italians had come from a suspicious group to an accepted one. The story never made any sense to us as children. We wondered why people would throw away perfectly good fruit, especially if everyone was as poor as they were always portrayed."

"You felt no prejudice growing up?"

"No," I replied honestly. "Unless you count my pals hanging around the kitchen when my mother made pizza or homemade bread. The prejudice they felt was against their own mothers' cooking. I believed having an Italian mother meant guilt accompanied by terrific food."

"Ah, it is no different here." Luigi laughed.

"Maybe it was our food that won the hearts of Americans," Sebastiano added.

"Maybe so. Americans find the Italian cuisine irresistible," I said, "and it's probably true; Italian-Americans did win over a lot of admirers for serving wonderful meals. And they earned respect for all the hard work that goes into running a successful restaurant. My grandfather ran a good business, hired his fellow countrymen, and worked hard. They had something to prove—that they could work as well and be as successful as any other American. And they proved it in almost every profession from acting to motor car racing."

"*They* proved it? You didn't have to prove anything?" Luigi prodded.

"My generation didn't grow up with the same sense of mission—the same sense of inferiority in a way. My grandfather was always pointing out heroes. His special hero was a Pennsylvania supreme court judge, Michael Musmanno. The judge had been on the Nuremberg tribunal at the end of the Second World War. Musmanno was the sort of Italian-American my grandfather wanted us to emulate."

"There were many Italian-Americans of fame from that time," Luigi said.

"Of course, there were. My Dad's idol in the thirties and forties was Frank Capra, who made his favorite movies, his favorites still to this day. Ironic, in a way, because a Sicilian immigrant defined what Americans wanted to think about themselves." I remembered fondly the many nights Dad and I would go to the classic movie house and watch Capra's films together.

"For some of my relatives, the greatest hero on earth was Joe DiMaggio. My generation would laugh when someone would point out he was 'Italian.' It was a silly distinction as far as we were concerned—DiMaggio was a baseball player. What could be more American? One slightly crazy cousin once told me that if he had the choice of making love or watching Joe DiMaggio take a turn at bat, sex would have to wait."

"Careful, insanity might run in your family," quipped Sebastiano.

"And you got along with the others when you were growing up, there was no 'friction' between the groups?" Luigi asked.

The thing I remembered most about ethnic relationships in Pittsburgh were the festivals—the fantastic foods of the Greeks, Poles, Serbs, Croats, Jews, the delicacies that would have been reserved in the Old World for special occasions. In America, the special occasions were frequent and the food beyond belief.

While I could find no empirical evidence of the same, I remained convinced that hyphenated Americans of my grandparents' generation became at least twenty to fifty pounds heavier than the cousins who stayed abroad. What was festival food in the Old World was commonplace in the new. And food was the first thing we offered a stranger and the first thing we accepted when making an acquaintance.

Another reason for the harmony I remember, in Pittsburgh especially, had its roots in the labor movement of the early twentieth century. The big steel magnates in the Monongahela Valley would play the differing ethnic groups against one another in an effort to keep the unions away from their steel mills.

It was during the deadly showdowns at the Homestead and Braddock sites, when dozens of strikers and strikebreakers were wounded or killed, that the idea of solidarity took firm hold. It was those events that cemented the Croats and Serbs in Clairton—a union in America that would have been impossible in their homeland. It was the union movement that united the Poles on Polish Hill and along Second Avenue with the Italians in Oakland and in the Hollow and the Jews in Squirrel Hill, along with the German and Irish of the Southside and Northside.

The goal of equity in the workplace bled over into the worker's social life as well. I recall a city in my childhood where the ethnic differences were truly celebrated. We loved one anothers' food and music. I recalled no friction.

We pulled off the Autostrada for five-dollar-a-gallon gasoline and went into the snack bar for a coffee. The snack bars on the Italian superhighways make the astronomical price of gas a little easier to take. They rival the best Italian-American restaurants. The traveler is offered a complete array of food, ranging from prepared hot meals to cold sandwiches, packaged meats, all sorts of sausages, huge round cheeses, fresh breads, pastries, packaged cookies and candies, and the usual assortments and types of coffee.

Luigi and I shared a bottle of mineral water and a fantastic-tasting slice of lemon-filled cake. Sebastiano sipped a *caffè macchiato*—coffee with just a "spot" of milk.

I asked Sebastiano to continue with the story of how the Romans chose their names, and how he knew the origin of my family name.

"The Roman political system was based on clients," he explained. "A powerful Roman had several men in his entourage at all times. His following, or 'clientele,' were expected to vote in favor of any legislation he proposed and do his political and social bidding. In return, they received protection and assistance ranging from financial help to legal representation."

"Did that mean wealth?" I asked. I fantasized lost fortunes.

"Not necessarily," Sebastiano replied. "Only men had the vote in Roman times, and then only free men. The average Roman was considered middle class if he owned at least one slave. The clients were generally in this middle class. They were mostly tradesmen or small businessmen. Your name came from this system—your great ancestors were clients."

I was impressed. "You mean, I have a name that is around two thousand years old?"

"Without a doubt," he replied.

"Wish I'd have known that in Catholic school. The Irish kids always acted a little superior," I remembered. "They seemed to be the better Catholics. If I'd have known all this, things might have been different."

"*Beh,* the Irish," said Luigi. "They were still painting their bodies blue and clubbing one another with sticks long after Rome faded. Your ancestors invented the modern world."

I had gained a whole new self-image.

"What about other names?" I asked.

"We know other names came into existence much later," continued Sebastiano. "Craft names, such as 'Bottoni'—buttons probably referred to a tailor. 'Pesci'—fish or fisherman. 'Pellegrino'—pilgrim."

"And DiMaggio?"

"Means, 'of May.' "

" '*Joe of May.*' What a perfect name for a perfect center fielder."

"The name came after the Middle Ages," added Sebastiano.

"So did center field," I quipped.

They didn't get the joke.

We sped east toward Metaponto, across the arch of the Italian boot. We followed the basic path of the ancient Via Appia, the original super highway built by the Romans over two-hundred years before the birth of Christ and constructed for rapid access to the Ionian Sea and points east.

The landscape was like something out of a Hollywood western: a range of dry, desert-like rocky hills, with sparse vegetation. The country was harsh, hot and flinty, and most uninviting. Sebash (we were now on a nickname basis) said the land had once been heavily wooded, but had become denuded of all its timber during the Middle Ages.

"Man made this desert, not God," he said. "Do you know about this area?"

"Not really, just the name of a town."

"This is *Il Mezzogiorno.* In Italian it means 'the middle of the day,' but for this region it means a sleepy, hot, backward place. The provinces Carlo Levi wrote about in his book *Christ Stopped at Eboli.* Levi was a political prisoner here. His book helped change this region after the Second World War."

"Why do many of the Northerners I've spoken with seem to hate the South so strongly?"

"The region is backwards. It is not very industrialized. When the government tried to change things, it was very expensive. The Southerners pay less taxes as a region and use more government resources. The Northerners who dislike the South feel they are paying for a people who are not motivated and cannot adapt to the modern world."

I studied Luigi's face while the professor talked. He stroked his beard as he listened to Sebash, his sunglasses hiding his expression. "What do you think?" I asked Luigi. "You're a Northerner."

"They say all the people from here with talent went to the Americas. Do you know how many?"

I told Luigi the references I had seen claimed 25 percent of Italy's population left the country between 1880 and 1920. What's more, the overwhelming majority of that percentage were the young and healthy. And, since the worst poverty was in the South, the greatest numbers of emigrants came from that area. The region lost an exceptionally high number of young men. At one point there were more American dollars used for money in the five Southern regions than Italian lire.

"You are learning well." Luigi smiled. "Do you know what we say? 'In Italy, the Southerners are our problem. In America, they are the answer.' "

I related reading an article in a Rome newspaper when Rudolph Giuliani was elected Mayor of New York City. It clearly implied just what Luigi had said. A subhead read, in part, "In America, the Southern Italians provide solutions. . . ."

"Just look at the sons of Southerners who are successful Americans," continued Luigi. "Almost every famous Italian-American name has Southern roots."

"Like Al Capone?" I jibed. "He was some answer."

"He wasn't Italian, he was born in America. Besides, we only claim the good. Lee Iacocca, he's Italian. Al Pacino won the Academy Award . . . he's Italian. Look at all the other popular Italian-

American actors, too. Their families went to America, worked hard, became good citizens. Now their children and grandchildren make lots of money playing Italian gangsters in the cinema. We take credit for the good acting, not the criminals."

"Yes," laughed Sebash, "but there's a more sinister side to this North-South battle as well. You have heard the word '*Terrone*'?"

I had. I understood it to mean that the Southerners were 'people of the earth.'

" 'People of the earth,' yes," he said, "but, in the idiom they call us *Terroni* or *Africani*. It means what racists in your country call African-Americans. I'm a Southerner and your family were Southerners. I don't like the reference."

"Yes," said Luigi, "but look at both of you. Where do you live now? The South cannot support the ambitious."

"Things are changing," Sebash said. "Things are changing, finally. After all, the national railroad didn't even come through this region until the First World War. It was a feudal state until this century."

"Funny," I said, "we were always told the family was from the North until we looked up Potenza on a map."

"I'll bet most of the Italian immigrants at the time of your grandfather claimed Northern roots. After all, once they got to America, who would know?"

"And I'll bet many of them had bones in the cupboard," Luigi added.

"Had what?"

"How do you say, 'had something to hide'?"

"You mean they had 'skeletons in the closet'?"

"That's it. How many had bones?"

We drifted off to private reveries. I was thinking about what this country must have been like in the early part of the century—what an incredible journey my grandparents had made to go to America. They had probably traveled through this same desolate, deserted countryside to get to Naples, board a ship, and sail to the New World. And they didn't ride in an air-conditioned Passat. I was gaining a new appreciation for my *antenati*—my ancestors. They must have been tough old birds.

Finding Family . . .

After twenty or thirty miles the landscape changed. We streamed through a valley. The mountains on either side became greener, more life-sustaining. Little towns and villages were sprinkled about the mountainsides. Exits became more frequent.

Then I saw it.

"That's it!" I shouted, breaking the silence.

"*Cosa?*" asked Luigi, startled from his nap.

"Miglionico. It's on this road, I just saw a sign for the exit. I had no idea . . ."

"Mill—what? What is on the road?"

"Miglionico. The town where my grandmother and grandfather were married. It's the only name I know. It's the town listed on their marriage certificate. The town that's *not* Potenza."

"We must stop," said Sebash.

"Oh, no, I'm not prepared at all. I don't even know what questions to ask or where to start to ask them. I wasn't ready for this—I had no idea we'd be in this region."

"Nonsense," said Luigi. "Of course we must stop. You've been preparing for this for a long time."

"But I don't know where to go, it's late . . ."

"We start at the *Municipio*—the town hall. They'll know if your grandfather ever lived there. Or his family." Sebash pointed to the dashboard clock. "They will be open for another hour or so."

"Oh, sure," I said, "I'll just waltz in and say, 'Hi, I'm from America and I'm trying to find out about my grandfather,' and they'll jump in circles with delight."

"The exit is soon," said Luigi, "pull over and take this next road."

The exit was for the "Via Appia Antica," or the original Appian Way and the village of Miglionico. In a matter of minutes my Volkswagen was rolling along on the same roadbed the Romans had originally built over two thousand years ago.

We neared the village. I followed the signs for the city hall and, midway up a steep hill, turned into the parking lot.

The building looked modern, an A-frame–type construction that contrasted sharply with the castle turrets towering above at the crest of the hill. It looked like a sleepy public building, only a few cars were parked in the lot. We saw no one coming or going.

"I don't know about this," I protested as Luigi and Sebastiano jumped out of the car.

"They will close soon," said Sebash, looking at his watch, "we must move quickly."

The building seemed deserted. We found a sign for the records office and Sebash guided us there.

A wide counter separated the public from desks and file

cabinets in the office. A middle-aged man sat at one of the desks. He looked up as we entered and seemed pleased to have visitors. He came to the counter and greeted us in a dialect I couldn't completely understand. A second, younger clerk from an adjoining office stood in the doorway as we talked with his colleague.

I told the older clerk, with Luigi and Sebash's help, that I was looking for the birthplace and records of my grandfather and that the only document I had for him—a copy of a marriage certificate from the local Catholic diocese—listed this town.

"What was his name?" he asked and broke into a broad smile, revealing a pleasing nature and a gold bridge.

"Paolicelli. Franceso Paolo."

"*No.*" he said abruptly and matter-of-factly, still smiling. "Not from here."

"But wait," I said, "this was in 1908. It was a long time ago. I don't mean recently—"

"Not from this town," he repeated.

I looked at Luigi. "How can he possibly know that without checking a record?"

"Believe me," said Luigi, "this is a small village. This man would know who was from here and who was not."

"But I'm certain he was married here."

I dashed to the car and retrieved my laptop, turning it on as I hurried back into the building. By the time I reached the clerk's counter, I had the family history program booted. I turned the screen toward the clerk and showed him the relevant entries.

He was obviously amused by my enthusiasm. Suddenly, his

eyes widened as he recognized something on the screen. "Ah," he exclaimed as he scanned the program, "Your grandmother is *Buono.*"

The word means "good" in English.

"Yes," I said. "Do you know the name?"

He said a sentence in Italian I will never forget: "*They are our village's most honest and 'best'* [the wordplay in Italian on the phrase for best—*più buono*—literally most good] *family in both senses of the word.*"

"There are Buonos still here?" asked Sebash.

"Of course," replied the clerk.

"Still here?" I heard myself asking. This was astounding news. My father told me he thought Grandma had a brother who stayed in Italy—a farmer in Potenza—and had died years before, his children scattered somewhere in Naples.

"Not in Potenza? Or Naples?" I asked.

"Potenza," said the clerk. "No one from these people comes from Potenza. The Buonos are of Matera and our Miglionico. The Paolicellis live in Matera."

"Then you know the family?" I asked.

The man laughed. "I know the name. It is quite a famous name in Matera, but not in this village. You must go there to find your grandfather."

"But there are Buonos here? In this village?"

"Yes," he said smiling broadly and flashing gold again. "Here, let me show you . . ." He pulled a pink file card from a box and showed me the typed information. The card listed an Angelo Raffaele Buono, his date of birth, address, and phone number.

It appeared the man was my father's first cousin—both men born in the same year and named after the same grandfather.

Until this generation, when the more modern or designer names have taken over, the tracking of Italian family names was simple; firstborn sons were always named after the father's father. Second-born sons, like my father—also Angelo Raffaele—were named after the mother's father. The same system applied to daughters. Thus the Buono whose file card I was studying and my father undoubtedly had the same grandfather.

The clerk copied some of the information from my computer program. "Wait here," he said, "I'm going to look up your grandmother's records." Both clerks disappeared.

The older clerk returned alone a few moments later, carrying a large black record book. We leafed through the brittle, yellowing pages and found the original, handwritten document certifying my grandparents' marriage. Not the extract copy that I had, but the full and original certificate.

We also discovered birth certificates for my aunt and uncle, the only two of the five siblings born in Italy and, obviously, in this very village.

"Would you like copies?" he asked.

"Yes, very much," I quickly replied.

The information in the big black book was written in Italian, the entries made by the town's *sindaco,* or mayor. I knew the documents would have firsthand information and clues. The clerk returned a few minutes later with photocopies, several pages for each document as the old book size was much larger than current copy-machine paper. I helped him tape together our impromptu jigsaw puzzle.

I quickly read over the marriage certificate, asking Luigi for help only on the antiquated words I was unfamiliar with. In a very clear hand the taped-together page read, in part:

Francesco Paolo Paolicelli married Caterina Maria Buono on September 9, 1907, in the village of Miglionico, Province of Matera, at 11:15 A.M.

The mayor, Michele DiRuggieri, recorded the event in the official state documents.

The groom was twenty-six years old, worked as a *"conta-dino"* [or farmer], was born in Matera and was currently living in Miglionico, son of Emmanuele also residing in Miglionico, and son of Filomena (Pizzilli), also a resident of Miglionico.

Now, for the first time, I had the name of my great-grandparents and an age for my grandfather, always a great source of debate when the subject arose. There was also my first "bone" in the next paragraph; Grandma had claimed, or so I remembered, to have been only sixteen when she married.

The Bride was Caterina Maria Buono, nineteen years old, a *"cucitrice"* (or seamstress), born in Matera and living in Miglionico, daughter of Angelo Raffale who resides in Matera and Vicenza (Volini) of Miglionico.

After my grandfather died, Grandma made her living in New York as a seamstress, obviously a craft she had learned in this very place before leaving for America. I was told by Aunt Mamie many times as a child, Grandma could make "coats without a pattern," apparently high praise for her skills. Aunt Mamie said Grandma made clothing for actors and many famous people of the period. The hoi-polloi, she said, used to like to come down to Greenwich Village when the Village was still, more or less, an Italian ghetto and filled with artisans like my grandmother . . .

Present for the event as witnesses: Fiore, Pasquale, forty years old, bricklayer; Signorella, Antonio, seventy-six years old, shoemaker

I had never heard these names. I wondered if they were family friends or if, as I had heard was sometimes the custom at the time, they were paid witnesses—a sort of alms giving. A bricklayer and an old shoemaker legitimized my grandparents' union.

DiRuggieri certified signing the certificate after reading all the pertinent information to those assembled *"perchó analfabeti."*

I studied the last two words. *"Perchó"* an antiquated form of "because," and *"analfabeti"*—literally, "without letters." In other words, illiterate.

My grandmother had always been ashamed of her lack of literacy. Suddenly it hit me that the system of poverty in which she had been raised had failed her—Grandma had not failed. She had gone off to a new world, learned a language, earned a living, and protected her children.

What kind of a system couldn't educate its children? What sort of a culture would allow for illiteracy? I, too, was beginning to have doubts about the South. I was beginning to fully appreciate the impact on my life of their leaving this place.

The clerk interrupted my thoughts.

"You should go visit your cousin," he said.

"Yes," agreed Sebash, "we should go visit."

"I have no intention of showing up on someone's doorstep claiming relationship." I was adamant. I needed more time to prepare questions. I had been taken by surprise with the very existence of this family.

"But they will be anxious to meet you," argued Luigi. "This is a small village. They don't get a lot of visitors."

"I will write them a letter and ask them for a convenient time," I said.

There was no way I was going to a complete stranger's home and announce myself as a long-lost American cousin.

Luigi shrugged, Sebash smiled, and I thanked the clerk profusely for all his help. I promised a quick return once I'd had time to process this unexpected information. We started for the door.

As we crossed the threshold I spotted the second clerk, missing since the records search. He walked toward us arm in arm with an older gentleman. As they neared us, I saw my grandmother's smile beam from the old man's face.

"Mr. Paolicelli," said the clerk in very formal Italian, "I present your cousin, Mr. Angelo Buono."

"Our Best Family . . ."

"You are my *Zia* Caterina's grandson," Angelo said. We shook hands and embraced. It took me a moment to find words and return his greeting. Angelo said he knew my name because I was named for my grandfather, who had been killed in America. He pronounced the name "Pavlo."

Angelo quickly recounted that my great-uncle and grandfather had been killed in accidents in the United States. I was amazed at how much he knew about the people on the other side of the ocean—people who knew nothing about him.

"You must come with me," he said. "We will go to my home."

I didn't want to disturb his family. I offered to take him out for coffee or a drink.

He laughed. "Where?" he asked. "This is a village, not New York. You and your friends will come with me."

Luigi and Sebastiano eagerly nodded in agreement. They seemed to share my curiosity and enthusiasm.

I thanked the two municipal clerks for their help. They smiled and repeated the comment that I was now with the most "honest and good" man in the village. I found it amazing praise coming from strangers. I hadn't known these "relatives" were alive two hours before on this Saturday afternoon. But now, I felt proud to be related to Angelo Buono, however tenuously and distant.

We followed the spry old man on foot up the steep hill. As we walked, the word "Pavlo" rang in my ears.

One of my earliest memories is of a visit with my father to my grandfather's grave. His name—our name—was misspelled; spelled with a "v" where an "o" should have been. I had to have been just old enough to read. I asked my father how this mistake could have happened.

He was evasive. His parents' illiteracy was never a comfortable subject for him. "That's the way they pronounced the name," he said. "I guess it was the way you said 'Paolo' in my father's dialect."

I hadn't heard or thought of the "v" pronunciation in a long time, yet here it was again in Italy on the lips of those who hadn't left.

In a few minutes we reached the Buono home on a little

street that ran along the top of the ancient city wall, just yards from what I learned was one of the seven ancient castle turrets.

Mrs. Buono rushed to the doorway to greet us. She threw her arms around Sebash, and welcomed him as one of the family.

Sebash reddened. "Here is your cousin," he said, pointing to me.

I, too, was embraced.

Angelo's house was filled with visiting relatives and friends from Rome and Naples. Everyone sat around a huge dining room table that miraculously seemed bigger than the little house itself. Within moments introductions had been made and Sebash, Luigi and I were fitted in with the group. They had been delaying their meal until our arrival. We were given plates and passed bowls heaped with food. We ate delicious pasta, cold cuts, and cheese, and there were several bottles of homemade wine. Everyone, it seemed, talked at once, and everyone had questions. Luigi and Sebash were obviously enjoying themselves.

I sat next to Angelo. He smiled like my grandmother and gestured exactly like my Uncle Jim. He pointed to a picture on the dining room wall. It was my grandparents' wedding picture, the same photograph that had forever occupied a space over my grandmother's mantelpiece back in Pittsburgh.

I was amazed at the many emotions the photograph stirred within me.

The group asked the usual opening questions about me, why I was in Italy, what I had done with my life and where I had lived in the United States? Was I married?

"Divorced," I said. I was getting used to both the question and the reaction.

"*Ahh,*" went the collective, sad sigh. "*Divorziato.* All the Americans do this," added Signora Buono and clucked her tongue. "Then you are alone," she said.

"Single," I replied. I hoped the subject would go away. It seemed Italians I met all had a way of getting to the heart of the matter.

"You are the first to come back to our little hometown," Angelo said as I munched on the excellent *penne al pomodoro.* "We heard that one of the Paolicelli boys was in Europe during the war. We expected to see him, but he never came." Angelo still seemed disappointed Uncle Chuck, who'd been fighting in Germany, hadn't "stopped by" at the end of World War Two.

"These olives are sensational," Luigi said. "Where did you get them?"

"From our farm," Angelo's son, Tommaso, said. "We grow most of our summer vegetables on our little piece of land."

Luigi's eyes moistened. "Sensational," he repeated.

After the meal, we set up an impromptu patio in front of the house on the little street and enjoyed the shade from the close-together buildings. I brought out my computer and tape recorder and asked as many questions as I could think of. I hadn't completed my language course as yet and felt unprepared for the task—my timetable would have been to wait for at least another several months before undertaking firsthand interviews. I had found the afternoon quite emotional and couldn't distance myself to think objectively.

And I could not get over my unexpected joy at Angelo's smile.

"Tell me the story of your family," I urged. "Tell me whatever you think is important so I can tell the rest of the family back home."

Angelo smiled. I could tell he was pleased by the attention. He began his narrative. Luigi and Sebash sat on either side and translated whenever I would look their way. With Angelo's Southern dialect, my pleading glances were frequent. Occasionally they would argue over the meaning of a word.

According to Angelo, the Buonos went to the village of Miglionico from Matera early in this century. His grandfather, the Angelo Raffaele he and my father are named for, countersigned a loan for some close friends. They defaulted. A.R. sold the house in Matera, paid the loan, and moved onto Miglionico, where costs were less.

All of the Buono men were businessmen, mostly in construction work.

"What kind of work," I asked.

"Construction," he repeated.

"What kind of construction?"

"Mostly roads, but just about anything that was available."

"Roads!" I exclaimed. "That's amazing. My mother's father, who is from a completely different region and never even knew of this family until my mother married, was a road-builder in America. He had a good business, too."

"So did the Buonos," a friend said from the corner of the group. "They have always been some of the best builders in this region." My grandmother, it seemed, was from a successful as well as respected family. It wasn't the background of poverty and depravation I had expected at all.

"My grandfather built this house I live in," Angelo continued. "He and his sons made all the buildings on both sides of the little walkway on top of the ancient city wall. But mostly they were road-builders as far back as anybody knows."

I thought about the nearby Via Appia. Was it an irony this family of road-builders lived hard against the furthest extension of what was, at one point long ago, Rome's most important road? I was also fascinated by the fact that now it turned out both sides of my family, from grandparents back, were involved in road-building.

Suddenly, another "bone in the cupboard" appeared.

Angelo talked about "Uncle Vito," who had been in the family business but who left to go to the United States with my grandmother.

I went over the list of names in my genealogy program; there was no Vito. Grandma's brother in the United States, and the man who raised my father, had been named Carlo.

Angelo never heard of anyone named Carlo. His uncle who had gone to America was Vito. He was insistent. I was confused. Then I remembered my father telling me Uncle Charlie had changed his name because his original name had been "too hard to pronounce." He died and is buried under the name of "Carlo Span." It never made sense to me as a boy that the name "Span" was any easier than "Buono."

Angelo continued—Vito was married to a woman from Miglionico who didn't like the United States. She left Vito in America and returned to the town with their son, Angelo. Vito never returned to Italy to claim her. The mystery deepened. Was Vito Carlo or Carlo Vito? If so, there was still another cousin Angelo somewhere.

"How was it here during the war?" I asked.

Angelo said it had not been particularly difficult in his region of *Il Mezzogiorno* during the conflict. He said things were pretty much in "the order of the day."

"I was a soldier, but because I was older and a father, they made me a guard at a munitions dump in Taranto. The Allies bombed us regularly." This, for Angelo, was "not particularly difficult." He laughed as he related the story.

Angelo said his wife and child had remained in Miglionico and things were fairly calm for them.

"Was there enough food?" I asked.

"There were no problems," he said.

"Things were awful," said his niece, who sat nearly opposite us in the semicircle we formed. "There was hardly anything to eat."

Angelo laughed. "I don't remember being hungry," he said. "I do remember the Germans throwing away their bread rations and stealing our local bread. The bread they had was awful Bavarian black bread. Who would want to eat that?"

Angelo said the only destruction in the area from the war had been four local bridges, mined and blown up by the Allies, to prevent the Germans from crossing en route to Rome. Because of the destruction, the Germans had to move troops and equipment overland to Salerno.

After the war Angelo went to Argentina to find work, but didn't like what he found. He had to take odd jobs for six months to save enough to return to Italy—during that time there was a coup in Argentina and it was hard to get full-time employment.

Most of the family had stayed in the area. Angelo had two brothers, Tommaso and Cosimo. Tommaso had died a couple of years before in a mental institution in Naples. He had been an Alzheimer's patient—apparently treated in Italy as a mental illness. Cosimo died in the war. He was a prisoner in Germany and died in a POW camp on May 31, 1944.

My grandmother could not have known about this, how could she have had nephews die in the war and not have heard? And so much for Grandma having a brother who was a farmer somewhere near Potenza. Her last remaining brother in Italy died in Naples.

I asked how the family felt when the older generation had left, emigrated to other countries.

"It was the way things were," Angelo said, matter-of-factly. "There were so many men leaving to find work, to make enough money to get by, no one thought very much about it. It was just what had to be done." He paused for a moment.

"I think it might have been harder for the women," he added, looking across the alleyway at his wife and niece. "Women like your grandmother were not happy about having to uproot their lives and move to a new land, but there wasn't much to be said or done. They understood the problems here."

"But you stayed, your father stayed?"

"We had work. My father owned his company. But your grandfather didn't have work. My aunt, your grandmother, went with her husband. Only a very few women like Uncle Vito's wife came back and refused to stay in America."

"Did people maybe go to America to get away from bad marriages?" asked Sebash.

"Bad marriages are a modern problem," said Signora Buono. "We didn't think of such things. Our problem was food for our children and proper clothing."

"I know of no one from here running away from their family," Angelo added. "We heard stories about how the immigrants in America had been treated badly. We were told our *paesani* weren't liked very much by the Americans when they first went over. No one would go to that unless they had to."

"Why didn't we know about the family here?" I mused.

Angelo said he felt they had lost touch with the American cousins because of the depression and the war. He said my grandmother had written him for some paperwork after the war. It was her request that resulted in the only document I had about her life in Italy until that very afternoon. She needed the document to remarry after being a widow for nearly forty years. I never saw her wear anything but black until I was a teenager.

"I'm sorry we didn't stay in contact," Angelo said, "but there didn't seem to be any interest about us in America. I never heard from *Zia* Caterina again."

"She couldn't write," I said. "I didn't know that for a long time. I think she tried to hide it from us. Maybe she was embarrassed by having to ask someone to write for her?"

I thought again about my grandmother feeling guilty for a system so shabby it couldn't educate its children in basic reading and writing skills. It angered me she had been denied such basic tools. My anger at the poverty of the Southern system surprised me.

3

Amendolara and Alessandria . . .

A small parade of well-wishers accompanied us to our car as we left Miglionico with promises to return. The day had been all but overwhelming—I had learned so many things, met so many people, heard so many stories. But I knew it would be a while before I would have the quiet time to review my notes and compose a letter home. There was a festival to attend.

We returned to the Via Appia, found the Autostrada, and headed southeast toward Metaponto.

"This part of Italy is still more Greek than Italian," Sebash explained. "The ancient Greeks originally settled along the Ionian coast in what is now the southern shores of Puglia, Basilicata, and Calabria. In Metaponto, in between Taranto where your cousin spent the war and my home of Amendolara, the Greeks minted coins. The remains of Greek temples are still there. The mathematician Pythagorus had a school for the study of geometry in the ancient town—today a sleepy, forgotten spot."

As Luigi drove, I studied the map. Taranto is at just about the point where the "heel" of Italy joins the sloping "instep." We were headed toward the little town of Amendolara at about midpoint in the "instep." It was also the easternmost part of Calabria, thirty or so miles down the coast from Taranto, where the Autostrada ended.

Aside from our surprise stop in Miglionico, all of my experience in Italy until this trip had been in Rome. I noticed a change in people and behavior as soon as we stopped along the coastal highway. At a little roadside bar, where we ordered coffee, a local worker struck up a conversation. No one in Rome strikes up a conversation with a stranger, maybe because, since the beginning of time, Rome has been filled with strangers.

The fellow in the bar was curious about my car. He wanted to know what kind of license plates I had. I explained I was an American and the car had German export plates. He asked where I was from and, of course, he had the inevitable cousin in Chicago. What stuck me most was his sincere curiosity—we were truly out of Rome.

We reached the little town of Amendolara just past sunset. We parked by a small hotel and Sebash used the phone to call his cousins and announce our arrival. It took a while for the call to get through. Sebash was puzzled because there was no answer.

"I am starting to worry," he said. "Angelo is the village doctor, he must always answer."

"Another Angelo?" I asked. "Seems to be a popular name."

Sebash called again and this time succeeded.

In a few moments, our hosts drove up in a Fiat filled with smiling faces. I was learning there is no such thing as a solitary Italian: they always came in groups.

I shook Dr. Angelo's hand, but found myself staring at his face. He was an exact double of my close friend and old college mate Mike Gibb. I couldn't get over the resemblance—both men are balding, very thin, and have Semitic noses and highly expressive eyes.

We were greeted cheerily and with an apology for the non-answering telephone, Dr. Angelo said he had turned it off. I must have looked confused; Mrs. Angelo explained, somewhat proudly, there are two doctors in the town but everyone wanted her husband. His vacation had begun that day. They had to force patients to see the other, perfectly competent, physician.

Angelo's beautiful wife, Carla, was from Milan. They have two children, Francesco and Carla. Two of Sebash's cousins were also with the little group—both named Giovanni, who rounded out the carful of smiling faces of two Carlas, two Giovannis, one Francesco, and one Angelo. None spoke English and I was actually pleased at the unexpected language test, though thankful Luigi and Sebash were completely bilingual.

I explained my surprise at Angelo's doppelgänger status with my American friend.

"Where is your friend from?" asked Carla.

"He was born in Chicago," I said. Then I remembered a key fact. "Wait a minute," I exclaimed, "Mike's mother's family was from Sicily."

"*Ecco,*" said Carla, "there you have it. They are from the same people. You know what they say about the people from

the Mediterranean? *Una razza, una faccia*—one race, one face."
The resemblance was truly uncanny—Angelo even spoke with
the same high and slightly raspy voice as Mike.

Later that evening we sat on the terrace of the doctor's beautiful new house overlooking the Ionian Sea. The orange trees
that grew about the patio were fat with fruit. The children were
well groomed and contented with their make-believe games.
This was a pleasant home. I felt a sense of calm with these
people. There was an aura of kindness and serenity surrounding the small-town doctor. The entire family seemed settled, at
peace. Just as the Buono family in Miglionico seemed to have
been happy and peaceful.

This certainly wasn't the problematic South I'd been hearing
about.

The family was curious about me and interested in my mission. Carla wanted to know my marital status and if I had
women friends in Rome. The younger Carla asked if I had ever
been to Hollywood. Francesco wanted to know about the motor in my car.

We had made a friendship.

The following morning, Sebastiano and I ran some errands
in the old town center, about two kilometers up the mountain
that lay just inland from Amendolara.

"Almost all old Italian cities, built after the Greek and Roman times, are on the high ground. They were put there for
defense and protection," explained Sebash. "There were suc-
cessive waves of invaders in this section of Italy almost every
couple hundred years after the fall of Rome until our *Risorgimento,* or unification, in the past century." Along the way we
passed crumbled Roman walls Sebastiano said were once a temple and a bath. The ruins were abandoned in a field. There

was nothing to mark the spot as special, no protection for the decaying bricks and mortar.

"There is no money for such things here," said Sebash. "It has taken the government all this time—since the end of the Second World War—to provide housing for needy people. Protecting antiquities would have been a great luxury." He was clearly proud of his native region and well versed in its history.

Later that day the entire family—two cars, three children, one doctor, one professor, one Roman, one curious American, two Giovannis and several bags full of baked goods and picnic items—left for the ancient hilltop village of Alessandria. This is the little town where Sebastiano's and Angelo's families originated.

We ascended steadily for over forty minutes, passing beautiful little hill towns and fortresses along the way. Sebastiano called out the names: Farneta, Castroregio, Montegirodano, and Oriolo.

It was a magical climb. As we gained altitude, we could clearly see the purple mountains to the north and east that were in neighboring Basilicata, the region where my father's family had apparently originated.

Carla the Elder, Angelo's wife, did not come with us. Sebash explained she was not all that fond of the celebrations in the old village; she was from a modern Northern city with very different customs and traditions.

"It is not uncommon for people from the North, like Carla, to regard the festivals in the South as old-fashioned," Sebash explained. "But some of us like being slightly out-of-date. Going back to our village is going back in time in many ways."

"This *is* another world entirely," said Luigi, who had been mostly silent during our drive. "But it is a very beautiful world,

71

at that." He smiled as he looked out the window at the passing landscape. We passed a shepherd in a meadow guarding a large flock of sheep. "Ah," sighed Luigi, "very beautiful, indeed."

The little *paese* was easy to find; it started where the mountain road ended. From Alessandria the view extended for miles and miles to the south and east. No invader in ancient days could have approached this town from the sea without having been detected well in advance. The air was pure and fresh—a good ten to fifteen degrees cooler than at sea level. It was a very small village.

"Only a handful of families live here year-round," explained Sebash. "But during the summer festival days we have hundreds return." He went on to explain that most of those returning were sons and daughters, and now the grandsons and granddaughters, of the native villagers.

"Few of the current generation have chosen to remain in our little towns throughout the South," said Sebash. "Mostly, only the old have stayed."

From the looks of the place I assumed the elderly that remained had long grown accustomed to the privations of country living and were, perhaps, somewhat fearful of modern city ways. Alessandria is not a town on any touring maps and few travelers ever found their way there.

We parked in the little town square before the village's only caffè. The square served as the town's main piazza. A dozen or so older men were gathered in the shade of a big elm tree overlooking the fantastic view. Angelo introduced Luigi and me. Everyone we met was somewhat vaguely related. They fussed over Angelo's daughter, Carla, and teased Francesco.

In the café we met another part of the family, Sebastiano's

brother Giovanni, who, now along with his two cousins, Giovanni and Giovanni, made for three Giovannis—all men of about the same age and with the same surname. There was obviously a paternal grandfather with three sons who, in turn, had sons at about the same time. I could see where this tradition could get cumbersome.

Only one of the contemporary Giovannis had remained in the area; the other two, along with all of Sebastiano's family, had gone to Rome.

Sebastiano was anxious to visit his grandfather and asked if Luigi and I would like to meet the old man. He wanted to relate our experiences in Miglionico the previous afternoon and ask if his *nonno* had any memories of my relatives.

"My grandfather knew just about every family in this entire area," he explained. We walked through a very narrow, old cobblestone street lined on either side with two-storied houses.

"How is that?" Luigi asked.

"My grandfather was an animal trader. He sold mostly mules, but also sheep and cattle. He's walked every inch of these mountains at one time or another."

We neared a corner house. A country door faced two intersecting *vicoli,* or alley-like streets. The top half of the door was open and Sebastiano poked his head through.

"*Nonno,*" he called. He peered into the dark shade of the interior of the home. Through the open part of the door, I could just make out a large room with a wooden ladder on the opposite wall leading to what looked like a loft.

From the far corner we heard a mumbled response.

"He must be sleeping," said Sebash. "He's ninety-two years old." Sebash opened the lower part of the door and we entered the ancient house. The old man lay on the bed in the corner of the room. He shaded his eyes as he looked in our direction. He appeared to have just awakened.

"Nonno, sono io, Sebastiano."

A toothless smile came to his grandfather's face. His reply was audible, though unintelligible to me. Sebash leaned over the bed and warmly embraced his reclining grandfather.

Luigi and I exchanged glances. He seemed as fascinated as I by the Spartan interior of the old man's home.

"Nonno, how are you?" Sebash asked as the old man stirred. They exchanged pleasantries in a dialect I found hard to follow. "I want you to meet my friends," he said, pointing in our direction. I stood in the center of the room admiring the reunion.

"This is my grandfather," Sebash said proudly. "Signor Giovanni Cessairo."

I smiled to myself. So *this* was the Giovanni responsible for the proliferation of Giovannis I had been meeting for the past couple of days. I walked to the bed and reached for the old man's hand. I was momentarily startled when I found myself shaking what seemed to be more claw than hand.

"I have forgotten to warn you," Sebash said, "my grandfather only has two fingers on his right hand. A mule bit off his two smallest fingers many years ago—long before I was born or my father was born."

The old man held up his right hand to show us the ancient injury, an obviously distinguishing and unforgettable trademark.

Sebastiano explained my situation and questioned his grandfather, who remained reclined on the bed. He asked his *nonno* if he recognized my family names. He did. He remembered the Paolicelli name from many years ago in the village of Miglionico, or was it Grassano? He couldn't remember the exact place, but he did recall the name.

"Can you tell me anything about the people?" I asked. Sebash had to translate, Signore Cessario couldn't understand my accent. He did not recall any specifics, only the name itself from when he was a young man and spent time "before the war" in the villages of Basilicata.

"Most of the Southern boys went off to fight at that time. The very few who survived never came back for very long," he explained. "Most went to the North or off to America." It took a few moments to realize he was talking about the *First* World War.

He explained he had been learning his trade from his father at the time. His mule-trading days had more or less ended with the coming of the Second World War.

His speech was difficult to understand; Sebastiano lovingly translated. "My grandfather is the last link in our lives to the way our families lived here for hundreds of years. He still draws his water from the well and lights by kerosene lantern. I don't think he would have lived this long if he'd lived in a big city."

"We should let him rest," said Luigi quietly.

"Yes," Sebash said. "This festival will tire him quickly."

We said our good-byes—the old man waved, apparently pleased by the attention we had shown him. *"Ciao,"* he said in a high, frail voice. *"Ci vediamo."* We'll see you soon.

We made our way back into the ancient narrow street. "He is starting to fade," said Sebash as we walked down a steep grade toward the plaza. "He was always so strong, so active."

"I think he's remarkable," said Luigi. "Imagine all he's seen in his lifetime and in this country. There, Mr. Journalist," he said turning to me, "there would be a story to tell."

I agreed.

La Festa di Alessandria . . .

A marching band formed up in the plaza. The group was from Amendolara and another town farther to the south in Calabria, and was a mixture of teenaged schoolchildren and adults. Only older men made up the elder members, but both girls and boys were among the young. The band tuned their instruments, practiced drum rolls, and adjusted their gear as a growing crowd mingled in the square. Children shouted and ran about as their parents laughed and greeted one another. The tiny bar did a brisk business in ice cream and coffee and an occasional beer.

At the stroke of noon a church bell rang the *Angelus*. When the last clang of the bell pealed, the band struck up a brassy hymn. A group of men struggled down the hill from the little chapel and entered the square, a statue of the town's patron saint, St. Alessandro, balanced on their shoulders. The crowd called out its appreciation. This was the "official" start of the ceremonies that were to last three days.

The afternoon was reserved for families to reunite. Most chose to go into the countryside, and, being Italian, made sure that food was not far from the agenda—they would picnic.

Sebastiano's family was no exception. By now, several additional cousins had arrived from various points on the peninsula, but mostly from other cities in the *Mezzogiorno*, including Naples. It now took four cars to accommodate our growing group.

We drove to the end of a dirt road. Sebash and his cousins swore us to secrecy. It was the family's special picnic spot. A natural spring at the foot of a mountain peak supplied cold water in a retaining pool. The bottled drinks were placed in the water for chilling and the women began preparing a meal. All the children disappeared into the surrounding hills and woods.

The entire group was in a festive mood; they joked about family quirks and teased one another over childhood pranks. The women asked what sorts of food I had known as a child— did my mother retain any of the authentic Italian cuisine or had she become completely Americanized? My answers seemed to satisfy them. The general consensus was, in diet at least, my immediate family had maintained some semblance of Italian sensibility.

In what seemed like only a few minutes, one of the most magnificent meals I'd ever seen was placed on a large blanket as we sat cross-legged around the edge.

We munched on homemade sausages, several breads, a couple of eggplant dishes, *Arancini*—wonderful deep-fired balls of rice, tomato sauce, cheese, and spices—cold pasta salads, roasted peppers, olives, and cheeses. It was a sublime feast.

The children had returned from their exploration carrying bouquets of fresh basil and oregano, which their mothers made a fuss over.

"They still look like weeds to me," I joked.

"Ah," sighed Luigi, "the basil here is beyond delicious. They say your grandfather's country was named Basilicata by the Greeks because of the basil. Either that, or there was a major basilica here, but no one has ever found the ruins."

"I believe it was the basil," said Sebastiano's cousin from

Naples. "Greeks, like Italians, think with their stomachs as well as their heads."

I laughed. I remembered my grandmother visiting our house in the suburbs of Pittsburgh when I was a boy. The same grandmother who had been born and raised in this very section of Italy where we now picnicked.

Grandma would go for long walks on the little farm and in the wooded area near our development. She would return with armloads of wild vegetation that she'd expect us to eat. We found the practice hopelessly Old World and slightly embarrassing.

"Grandma's picking weeds again," my sister would say. It would take years for us to learn to appreciate the delicacies of endive, dandelion soup, fresh basil, oregano, and mint. These children of the *Mezzogiorno* already knew what had taken me so long to learn—just as my grandmother had learned it as a child in hills not far from this very spot.

Il Professore . . .
Why Giovanni Couldn't Read

We chatted idly in the afterglow of our fantastic luncheon. Suddenly, the Cessario boys quickly, and in unison, jumped to their feet. They pointed to the roadway, part of which we could see down the slight grade leading from our "secret" clearing. An old man wearing a brilliant white snap-brim cap walked along the dirt road with the aid of a cane and the arm of an obviously much younger man.

"Professor Amati," the boys said excitedly. They ran down the slope and greeted the dapper old gent. There was a great wad of hugging and the kissing or brushing of both cheeks in the Italian tradition. The Cessarios escorted their friend slowly up the grade and settled him on a canvas chair under a shady tree. His young companion sat on the ground by his side. One of the Giovannis brought cold drinks to the visitors as Sebastiano made the introductions.

"This is Professor Amati, our 'master' at school in this province, and his grandson Emanuel," he said with obvious respect to those of us who didn't know the gentleman. "We were all his students. He is the reason we went on to the university."

Il Professore smiled a broad and fully toothed smile. He waved his hand and muttered a polite denial, obviously flattered by all the attention. "No, no," he said. "These boys made their own way to the university. I was lucky to have such a gifted group of students. I'm so proud of all of my boys . . . they have all done so well."

"No, no," said one of the Giovannis. "*Il Professore* made us pay attention. We were a playful group of young puppies, he showed us what was important, encouraged us to go on in our studies."

Sebash introduced the members of our group. As I leaned over to shake the professor's hand, he addressed me in perfect British-accented English.

"An American at our little festival? How unusual. What brings you to our hilltop village?"

By now, I had the spiel down to a succinct paragraph. I explained my search. Sebastiano told about our adventures the previous day in Miglionico.

"I see." The old man smiled, his startlingly blue eyes the color of the bright afternoon sky. "You are a research scholar searching for the past."

"Hardly." I laughed, "just trying to clear up some family mysteries, that's all."

"What are your sources?"

"Not much at all. For my father's family, just a photocopy of a marriage document and another copy made yesterday of the original."

"There were no letters, no documents of any sort to help you with your search?"

I felt embarrassed. Oddly, my grandmother's illiteracy seemed to be sitting uncomfortably with me, too.

"No, and there was obviously not much contact with the Old World either." I said. "I don't think the breakdown in communications was intentional. The problem, I think, was a generation that was, *'perchó analfabeti.'* " I used the wording from the certificate to explain.

"Ah," sighed *Il Professore,* "the legacy of our benighted South. Your grandparents were born in the 1880s." It was a statement, not a question. "Do you fellows remember your history lessons?"

"Garibaldi and Pope Pius IX," one of the Giovannis said.

"Precisely." The old teacher smiled. "See how bright my boys are?" He winked at his grandson. The boy's eyes shone as he looking up and smiled with obvious pride at this grandfather.

"Garibaldi?" I asked. I wondered what on earth this had to do with the price of pasta in Rome.

"Do you know about our revolution to nationalize Italy under one flag? The battle to get rid of all the foreign interests on this peninsula for the first time since the fall of the Roman Empire? About the same time as your American Civil War?"

I nodded.

"That's why your grandparents couldn't read!"

"Because of the Italian Revolution?" Now I was completely lost.

"Because of the issues it raised." He smiled broadly and looked at his former students. They returned respectful gazes. "My boys know the answer here. Your grandparents were political victims. They weren't lazy or unmotivated or even especially poor—though the region was the poorest of the entire country. They happened to have been born in the South at precisely the wrong time.".

The Professor glanced over at our picnic blanket, still strewn with the remains of our meal. "Should we have a little wine?" he asked no one in particular.

One of the Giovannis retrieved a carafe and poured the Professor a small tumbler of the dark red *vino di casa*. A few of the others joined him in a drink. By now, most of us sat on the ground and in the shade at the professor's feet.

He went on to tell a story he obviously knew well: Garibaldi and his Red Shirts had conquered Sicily, then marched north up the peninsula to capture Naples. Vittorio Emanuele's army marched due south, bypassing the inland regions, which were strategically unimportant and largely ignored. The goal was to eliminate the Austrians from the North, the Bourbon rulers from the South, and most of all the Roman Catholic Church in the form of the Papal States from the central part of the country. Garibaldi and Victorio Emanuele had united the peninsula, but the South was of little value to the new kingdom of Italy.

"Garibaldi expelled the Pope from government," explained *Il Professore,* "and made him what I believe you Americans call 'an offer he couldn't refuse.' "

The group laughed at the reference to the American film *The Godfather.*

"Garibaldi told the Pope he could have the Vatican as his territory, take it or leave it. If the Pope insisted on political authority he would be executed. The Pope took it, but refused to recognize the existence of the nation of Italy. It wasn't until Mussolini's famous 'Concordat' in the 1920s that the Catholic Church admitted to the political reality of an Italian nation."

"Some cookies with your wine, Professor?" asked one of the cousins from Naples. "I made them myself."

"In that case," said the old gentleman, doffing his white cap as the woman extended a tray, "I couldn't possibly refuse." He picked up a finger-shaped cookie and dipped it into his wine. He sighed as he nibbled on what we had called "*biscotti,*" a treat I recognized from my childhood. Now I knew their origin.

"Where was I..."

"Garibaldi made the Pope an offer he couldn't refuse," I said, laughing.

"Ah, yes... but there was a problem," the old man continued, his immaculate hat now resting on his knee. "Our famous first Secretary of State, Camillo Benso di Cavour, said the problem wasn't in *creating an Italy,* our problem was in *creating Italians.* We had no national tradition, no governmental systems in place... this is when and where your grandparents enter the story."

He looked appreciatively at the faces staring up at him. It had probably been a while since he'd been in a classroom and seen genuine interest on the part of his students.

"One of the first official acts of the new Italian government was to eliminate the Roman Catholic Church from the new nation's educational system. It became illegal for any prelate, or religious person of any sort, to teach our children.

"For the North, where a public school system already existed, this wasn't much of a problem. But here . . ." He shook his head sadly. "Here in the South, there was no educational system *except* for the Church. Thus, families had to decide how to best educate their children."

The old professor took a delicate sip from his tumbler of wine. "Your grandfather was not a soldier?" he asked.

"No, there was never any mention of military service."

"That was virtually his only chance for literacy in his time. The national government finally realized the extent of the problem during the First World War. The majority of the Southern boys who had been drafted into the military were also illiterate. The army came up with a special program; the normal draft time was three years, but if the Southern soldiers could learn to read and write, they were sent back home a year early. The program worked well. Any healthy boy would rather be with Mama than stay with his sergeant." The old man smiled and winked at his grandson.

"Communication at that time was also a big problem," Sebastiano added. "There were so many dialects in Italy—more than two dozen—that many soldiers from different regions of the same country couldn't understand one another. The army also had to teach the soldiers proper Italian."

Il Professore nodded agreement with his former student.

The conversation brought fond memories to mind of my uncle Dom, the only veteran of the First World War in our family. Dominic Falduto was from Calabria, the very region we now sat in. He had married my father's only sister and spent his many working years as a gardener. Uncle Dom's wide fingers and callused hands were magic. He could wrest beauty from any piece of barren ground. He could grow roses where nothing had been before, leave flowers where weeds had been the only living thing to flourish.

He raised figs in Pittsburgh. *Figs.* He had to bury the trees in winter to prevent the freeze from killing them, then resurrect them again each spring. He did so with joy. We celebrated in summer when the plump purple fruit ripened and was ready to eat.

Uncle Dom was one of the most simple, basic, and dignified men I ever knew. He seemed completely at ease with life, in tune with his world. His heart was broken when he lost his favorite dog. It took years for him to adopt another pet, a tomcat, and when the cat disappeared Uncle Dom never again risked his heart.

The summer I came home from the Army my family was invited to a welcome-home dinner at Uncle Dom's. During the meal our conversation turned to Europe. Uncle Dom wanted to know if I had ever seen the Leaning Tower of Pisa. I had, and told him about the visit.

"I saw it only one time," he said. "And that was from the window of a train. I've always wished I'd had time to see it closer." His diction carried the charming reminder of his Calabrian roots.

"Where were you going, that you didn't have time?" I asked.

"Up north. To the front."

My brother and I exchanged glances. "The front," we said, almost in unison. "What front?"

"The Italian front. I was a soldier. We were fighting the Austrians."

"You mean," I said, astonished, "in the First World War? For Italy?" No one in the room, except Aunt Mamie who had never said a word, knew Uncle Dom was a veteran. And no one, not even my father, suspected he was old enough to have been in the First World War.

"Yes," he said simply.

After some prodding we learned the full story. Uncle Dom had been in America, working in New York, digging the tunnels for the subway system. At that time, he explained, all the Italian laborers read the newspapers published in their native tongue.

When the First World War broke out, the King of Italy advertised in the journals for native sons to return and fight for their homeland. In return, and if they survived, they would be given a thousand-dollar bonus and free passage back to America. Uncle Dom took up the cause. His only regret seemed to have been the missed opportunity in Pisa.

Aunt Mamie said Uncle Dom was not only literate, but also trained in classical Italian, and fluent in several dialects. I wondered, now that the professor explained the background for the times, if Uncle Dom's literacy and fluency were the result of his military stint. He never said *he* read the Italian papers in New York. Was his literacy before or after his military service?

Uncle Dom died quietly and peacefully with his wife of more than fifty years by his side in the mid-eighties. He had a rich and full life, certainly not without sorrow, but, on balance, a life that had brought more beauty to his world than had been there before he passed by.

Now I had another question I could never ask.

The old professor interrupted my thoughts. He looked directly at me, his eyes clear and bright. "Is it fair to assume your grandparents had a craft?"

"Yes," I replied. "My grandfather was a teamster, he had his own business and, as part of his work, drove a horse and wagon in New York City. My grandmother was a seamstress."

"That's how your great-grandparents chose to educate their children. Like most simple people of the time, they believed a craft was far more important than general literacy. Our system was such that they had little choice. If children were to be lettered, they must enter the religious life. A literate education in the secular world meant going far away and great expense. Not surprisingly, the children were taught trades by craftsmen and women. They learned how to survive.

" 'Perchó analfabeti,' " he repeated wryly.

The Tarantella . . .

We returned, exhausted, to Alessandria later that afternoon. Siestas were the order of the day. Each of us retreated to our accommodations to enjoy the delightful custom of the afternoon *pausa*.

Luigi and I stayed with Sebastiano, one of the Giovannis, and the Giovanni's mother, in what had been her home as a child. It was surprisingly modern, well furnished and, with three separate floors, much larger than it appeared from the street. The only major lack of modern convenience was running water; the water was pumped for only a few hours per day. All water business needed to be conducted during the pumping window.

A few hours later, refreshed from our naps, we gathered in the dining room. A large bowl of fruit and tray of cookies sat on the beautiful old wooden table, along with carafes of wine and mineral water.

"The first event is tonight," said Sebash as he laid out the logistics for the evening. "There will be a concert in the church plaza, then fireworks after the music." He sipped from a glass of mineral water. "We will eat at the festival. There will be several stands for food." Eating, of course, was a priority item.

"In my hometown the festival lasts three or four days," said Luigi. "The same here?"

"Yes, and every year we try and raise more and more money to get better entertainment. This year we will have three different musical groups and a couple of locally famous singers." He went on to explain there was a great competition among the local villages to stage the most popular and opulent festivals.

The cousins started filing into the house. Soon the room was filled with Giovannis, their spouses, children, and other relatives. It was time to move on.

"Bring chairs," Giovanni's mother called out. "There will be no place to sit, just the stones in the *piazza*." Several family members followed her suggestion. Folding chairs, apparently rented for the occasion, had been stacked by the front door.

Sebash, Luigi, the Giovannis, and I formed a separate group and headed off for the church plaza; Sebash wanted to stop by the home of an old school friend.

Night was falling as we walked the narrow streets. We could see into the homes as we passed; the town had been electrified since just after World War II. The light through the windows of the little houses cast long, yellow patches onto the ancient cobblestones.

A man and a donkey stood by an open door. The man was old and wore tattered clothing. He was in conversation with the lady of the house. The donkey stood loaded with what looked like hay. Everyone exchanged smiles and greetings as we passed.

"He's a peddler," explained Sebash. "He's selling herbs and spices he's picked from the fields. My mother said he's been doing this since she was a little girl."

Behind us we could hear the donkey's hooves against the stones as the peddler moved on. The animal's steps echoed in the canyon between the houses. How often, I thought, have these homes heard the clopping of hooves throughout the centuries? It would be easy to forget time in this village.

As we rounded a corner, Sebash spotted his friend through an open dining room window. The young man sat before a bowl of steaming pasta. We talked through the window frame for several minutes as the friend continued his dinner. His mother waited on her son as if he were a highly prized diner at an expensive restaurant. The woman smiled and invited us to join the meal, a tempting offer we declined as we stood in the street and watched the arrival of each new mouthwatering course.

After several more greetings of old friends and a few more open-window conversations, we reached the *piazza* in front of the village's only church. It was a large, flat, level area completely closed in by the surrounding buildings. The church sat at the far end of the plaza. All of the edifices, including the church, were constructed of the stone native to the regional mountains. It would have been impossible, in the long-ago centuries when these structures were made, to have imported building materials to such a high and remote village.

Directly in front of the church's main entrance, a large wooden stage had been constructed. Technicians hustled up and down the stairs leading to the platform, checking various instruments and settings. The paraphernalia of a music group sat on the stage; guitars leaned against stands, huge black speakers sat menacingly silent at the corners. Amplifiers with dozens of wires running to and from were being checked as little red and green lights blinked in electronic anticipation.

"Looks like a rock group," I said.

"Yes." Sebastiano smiled. "It's a very popular group from Sicily."

"A rock group?" I repeated. Somehow I had expected something else—more traditional, more religious, especially since the festival was in honor of the town's patron saint.

"You wanted the *'Tarantella'?*" Luigi laughed. "You've seen too many movies."

The incongruity of a rock group hard against a church edifice was jarring to me, even more so when the group actually appeared. Three young women jumped onto the stage, wearing bright, primary-colored acrylic costumes. Their hair was coifed with streaks of orange, blue, and green. They strummed unbelievably loud guitars. Artificial smoke poured out from the huge speakers, creating both an incredible din and blinding fog in the little plaza. In an earsplitting volume, the women shouted lyrics about tortured love.

I looked about the place. The younger members of the audience seemed to be enjoying the program, but even more surprising, so did the elder members of the crowd. An old woman, at least eighty, sat in the front row, catercorner to the stage. A shawl was draped over her stooped shoulders. Her gray hair was neatly pulled back into a bun. Her cheeks were rosy with the flush of these mountain people. She was, in every appearance, the very stereotype of the Italian grandmother.

And she was nodding her head in time to an acid-rock tune.

I could only wonder at what thoughts were going through her mind.

I guess I had expected the *Tarantella,* after all.

4

Rome, Ancora

Dances with Luigi

When I told him I was not very pleased with my German car, Luigi cheered up.

"I am happy to hear that."

"Well, I'm not happy to report it."

"No, no," Luigi continued, "I'm not happy you are having problems, I am happy that it is not only the Italian cars which have problems. My colleagues think only the Italians make lemons and the Germans never make a mistake."

My Italian vocabulary was increasing daily, but not in the way I'd have wanted. I was developing, with Luigi's help, an amazing array of words to describe my Passat's problems.

The car was equipped for use in the United States; it came with power windows—unheard of in Italy, air-conditioning—

no self-respecting Italian would sit in cooled air and get stiff joints—and a factory-installed security alarm.

The design of the anti-theft system couldn't take Rome's stray cats into account. Most Romans believe cats are outdoor animals. While they'll feed them and, like our neighborhood butcher, build elaborate cardboard houses for the females to have their litters, most Italians are firm in their conviction that cats belong outdoors. And cats, being cats, are in constant search of a warm place to sleep.

My VW apparently conformed with basic feline comfort standards.

As a result, my car was always beeping, flashing, honking, or making a nuisance. I developed a system to handle the problem at night; when I'd hear the alarm sound, I'd jump into sweat gear, run barefoot down four flights of marble stairs, tear up the hillside next to the apartment building, jump over a small prickly hedge, find the car, jiggle the key in the lock—when I didn't forget to bring the key in the first place—and disable the obnoxious noise.

The system worked fairly well at night, but during the day I went into the city by bus and attended language class. The car remained parked in Portuense. Romans still keep the tradition of the siesta, or *pausa,* in midafternoon. It seems the cats in Rome have the same tradition. When they'd hop onto my hood or trunk lid to catch their afternoon nap, no one—or thing—living in earshot of my hollering Volkswagen could rest or sleep.

My neighbors were clearly unhappy with their new tenant. They were leaving interesting notes on my apartment door that taxed my translation skills. Something had to be done.

The men at the local VW dealership seemed confused. I had

a problem with the power windows, which they'd never had before; my windshield wipers had quit working. It took repeated lessons with Luigi to get down the correct pronunciation for *tergicristalli;* I had to learn the ever-popular Italian phrase "squeaking speedometer," and, of course, there were the constant alarm problems to relate.

This was the real world of the Italian language, not the sort of things we were learning in our lessons. Half of this communication was done in pantomime. I was, I'm sure, the crank customer the mechanics told their wives about at night.

A young, lanky mechanic in starched, clean blue overalls listened to my lament. He seemed sympathetic. I begged the young man to disable the alarm—to just unhook the apparatus so my neighbors, the cats, and I could all get some rest. He asked to keep the car overnight.

The next day I returned. The man said he couldn't do the work. He didn't have a *schema*—another interesting word. Because the car was made for the American market, he had no idea how to make the changes. He needed a set of detailed instructions.

The mechanic explained he couldn't simply disconnect the anti-theft system. The security program was designed to allow the car to run only a short distance *if* a thief went under the dashboard and cut the wires to disconnect the alarm. The motor would soon cut off and the car would die in the middle of the road.

He was speaking *conditionally.* I hadn't learned the conditional verb forms as yet. He was saying *if* this was to occur. What I heard, however, was that it *had* occurred; my car had been stolen, a thief had gotten in, cut the wires, and my VW was now dead and abandoned somewhere in a Roman alley. I demanded to know why in the hell the car hadn't been locked up. How could he have let some dashboard-cutting thief steal my wheels?

He gently led me to a nearby lot, where the car sat shining in the afternoon sun.

The young man brushed his overalls and asked if I had ever been to Los Angeles—he was getting married soon and planning a honeymoon in California. What sights did I recommend? After a brief discussion of L.A. areas of interest, I suggested we call Germany and get a copy of the missing *schema*.

"I have an idea," he said. "I'll call Verona."

"Why Verona?"

"It's the place for Volkswagen headquarters in Italy."

So, instead of receiving a schematic from the factory in Germany, we got a fax from Verona saying they didn't have the designs for an American-made model, please contact Wolfsburg. This, I was learning, was normal business practice in Italy.

I stopped locking the car. The alarm stopped going off.

La Seconda Guerra Mondiale . . .

It was fall. The festival season was over and the Romans had returned to their city and their work. My language classes droned on, but at least more comfortably now; the searing heat had finally broken.

The summer had ended with a long, overdue rain. It came one evening with great fury. It sounded as if the lightning cracked and thunder rolled directly overhead.

I went to the window facing the little courtyard five floors below. I could see my neighbors standing in their window frames as well; an elderly woman stood across the way wearing only a slip; two young girls peered out shyly from behind the wooden shutters of a corner apartment; a potbellied man in a strapped T-shirt smoked a cigar as we, the tenants, formed a welcoming committee for the long-awaited respite from the heat. We watched as the rain splattered and poured noisily in the gardens below.

As I stood, storm-surrounded and grateful for the great cooling of things, the aroma from the basil growing in my window box mixed with the ozone from the rain. It was the earthiest, freshest thing I had ever smelled.

I realized, in that moment, my senses of smell and taste had come alive in Italy. I don't know if they'd been dormant or just forgotten, but there was an aura of newness each time I tasted a tomato, or peach, or delicately seasoned bowl of pasta. I had found the city to be a great trove of tastes. I had never had a bad meal.

Standing by my window box on the night of that great, cool rain, I celebrated the simple seasonings of my Roman experience.

But I was learning a far more serious side to the city, as well.

There was evidence—more each day—that in Rome and in Italy, World War Two was never very far away. Despite all of the seemingly modern high-tech appliances; the young men on street corners shouting into cellular phones; the ubiquitous message T-shirts and the constant roar of traffic made from an endless parade of shiny new cars—still, there was an undercurrent, a fine-lace touch of sadness and memory that doesn't exist in the States.

On countless street corners in Rome little shrines or altars had been erected bearing pictures of a favorite saint or the Virgin. The custom dates back to ancient Rome, when cross-roads were considered spiritual places. Some of the modern altars had electric candles; most had fresh flowers, memorializing some event from the *"la seconda guerra mondiale."* The altars and memorials scattered about Rome were very subtle and blended into the natural background of a city filled with religious statements.

On a memorial near my neighborhood, a marble plaque simply read, "In memory of the liberation of Rome, June 5, 1944." It didn't mention the liberators. Nor the captors. Nor the fact that the world remembers early June 1944 for D-Day. Rome's liberation was a conquest quietly slipped into the historic landscape. But the message was clear.

I have seen Moscow and have found in Russia there is a monument or memorial on virtually every corner, overstated in heavy-handed Russian Communist–era fashion. But the memorials in Rome are not Russian, they are Italian and, more specifically, Roman. They are simple, yet forceful.

And they raised issues still not completely settled.

The story of Rome's liberation is one of the most overlooked in all of the Allied victories of World War II. Rome officially fell to the Allies on June 4, 1944. The American-led force formally marched into the city on June 5. While a major event in itself, it came only one day before the largest naval armada and armed invasion anywhere, at any time, in all of history. Rome's story got lost.

It had taken the Allies in Italy tens of thousands of lives and nearly a year to march up the peninsula from their invasion points at Reggio and Salerno, south of Naples, and Anzio, south of Rome.

The Allied invasion was the first to march *up* the peninsula in more than two thousand years. The Carthaginian, Hannibal, nearly two hundred years before Christ, and all subsequent military strategists until General Mark Clark of the U.S. Fifth Army, knew the key to taking Rome was in coming *down* the peninsula from the north. From the south, an army—any army at any point in time—had to storm innumerable hilltop fortifications and provided an easy target for anyone defending those hilltops.

The World War II Germans, if nothing else, knew history. They weren't about to concede the Italian peninsula without a fight. The Germans knew they couldn't defeat the Allies; they had been ordered to slow their advance and keep them out of Germany for as long as possible.

I was to learn sometime later that the hilltop birthplace of my grandfather, Pietro DePasquale, was one of the many defensive positions key to the Nazi-stalling effort.

Thousands of Soldiers—American, French, Moroccan (who fought under the French flag), English, Canadian, and Polish— died in what some still argue was a foolish effort. When the fighting was over and the Germans routed, they marched into Rome, got one day's headlines in the papers back home, then disappeared to history. The very next day was the long-anticipated D-Day, and Normandy's embattled beaches justifiably captured the world's attention and imagination.

When the Allies entered Rome on June 5, they marched into the city along the Via Appia, the same route Scipio Africanus must have used when he returned from the destruction of Hannibal's troops to end the Second Punic War.

The American-led force marched into historic Rome through the ancient city gate. They continued down the Via Appia to the remains of the Circus Maximus, turned up the slight rise along the Via di San Gregorio, and marched through the Arch of Constantine, next to the Colosseum. Another left brought the troops along the Via dei Fori Imperiali and the place where Mussolini loved to show off his Fascist troops before Adolf Hitler. The parade ended in central Rome's largest piazza at the base of the huge, garish monument to Vittorio Emanuele II, the Risorgimento leader and first king of modern, united Italy.

It's always seemed strange to me that a country, which as far back as Roman times adamantly opposed the concept of royalty, and which didn't institute a constitutional monarchy until the time of America's Civil War, should dedicate so much marble and space to an institution that lasted less than a century and failed them miserably.

In fact, if Vittorio Emanuele III, the grandson of the Risorgimento king, had had his act together during World War II, he could have surrendered Rome to the Allies without a shot being fired. After timidly dismissing Mussolini as dictator and placing him under arrest, the king was so unsure of his powers that he made a hasty retreat to the south and didn't maintain proper communications with the outside world. Dwight Eisenhower had demanded assurances from the king of unconditional surrender. Had Vittorio Emanuele been able to reply decisively and effectively to the Americans, the entire Italian campaign might have been avoided.

Another of the endless Roman contradictions.

And no less a contradiction than on June 5, 1944, when thousands of Italians gathered in the grand piazza honoring a failed dynasty to cheer the American-led armies and celebrate their own defeat.

Italy was the only country during World War II to change governments and sides while the war was in progress. That revolt against Mussolini's Fascists cost them not only prestige and international respect, but also a bitter civil war that ravaged the Italian countryside for over two years.

Every American growing up in post–World War II America had heard countless jokes about the Italian military. Yet I couldn't help wondering when I learned the details of the overthrow of Mussolini, What if the Germans had changed governments in 1943? What if it had been Germany, and not Italy, that threw out its corrupt dictator? One can only wonder if folklore would have treated the Germans the same as the Italians, created as many humorous jibes at the German army—which was committed to defeat—as the Italian army has suffered even to this day.

A "Little Mother's" Memories

Luigi's mother was in town for a visit. I was invited to Sunday dinner.

"It won't be any good," she said. "I couldn't find anything I wanted at the market today."

She and Luigi bickered as she prepared the meal with help from her granddaughter, Laura. Luigi was a man of definitive tastes. His mother was still trying to convince him he should like a certain cheese that she had bought that morning. The aroma of cooking filled the apartment.

La Signora asked about my family and how I was enjoying Italy. "Very much," I said. "Especially the food."

"I wish I had time to prepare a better meal," she apologized. "I just couldn't find the right things."

"*Nonna,* it will be wonderful." Laura laughed. "You always say your cooking isn't any good and it's the best in the world."

La Signora wrung her hands, as if seriously concerned over the meal's preparation. "Ah," she exclaimed, "the pasta . . ." as she ran off to the kitchen.

"My mother loves theater," said Luigi with a grin. "We call her *Tosca,* especially when she cooks. This is a woman who has seen war, yet she worries about the maturity of artichokes."

Meanwhile, I watched as Laura divided into two people. When she spoke with her father or grandmother she spoke in rapid Italian. She was animated in her grandmother's language and used facial expressions and hand motions to emphasize points. When she spoke to me, she used only English, spoke calmly, and seemed almost reserved. I was enjoying the performance a great deal.

As we took our places in the dining room, I asked *La Signora* about the war. Luigi told me she had lived through the occupation of her hometown in Umbria, and he had been born in the bad times for his family and the country.

"What was it like then?" I asked. "What happened when the Germans were here?"

"*I Tedeschi,*" she clucked. "The Germans." She shook her head slowly, as she called up the memory. "They killed hundreds here in Rome. And in the countryside, up in the Abruzzi, where your mother's people are from, it was even worse."

She lovingly lifted the bowl of pasta from the center of the table and offered it to her granddaughter.

"They called me 'little mother,'" she said, as we passed around the delicacies and helped ourselves to the food she had prepared. "They were in our town of Foligna until the Americans came. Sometimes we would give them food. They were just hungry boys away from home, really. They liked the Italian food."

"Everyone does," I joked, "especially if it was as good as what we're eating." The pasta was done perfectly, of course, with a fresh tomato and basil sauce that reminded me of my window box.

"Italian food is especially good if your main diet is cabbage, sausage, and potatoes." Luigi laughed. He, like most Italians I had met, found the German diet more comical than appetizing.

"They didn't have enough to eat," Luigi's mom continued, "but they seemed to believe what they were told, what their government wanted them to think."

She recalled a story as she insisted I try more of her fabulous homemade bread. "The German soldiers would tell us the Americans had black troops straight from Africa in the front lines—ape-men who had tails rolled up in their trousers. They said we'd all be raped and slaughtered if the Americans weren't stopped."

She laughed at the memory. "You know, not only do I think they believed that, they actually wanted for *us* to believe such nonsense."

"What happened when the Americans did come, *Nonna*?" Laura asked.

"The first American I saw wasn't an ape-man. He was an Italian boy from Brooklyn whose family was from the Abruzzi. He spoke perfect Italian and made sure we had enough food, especially when he saw I was in a family way with Luigi." She paused and looked off into the distance, recalling the long-ago American visitor. "He would come every day to check on us.

He brought us chocolates and milk. Then, one day, his unit went away, we were told to Belgium. I never saw him again."

"There was no destruction, *Nonna*?"

"Some bridges were blown up. Nothing to hurt the people. Not like here, in Rome. Not like in the mountains." She passed me a huge bowl. I helped myself to a big plate of salad made from romaine lettuce, endive, and radicchio, lightly seasoned with olive oil, a touch of garlic and balsamic vinegar.

"In the mountains, where your grandfather is from," she said nodding in my direction, "there was much destruction. There were many partisans at that time and the Germans tried to kill them all." She was a simple woman and seemed truly saddened by the memory.

"It is very easy to like the young Germans who come here now." She stared down at the table and slowly brushed crumbs from the linen. "They are generally very nice people, very polite to the Italians. They spend a lot of money here on holiday. I know they are not the Nazi murderers of so many years ago." She sighed heavily.

"*I Tedeschi*—the Germans," she repeated.

It was more a question than a statement.

And it was one that I knew had been asked before.

5

Gamberale . . .

The Search for Pietro's Past

The village of Gamberale is about a three-hour drive from Rome, but it had taken me over a year to get there.

The little village lies high in the Apennines at about nine thousand feet. It is one of those postcard-perfect places—an almost-miniature town situated at the top of a sheer bluff, with clusters of houses clumped together about the hillsides, their peaked tiled roofs and the spire of the town's only church breaking into a cloudness sky. At the very end of the cluster stood a rebuilt Dark Ages castle.

I'd come to appreciate the Volkswagen's performance. The little engine had surprising power on the steep hills that led to my grandfather's birthplace. I had stopped to take a picture of the first road sign I passed, the town's name printed in black lettering against a yellow arrow.

I still didn't have complete confidence in my language skills, but it was time to get on with things. I made the trip alone; Luigi was unavailable. It was a crisp, beautiful Saturday morning.

Only one paved road leads to and through the town. It meets a single cross street at the town's main fountain in a little square opposite the church.

It had taken me so long to get there because I had needed time, not only for Italian lessons, but also to research the area. I had quickly learned Italian history is no easy subject—especially when one is trying to learn about small, remote villages.

All of my information about Gamberale before coming to Italy was anecdotal; my grandfather Pietro left his village, returned often before the Second World War, and never spoke of it again after the war.

My mother had visited with Pietro on one trip. She had pictures of that visit somewhere, but they, along with most of my mother's things, had been lost in the many years since her death. My factual knowledge of the town was hazy at best.

My readings—mostly reference books I'd found in libraries or with Luigi's help—hadn't given me much. I had read about the region in histories that dealt from pre-Roman times on. But the modern journals I found, and the two very detailed books on Italian towns that Luigi kept in his apartment, only listed the name of the place, its elevation, the very small population of 325—which proved to be too high—and the fact that the local economy was tourism-based.

The Italians I talked with all thought of the *Abruzzesi* as "tough" people, a people who have been hardened by time and the elements. They still recalled the ancient tribes who lived there as stubborn and the only native people to ever defeat the Roman army on Italian soil—which might account for some familial hardheadedness. They talked about rumors and some vague historical references that the Romans might have fled to these hills when their defenses collapsed and the barbarians crashed their ancient party.

My interest, however, wasn't in ancient times. I specifically wanted to know what had happened here since my grandfather's last visit in what I believed had been 1933. A more manageable time frame, given the long sweep of Italian history, but no easy question nonetheless.

It had also taken me such a long time to get there because of my hardheaded decision to learn Italian. I have never been a linguist. Friends have described my German as *Gasthaus Deutsch,* or "beer-hall German," learned in rather obvious places during my stationing in Germany as a soldier. My Italian was no better at this point, but my determination was fierce. I was going to return to the village of my grandfather, speaking the language he had spoken when he left for America.

It was an emotional moment. In Pittsburgh, the St. Lorenzo Club on Bouquet Street, just a couple of blocks down the hill from where Forbes Field once stood, had been founded by my grandfather. The club was named for the little church in the village square, and both are named for the town's patron saint.

I could clearly remember my mother's description of her arrival there so many years before my own. She laughed as she recalled riding a donkey up the mountainside. It was a picture that implanted itself in a small boy's mind; my mother in a dress on the back of a donkey, climbing a steep hill. For my mother, the story was a parable of how out-of-date the Old Country was. She was a second-generation American and greatly amused by her trip into the past.

She often told the story of a dinner, held in my grandfather's honor at a neighboring village during her visit. Breaking open a dinner roll, she found a cockroach baked inside. She quietly told her father, in English, what had happened. He explained, quickly and firmly, it would be a great insult to the hostess not to eat the bread.

"So, I had to eat that roll," she'd say.

We pretended to gag when she reached the end of her story, and would always laugh. I remain convinced she only ate part of that roll—and certainly had nothing to do with the disgusting bug—but it was a good story and we always enjoyed hearing it.

She and her father had visited Italy at what was probably the height of Mussolini's rule, and the same year Hitler came to power in Germany. My grandfather Pietro had come to the village after meeting with Il Duce in Rome. My mother wasn't invited into the session with Mussolini. Popa hired a motion picture photographer to record the event on 35mm black-and-white film. A photographer also accompanied him and my mother to Gamberale. He undoubtedly wanted the film to record their travels for family and friends back in the States.

This was long before the age of home movies and video cameras. Viewings of these films were anything but casual; a projectionist had to be hired, the hall arranged for, invitations made. It was an *event*.

I remember as a very young boy the excitement of spending a Sunday afternoon in the St. Lorenzo club, set up as a movie hall, to watch these same films. By the time I viewed them, probably sometime around the mid 1950s, they were not complete. According to my mother, Pietro became so enraged at Mussolini for declaring war on the United States the day after

Pearl Harbor, he destroyed all of the segments containing the dictator.

That was the only time I ever saw the Mussolini-less films. It was a very old memory. The movies had been also the only insight into the Old World for virtually all of my family who had been born in the United States. They had been made on silver nitrite stock, and now even they were but a memory.

His Name Was Pietro DePasquale...

So, here I was, nearly sixty years after the last member of my family had been there, returning to an ancestral homestead. An American pilgrim, middle-aged wanderer, and curious grandson interested in the origins of his dark-eyed, laugh-filled, and robust Pittsburgh family. This was a trip I had been imagining, in one way or another, for a very long time.

I drove my Volkswagen into the little village square. The day became chilly, especially at nine thousand feet.

Only a few people were out and about. Two elderly men conversed in the plaza; one stood by the church, the other across the way by the fountain. I drove up to the man at the fountain, lowered the window, sucked in a deep breath, and went off in my best school-taught Italian.

"Mi scusi, signore, ma dove e il municipio?"

His response was typical of most Italians when I tried to speak their language. He wrinkled his nose and narrowed his eyelids, making it clear, without using a word of the language I was trying to speak, he didn't understand.

"Cosa?" he asked—the Italian catch phrase for "eh," or "what's that?"

I repeated the sentence, paying particular attention to pronouncing the vowels correctly, especially on the word *municipio* or city hall—a real tongue twister for me.

He smiled. In nearly perfect English he said, "Say, where are you from?"

I told him I was born in Pittsburgh.

He laughed. "I'm from Pittsburgh, too," he said, and we both laughed. The value of my year of Italian lessons had become a questionable expense.

He was a Sculli, a name and family I knew well. He had been in Pittsburgh for twenty years but had returned to Gamberale after a disabling accident during construction work. He asked the name of my family.

"Oh, you mean Pete, 'The Animal.' I knew your grandfather," he said.

This man definitely did *not* know my grandfather. No one who ever knew my grandfather would have dreamed of calling him anything even remotely resembling this nickname.

My grandfather was an old-world gentleman. He died when I was twenty-seven years old. In my entire experience with him, the only time I had ever seen him not wearing a jacket and tie was when he lay on his deathbed.

This Sculli was clearly mistaken. He went on to describe a character who was large and burly who had worked construction jobs. A fellow who shared the name or, *more probably,* had been named *for* my grandfather.

I was surprised, given all of my grandfather's involvement with this village, his name wasn't instantly recognized. I repeated my request, in English this time, for directions to the municipal offices. I was sent a few blocks away.

Two young men stood behind the counter in the small office.

I explained that my mother's family was from this village and I would like to research the records for any information concerning these people.

What records did I mean? they asked.

I told them any documents regarding birth, death, property and real estate, or any other city records that might give me some picture of the community in their times.

They seemed uncomfortable with the questions and suggested I talk with Signor Caruso, the unofficial local historian. They called to a man in the back of the office.

Signor Caruso, an older gentleman with a round face and receding hairline, and who looked much like my uncle Al, came over to the counter. I began the conversation again. He asked my grandfather's name and, when I told him Pietro De-Pasquale, he replied the name was a *famous* one from this town.

Now we're getting somewhere, I thought.

Caruso told me there was one DePasquale family still in the village, the descendants of the only brother of my grandfather to return to Italy. He suggested I visit with them, but my interest on this day was not social. I still had my hang-ups about dropping in on strangers and announcing myself as family.

I asked about the records.

There are none, he replied.

I was sure I had misunderstood.

"Niente," he repeated. There was no mistaking the word. *"Tutto bruciato,"* he added, obviously seeing my confusion.

"Bruciato"—*burned.* It took a second for the meaning of the word to hit me.

"Burned?" I repeated. "There was a fire?"

"Of course." He acted as though I should know this. "The entire village was burned."

"When?"

"The war," he replied. He seemed surprised at my reaction. "The record hall was burned during the war. Everything was burned."

"How?" I asked.

"The Germans. The Germans burned the town."

"The Germans," I said incredulously. "The Germans were here? They burned the town?"

I couldn't help but repeat Signor Caruso's words. "But why?" I was completing my list of basic Italian interrogatives.

He looked at me, his eyes dancing over half glasses. He smiled a slightly exasperated smile. He was telling an old and apparently well-known story to a naive American who barely spoke his language. He explained that the partisan movement had been very active in this area and many men from the village had been killed. I understood him to say thirteen men were killed one day alone.

"Look," he said, "the Germans burned the town when they left. They burned all the records. But there is another set of official records for the town in this period in Lanciano, the county seat. You should go there."

Disappointed, I left. I had no idea the town had been occupied by the Germans. I had heard that some of the villagers had died in the war, but there was never any mention of an occupation. Or burning. I wondered if my grandfather had known this.

It was lunchtime. I stopped at the Hotel La Fonte, the town's only lodging and restaurant. I decided to return with Luigi as my translator before visiting the family relations Signor Caruso had mentioned.

The hotel seemed deserted. It was built in ski-lodge fashion, the alpine sports trade undoubtedly its main source of customers. At the back of the building I found the dining room. It had three glass walls offering a dramatic, panoramic view of the mountainside.

A small group of people sat next to the fireplace. The day was crisp and clear and just cool enough for the early-autumn fire crackling in the Franklin stove.

I asked the man who looked most senior if lunch was being served. He jumped to his feet. I was offered what was obviously the prime table.

A younger man came to the table and recited the special of the day. I asked about a poster of Pittsburgh I had seen in the lobby.

"My father was there last year," he replied.

"Pittsburgh is my hometown," I told him.

"Yes, I know, your grandfather was Pietro DePasquale. Your grandmother was a Diulius and so am I. I think she was a cousin to my father."

News travels fast in small towns.

I learned from the young man—Stefano—that the main business of the village, aside from those who still farmed or tended herds of sheep, was that of part-time ski resort. The government had helped pay for some of the newer lodge construction. Christmas season was the busiest time of year.

Thinking of my immigrant grandfather having been born in a ski resort changed my perspective. I wondered what he would have thought of this turn of events.

I asked Stefano if he had visited the United States.

"No," he said, "I haven't, but I would one day like to see Pittsburgh. I have heard so much about it."

Stefano gave me a map of the Abruzzi, which he thought would be helpful. After a few minutes' study I pointed out that Gamberale was not shown on the map. He shrugged the shrug of a man used to slights.

On the way back to the main road I stopped at the little cemetery at the foot of the mountain and walked among the tombstones. It was like being back in the Oakland section of Pittsburgh. They were all there, all of the names I had ever known as a young child: *Sculli, DiNardo, Bellisario, DePasquale, DiIluiis,* names so familiar to me despite the endless variations in spelling.

It seemed strange none of the tombs or markers were older than the early 1920s. The cemetery was built on a sloping hill. At the top of the hill, next to what looked like a little chapel, was a marble plaque. It read:

S.M.S. S-ANTONIO
EROI CADUTI CAUSA EVENTI BELLICI
NOVEMBRE 1943

Thirteen names were listed on the plaque along with the names, birth dates, and fathers' names of the "fallen heroes as a result of the hostilities": two Buccis, four DiNardos, five Scullis, one Pollice and one DeIulis (who also had the distinction of being the youngest killed, at twenty-one).

Obviously, these were the men Signor Caruso had been referring to. It was fifty years after the event, yet my heart still went out to their mothers and wives. Young men killed in the prime of life.

It was troubling to see these names, so very familiar and, in at least two cases, probably related, and to have only learned of their fate some fifty years after the fact. I knew these families, knew their relatives, knew that they were a simple people more prone to laughter than anger.

I lamented the fact that communication had been lost, that we hadn't known of or about one another, that apparently no one in Oakland could have helped ease the suffering of the Signori Scullis and DiNardos and DiUliis.

I was beginning to fully comprehend how the Second World War, more than any other factor, had separated the people from this village. It was the war that had fully Americanized the Italians who had moved to the States. It made the complete break with the Old Country an inevitability.

Still, I couldn't shake the feeling, standing in that small, sloping cemetery in the middle of the Apennines, that something had been lost.

Lanciano . . .
Yet Another Language

Luigi offered to help with the records search in Lanciano. He perked up from his normal gloom the second we left the Rome Autostrada and headed into the hills.

"This is the *real* Italy. The villages and mountains are the true country," he said.

Like most big-city people I know, Luigi believes rural people are an honest and hardworking stock, simple and uncomplicated, and the country offers an easier solution to the inevitable complications of life in a city like Rome.

As we drove along, Luigi named every flower and plant we passed; his botanical knowledge seemed endless. He became nearly ecstatic when, somewhere near Roccaraso, we passed a herd of sheep guarded by a shepherd and a big dog. He spoke two of the few English words he had difficulty with. *"Sheps,"* he said, "I love *sheps.* I've loved them ever since I was a *guy.*"

"Sheep," I corrected.

"That's right," he replied as we sped along the country road, "I love *sheps.*"

In Lanciano, Luigi and I were met by a very officious young Ph.D. who obviously took her job as records keeper very seriously. She wasn't about to admit just anyone to the records stack. She demanded an explanation; exactly what records did we want to see and why?

The woman was condescending and abrupt. It was the first time I'd even been spoken to by an Italian in a manner that was neither charming nor civil. She told us to wait in an outer office. She then proceeded to take phone calls from friends for the better part of the next hour.

Luigi was getting angry. He explained that in small provincial towns there is a distrust of Italian-Americans rummaging about old records—a constant fear of distant and unknown American cousins returning to make property claims. That might have explained our reception and the young woman's attitude.

"But there's no excuse for her rudeness," he muttered. It was a *"brutta figura."*

A clerk arrived. The bureaucratic *Dottoressa* told the young man to go and look for my grandfather's birth certificate. I had made no mention of any specific records. I certainly didn't need and wasn't especially interested in a birth certificate—I knew when and where he had been born. I had wanted to trace my grandfather's family as far back as possible.

The records search would have to be made by hand, and by

114

going through whatever volumes lay on the shelves. "Is nothing on a computer?" asked Luigi.

"A *computer,* Signor?" The young woman smirked. "Do you realize how many records we have? It would be impossible to put them on a computer."

"Beh," said Luigi. "The Italians invented record keeping. Certainly they know how to enter data into an Olivetti."

The woman said nothing and shook her head as if to say the idea wasn't even worth commenting on.

We decided to slip away with the clerk, despite the fact our bureaucrat friend had made it clear we were expected to wait in her office. We sneaked into the hall and down the staircase. We were taken to a large, damp basement room filled with mildew and dust.

The assistant said plainly he was embarrassed by both the attitude of his superior and the condition of the room. He told us that, technically, we weren't permitted to enter but he wanted us to see for ourselves what bad shape things were in. He apologized a second time for his boss's behavior.

The record books were kept on metal shelving about ten feet high. Several stacks ran the length of the room, which was about thirty feet long.

We went to a shelf where the handwritten label read, "Gamberale." There were about twenty or so ledger journals and, from the amount of dust on them, it was apparent that no one had gone through these records in a very long time.

Luigi said we owed a debt of gratitude to Napoleon; the Napoleonic Code required duplicate records for all villages to be made and kept at provincial capitals. These were the only records left for Gamberale for the period prior to the Second World War.

The records we saw were both fascinating and disappointing.

The region had been under Napoleon in the early nineteenth century. Then, after Garibaldi unified the country in the 1860s, national Italian record keeping had become better organized, and the later documents reflected this enhanced national policy—there were triplicate records from the Italian unification period on.

The political makeup of an "Italy" that didn't exist before Garibaldi's time was a mishmash of Papal States, Duchies, Provinces, and regional governments in the long, long string of foreign or outside powers who controlled different regions in various times.

Searching through provincial Italian records, I learned, is an eye-crossing puzzle that requires the skills of journalist, historian, detective, and snoop.

I was also later to learn the best records have been maintained by the Roman Catholic Church, only *if* you can find a cooperative priest. In Lanciano, we found most of the records were duplicates of church records—mostly certificates of birth and death.

I went through the handwritten stiff and yellowing pages, the old ink fading. The same family names repeated over and over in the official markings of lives long gone.

There were, of course, language problems. For both Luigi and me. I had spent over a year trying to learn enough Italian to cope with a records search. Luigi was a native speaker. The records had been kept in Latin. *Only* in Latin. I cursed my lazy, unmotivated fourteen-year-old self for not having studied harder; for having ridiculed a "dead" language.

We managed to track my grandfather's family back through the volumes for five generations to Domenico DePasquale, who had been born in 1805. Domenico's son, Raffaele, had become mayor of the village and, during his long life—he lived to age eighty-seven—his name appeared as the official signature on many of the official birth and death registers.

The DePasquales over the years married with the Scullis, Buccis, DiNardos, DiUlius—my grandmother; all the names I grew up with. These same families had been intermarrying for at least a couple of centuries. And for each time period, almost for each decade, there were different spellings for each of the names.

In the twentieth century they went to America, mostly to Pittsburgh, where they *continued* to intermarry—and finally decided on fixed spellings. As a child, I found it impossible to describe family relationships to my friends; two uncles (DePasquales) married two sisters (Bellisarios); a third sister (Bellisario) married my father's brother (Paolicelli).

We then found another document that granted a dispensation to my great-grandfather (DePasquale) to marry a (second) cousin (DiNardo), which may have been responsible for the rather odd behavior of a cousin or two.

The death records listed the age of the deceased, but not the cause of death. The records also list the ages and occupations of the two required witnesses.

In Gamberale there were only three occupations: proprietor, farmer, or field hand. My relatives were all property owners; they had houses and farmland.

In the more recent journals—the ones from 1910 on—there were occasional death certificates issued by the City of Pittsburgh. The papers were apparently necessary for some legal situation or, more probably a benefit claim. It seemed strange and out of place to see the formal documents printed in English with the gold seal of an American city and a physician's report on the death compared to the simple, handwritten village documents.

Our search was interrupted; our Ph.D. friend had learned we were rummaging around in the stacks. She was demanding we leave. She claimed to have another assignment for our clerk.

The young man seemed resigned about this information but insisted on taking us to see the bathroom before we left—he was determined to show us the leaking pipes and water-stained walls.

"This is how we keep our records," he said, shaking his head in disgust. "This is what the big-shot professors upstairs allow to happen."

We returned to the official's office. She asked if I had found what I had been looking for. I told her I would have liked more time, but would like a copy of the mayor's document listing my grandfather's birth—not his official birth certificate. The young bureaucrat said I could have either a photocopy or an official typed copy but could not have both. Then without waiting for my response she assigned the clerk to make a verbatim copy of my grandfather's birth certificate—exactly what I didn't ask for and certainly didn't need.

I suggested to the Signora there was a danger of losing all the information in the basement. I pointed out the damp conditions and repeated Luigi's earlier suggestion that the records be computerized.

She looked at me as if I were speaking a Tibetan dialect.

"That's crazy," she said. "You could never transfer all those records to a computer. Who has the time to do such a thing?"

I wanted to suggest the Mormons, but thought better of any further conversation.

. . .

Luigi and I spotted a small arrow-shaped sign advertising a local trattoria and promising a view. We were hungry. It was late afternoon and our minds were numb from record reading and Latin scanning. A meal was just the thing to stir the senses.

We parked the car off the side of the curving highway, backtracked to the sign, and walked up a long and steep staircase cut into the hillside.

The trattoria sat at the top of the hill and resembled an American country inn. We entered and, not being greeted, seated ourselves at a window table. It was late afternoon and we were the only customers in the place.

It was not false advertising. The view from the top of the hill was spectacular; we looked out over a lush, green, and heavily wooded valley that ran to the eastern horizon. The cliffs on both sides of the valley were craggy, sheer, and majestic, the leaves just completing their spring greening and a wide variety of wildflowers bloomed in a rainbow of primary colors.

The proprietor, a heavyset man with dark thinning hair, came into the dining area from the kitchen and seemed surprised to see us. He rushed over to our table and greeted us warmly in the local Abruzzese dialect. Luigi asked if lunch were still available.

"*Ma, certo.*" The man sighed. "Certainly."

"Do you have a specialty today?"

"Today like every day in spring—the lamb. I have some fresh artichokes. Maybe some spinach. And, of course, pasta to your liking." He straightened out his apron as we made our decision.

We ordered marinated artichokes for an appetizer. I ordered the lamb, Luigi ordered a *penne pasta* with marinara sauce and we both ordered a mixed salad to follow the meal in the Italian fashion as a "digestive."

"You passed up the man's specialty?" I asked when the proprietor disappeared again into the kitchen. "*Penne marinara* is rather pedestrian."

"I can't eat lamb. It upsets my stomach." He quietly belched, holding his fist in front of his mouth as if the very thought of lamb could upset him.

"But *sheps*," I joked. "I thought you loved *sheps*."

"In the field with the shepherds I love them," he said, "not on my plate."

We devoured our *antipasto* hungrily, the artichokes were tasty and the local bread light and airy. Luigi's pasta and my lamb arrived.

It was then I had one of those extraordinary culinary experiences that happen only rarely and, even in a country of unbelievably good food, was still remarkable. The lamb I tasted exploded with flavor in my mouth. It was the most perfect tasting, seasoned, and cooked piece of meat I'd ever had the pleasure of ingesting. I almost swooned, and for the first time I understood what the word "swoon" meant.

Luigi munched contentedly on his pasta. He didn't notice my profound involvement with my entrée. The proprietor came over and asked about our meal.

"This lamb is sensational," I raved. I couldn't find enough Italian adjectives, I starting adding vowels to English ones, "*delisioso, fabuloso, wonderfuloso*," I babbled. "This is the best lamb I have ever tasted."

The proprietor smiled broadly and bowed in my direction. "*Grazie*," he said softly, "*mille grazie*."

"Just sensational," I repeated. "Where do you buy your meat?"

The man's eyes widened as he stood fully erect. "Buy, Signore?" He smoothed his apron again. "Signore, I do not 'buy' this lamb. It is my lamb. I grow this lamb." He was nearly indignant at the suggestion of foreign influence over his specialty.

"It is magnificent," I said, "You are obviously a great artist as a chef *and* as a farmer."

The man slicked back the few remaining strands of black hair over his broad brow. He thanked me again and strode off toward the kitchen much in the way I assumed a general would strut after winning a military battle.

"He raises his own livestock," I said to Luigi in amazement. "The man grows his own specialty and you're missing it."

Luigi sighed. "This is the country I love," he said. "This is the true Italy."

"But you're missing one of the greatest taste sensations I've ever had."

"Beh," Luigi sniffed. "I have the Abruzzi outside this window, this clean mountain air to breathe, and my pasta. It's enough for one day."

The Heroes of Gamberale . . .

I returned to Gamberale a couple of weeks later, this time with Luigi as chief translator. We reached the village just as the Sunday service ended at the church of San Lorenzo. Luigi insisted our first stop be a visit with the parish priest. We parked the Volkswagen next to the church and went in.

Don Riccardo had just finished Mass and was delighted to

have visitors. The service had been poorly attended, with only a smattering of older women in the first two pews. There wasn't a man in the place except for the priest.

The little church had recently been beautifully renovated and redecorated; the smell of paint was fresh. Don Riccardo proudly pointed out the renovations and invited us into the cramped vestry off the main altar. I told him I was searching for any and every record I could find. He seemed a little saddened.

"There aren't many records here," he said.

Luigi and I explained we knew of the fire and the destruction of the *paese*, but wondered if the church may have any additional records concerning my family. Don Riccardo went to a small cabinet and pulled out two ledger books, smaller than the ones in Lanciano. We began to page through.

As we opened the books, I took out my laptop from a tote bag. I turned the computer on. Don Riccardo found this very humorous.

"Ah, the Americans are here," he joked. "We old priests write with pen and ink, in Latin, while you Americans enter data in your little computers."

We pored through the records with the hopes of finding new information. There was none.

I had known the name of San Lorenzo, of course, all of my life. The patron saint, very popular in Italy, was an early Christian martyr. A Roman, he had been a deacon of the then new Christian religion and, according to the legend, sold church property in order to help the needy.

When the Roman officials learned of his activities, they demanded he present the church's treasure to the emperor. San Lorenzo pleaded for time. Three days later he returned, accompanied by the blind, crippled, and poor of Rome, whom he presented as the church's wealth. For his defiance he was ordered to be burned to death and was placed on a red-hot griddle.

As the story goes, he told his executioners to turn him over, he was done on one side. His death and his defiance of the Romans inspired other Christians.

The sense of determination in the face of overwhelming odds was a theme repeated again and again in Italy over the ages, particularly in the smaller Southern villages. I wondered if it had been San Lorenzo's sense of defiance, or his dedication to the poor, that my ancestors found most attractive and wanted to honor in naming their church after this man.

My grandfather and a group of his compatriots had built the San Lorenzo Society Hall on Bouquet Street in Oakland during the late 1920s. For many years it was the meeting place in Pittsburgh for the people who had immigrated from this village and the many places like it. But, even more important to the first generation in particular, the Society raised money and sponsored other villagers and their relatives in immigrating to the United States. It guaranteed them a place to live, employment, and a community when they arrived in America.

My grandfather would repeat over and over, "We never asked for a handout, only an opportunity." He was very proud of the San Lorenzo Club.

It was also the only hall in Pittsburgh where all of my mother's family weddings, communions, confirmations, and general parties were held.

I asked Don Riccardo about the little church whose name I knew so well. This was the "new" building, he explained, having been built in 1709. The priest was happy to add that the first permanently assigned priest to this village was one Don Gaetano DeJulius. This possible relative of my grandmother had been assigned to the village in 1726. It must have been a great honor to the village to have a native son assigned as pastor.

The "old" church had been incorporated into the ancient castle on top of the hill, but it had fallen into disrepair in the late seventeenth century and the decision had been made to build a separate place of worship. This had been a big moment in the long life of this little village. The priest explained that for a village to have its own church was a great distinction at the time.

Don Riccardo was especially proud to show us a statue from the "old" church, the last remaining article from the original sanctuary that hadn't yet been placed on display in the "new" one. It struck me as unremarkable, a wooden statue about a yard high of St. Michael the Archangel. It had been crammed into the back of a cabinet in the vestry and had been sitting there for around 290 years. Don Riccardo explained that there had been no money to make repairs.

I could only wonder what was so wrong with the thing— why it had taken three hundred years without the wherewithal for repairs to be made. From what I could see of it, craning my head about the shelving and squinting into the dark cabinet, it was nothing more extraordinary than a carved wooden and painted figure of an angel.

I asked Don Riccardo why I couldn't find any grave markers in the little cemetery dated before the 1920s. He found it an odd question. I explained that I could find neither crypts nor tombstones marking any graves much older than seventy years.

"There were no such things as graves before that," he said.

"How did they bury the dead?" I asked.

"They would put the bodies of the deceased under the houses and, after some time, when they had turned to bones, collect the remains and bury them in a common grave."

"There were no records of any of this, no records of whose bones are in that little yard?" I asked.

The priest stuck out his chin in the Italian fashion, a popular gesture meaning, "Eh, what can I say?"

I asked Luigi what he made of this information. "These were poor people," he replied. "Only the rich could afford marble markers."

I found the practice barbaric. I was amazed there was so little interest in record keeping or memorializing the dead. It was even more surprising in a country where people still burned candles or brought flowers to the remains of saints dead for centuries.

The priest had used the word *"cassetta,"* or little box, to describe where the bones had been placed. I found the concept of a box full of unidentified human bones—my ancestors—unsettling.

We left the priest and watched as he headed down the steep hill in his little black Fiat on his way to another village for an afternoon Mass. He had told us to visit the town's only bar, The Eagle's Nest, which was owned by the DePasquale that Signor Caruso had mentioned.

Don Riccardo invited us back to visit anytime we were in the area. He had seemed genuinely happy to spend time with us, particularly amused by the rapping of my laptop keys.

Before visiting the bar, we climbed to the top of the hill to inspect the old castle and former church. As castles go, it wasn't very impressive—a big building with a square watchtower at its nearest corner to the village, and made from wood and plaster—not the traditional heavy stone. It had a fresh coat of paint and was not open to the public.

Above the main door was a small marble plaque, in Latin again, which read that the building had been restored by "DePasqualis" and "Buccis," the Latin equivalents of the same names. The restoration had either been paid for or the work actually done by the two families. The restoration had occurred in the year MLCCCI—1801—a hundred years after the people of the village built the new church. Growing up in Pittsburgh and in Southern California, I had never thought that I would one day see a family name on the nameplate of a castle, but here in Gamberale as well as on the plaque of the San Lorenzo club in Pittsburgh, the name seemed to endure.

From the castle we made our way past the main square and the public fountain to the Eagle's Nest. Inside, several tables lined the wall opposite the long bar. We were welcomed by a smiling bartender. Three or four elderly gentlemen sat at the back table and shared a drink.

One of the older men approached us as soon as our drinks arrived. He asked where we were from, but I suspected he already knew. He had lived in Pittsburgh for several years and knew my family well. He spoke lovingly of "Al the insurance man," my favorite uncle. Like his father, Pietro, Uncle Al had always seen to the needs of newly arrived immigrants.

Our elderly friend explained that he and a few friends had returned to their village from Pittsburgh to retire. I asked when they had gone to the United States. He said it had been well after the Second World War, that for a long time before the war it had been impossible to leave.

Our companion was a courtly gentleman, impeccably dressed in a jacket and tie with a sporty cap on his balding head. He was reserved in his speech and very formal in his form of address. I could hear my grandfather's manner in his speech.

"You were in Gamberale during the war?" I asked.

A sadness seemed to come over him like a cloud passing in front of the sun. "Yes," he replied, "I was here during the war."

"Then you must have known the thirteen men who were killed by the Germans, the names I have seen in the cemetery."

"Yes," he said, "we all knew those men."

"That was a terrible toll for a little town, thirteen killed in one bombardment," I mused.

He looked at me sharply and said, "Do you think that is what happened?"

"What do you mean?" I asked.

"When the war started," he went on, "there were over six hundred people in this village. Then the Nazis came. When they left, one hundred and five were dead. The thirteen that you speak of were killed on the same day and in the same place. But it was not a bombardment."

Luigi and I exchanged glances. I was not aware of anyone in Pittsburgh ever discussing the effects of the war on this little place. Our older friend maintained his reserve, but was even more solemn as he recounted the horrors of his youth.

"The Nazis came into this village and stayed here for six months in the winter of 1943 to 1944," he went on. "The English were on the opposite mountain to the west in the town of Capracotta. On the first day the Nazis came they didn't come as Nazis."

Luigi and I asked questions at the same time, trying to clarify his meaning.

"The first Germans to reach the town came dressed like British soldiers. They spoke in English and asked for assistance. 'Did anyone know the language? Would they help maintain contact between the British and Americans?'

"Thirteen men came forward. They had all been to Pittsburgh and spoke at least some English. The 'British' soldiers rounded them up and marched them into the town square. You know the square by the fountain?"

We nodded.

"A truck came by, backed up to the square. There were soldiers in the rear of the truck with a machine gun. They shot all thirteen of our men. Killed them all in just seconds." The old man paused his narration, took a sip of beer, and added quietly, "It was then we knew they weren't who they said they were. The English would never do such a thing. We knew then the Germans had come."

Luigi and I were silently absorbed in the story. The plaque in the cemetery made no mention of a massacre.

The old man seemed pleased in a way that someone was interested in the story of the town and his people. He continued in his soft gentlemanly voice. "The English across the way bombarded the village, but they were shooting at the Germans, not the Italians. The Germans fired back. Many people were killed as they tried to escape the shellings. Most of the villagers hid in the mountains, but it was winter and there was no food, so they couldn't stay there for very long."

He paused and looked into his empty glass. We ordered him another drink.

"The Germans defiled our church," he said, after a long draw on his beer. "They used our beautiful San Lorenzo as their stable. They put their animals in our church. And in our cemetery. They covered our most sacred places with manure."

There was obvious anger in our friend's voice—anger oddly blended, I thought, with resignation. He told the story slowly, and watched the effect of his words on us as Luigi translated.

"They put their animals in our church, shot our men in the square, and people starved to death in the woods. And they burned the town when they left." He spoke very softly now. "And when the war was over, many of our young men tried to leave but couldn't. We had been America's enemy. There was a price to pay for this treachery."

We stood by the bar. No one said a word.

"And how many people live here now?" Luigi asked, breaking the silence.

"Only about two hundred year-round, but a few are coming back and there are wealthy people from Rome and Naples who are now buying some of the old houses for winter apartments. They ski here now in winter, you know."

It was an incongruous notion—a shelled, burned-out village in 1945, a place where such misery and human loss occurred— now a winter playground. Did my people know about this? Did they not want to know? Surely these stories had crossed the Atlantic; our friend in the bar had carried them with him. Why hadn't we known? Had my grandparents lost interest by the time they heard of these events? Or were they still embarrassed by Mussolini, still uncomfortable to be identified with his Italy?

Or, like me, were they so thoroughly Americanized, the story was only one more about the horrors of war in Europe in a war of incalculable horrors?

I asked about our last relative here in Gamberale, my grandfather's brother Bartolomeo. The bartender finally spoke up; Bartolomeo was the barkeeper's grandfather. Another distant cousin discovered.

"What happened to him," I asked.

"Killed," he said in English. "The Germans left in the summer of 1944, but they left behind many mines. My grandfather stepped on one of those mines in February or April of 1945 and was blown apart."

I studied my distant cousin's face. We were of the same generation in this family, our grandfathers had been brothers, yet our stories and the stories of our grandfathers are so very different.

Part of Bartolomeo's story I had learned from my uncle Al. He was my grandfather's older brother and had returned to Italy after working in the United States and Argentina. He had worked for a time with my grandfather in the construction business in Pittsburgh, then had gone on to South America to try his hand at farming. He was apparently the only one of his brothers and sisters unable to adjust to the New World. He returned to and died in the Old.

I was hit with one of the ironies of history. At about the same time Bartolomeo was killed—in essence, by the retreating *Wehrmacht* in his small village high in the Italian mountains— his nephew and namesake was in far-off Iwo Jima, landing with the American Third Marine Division.

My uncle, also named Bartolomeo but called Eugene, was a U.S. Marine corporal. He would survive one of the bloodiest battles of the war. His uncle and namesake, a civilian, would die a soldier's death far from any combat.

. . .

My mind goes to a memory of a complete scene in Pittsburgh's Oakland section. It is summer in my memory. It is always summer when I remember that place. It was the season when I spent the most time there with my mother's family. It is always evening in that scene. The men are in short-sleeved shirts and drink from small green "pony" bottles of "Rolling Rock" beer.

And they talked in an animated and fervent fashion.

To anyone outside the family the conversation would have sounded like an atonal symphony, almost an argument. But I was an insider and not frightened, almost nonchalant about the level of noise. They discussed the most amazing gamut of subjects ranging from astronomy to zoology in passionate voices.

There is always a Sculli there in the memory; we called him "Elmer," but his birth name was Anthony. I see his pleasant face heavy with five-o'clock shadow, his dark, dancing eyes hinting at some merriment contrasting with an otherwise hangdog look. I hear his voice—sharp-edged and deep, yet subtle.

Elmer Sculli was a postal worker. He had been an American GI in the Second World War. An infantryman, he fought in North Africa, Sicily. He was sent to England, participated in the D-Day landings at Normandy—then wound up in the Battle of the Bulge in Belgium in December of 1944.

It was during the last battle that something broke in Elmer. He was sent to a hospital in England for a time, where apparently they could not fix what had been broken. He went home to Pittsburgh.

One Fourth of July, a couple of years after the war, Elmer went golfing with my father and uncle. Someone, probably children, set off firecrackers near the golf course. Elmer became nearly hysterical, threw his clubs into the air, and dove into the nearest sand trap. He shouted for my father and uncle to do the same.

My father would tell me that story quietly and privately. It was a lesson about war. His respect for our cousin was obvious, as well as his understanding.

I never knew Elmer very well. He would seldom talk directly with anyone other than my uncle Al. Most of the time he only wanted to discuss Shakespeare or Thoreau with my uncle, who was the family's expert in music, literature, and baseball.

Once, though, when I was in college and back in Pittsburgh for a brief summer visit, we sat on the porch of my uncle's apartment one hot, humid evening and talked about "On Walden Pond." My cousin was fascinated with Thoreau's concept of the individual. Elmer, who never married, carried a copy of Thoueau's work, dog-eared and underlined, with him at all times. It seemed to be his only hobby. That, and betting on the horses, where he always lost and seemed forever marooned in serious debt.

In my mind's eye of that time, in the summer in Pittsburgh, Elmer is always one of the men in shirtsleeves. A simple soldier who managed to see most of the important fighting in Europe, yet came home silently, his exploits told from father to son in respectful quiet.

He, too, was a grandson of Gamberale, a relative to the five other Scullis shot in the square when the Germans came. Was that why we hadn't heard the stories of this place? Weren't there enough troubles of our own? Was it just too much pain for people to recall?

The people from this little village, on both sides of the

ocean, participated in that bloody war, played a role in history, were deeply affected. In the end, the war would destroy Gamberale—and everything that came after the war would be different from everything that came before.

In America, where many of the villagers had emigrated, the war ended many of the ties to this village, this country, and to Europe in general. Because of the war the people in America changed. Their attitudes and their outlooks were thoroughly American now. A new generation took over—a generation born in the United States, whose primary definition of themselves would be simply "American." The birthplaces of their grandparents would become only distant curiosities.

For those first-generation Americans, Europe had become an embarrassment. The new third generation, those of us from the noisy, self-centered, postwar group called baby boomers, were far more interested in being the envied and victorious Americans than in identifying with any of the war's losers. We spent our childhood riding in the backseats of huge American gas guzzlers, studied abundant textbooks in what was then the world's best school system, and watched gripping American TV dramas like *Father Knows Best* on an unbelievably broad distribution of television sets.

All the while people in the towns of our grandparents were still finding the bones of loved ones in the fields.

And though I didn't realize it at the time, it was going to take several more trips and nearly two more years for me to get beyond the surface of that town and its story.

The drive back to Rome was quiet, Luigi and I lost in thought as we twisted and turned our way down the mountainside in the lingering twilight.

I had been most struck by the calm and equanimity of the villagers when they recounted the stories of their past. They told their stories factually, more like journalists than participants. And I was feeling guilty over driving a German car with German tourist plates in the area. I asked Luigi how his countrymen felt about the war, about the Germans.

"Do you know about the Moroccans?" he asked.

I didn't. It was going to be another of Luigi's circular answers.

"The Moroccans were part of the Allied troops who landed in the south of Italy and fought their way up the peninsula. All the way up they would take over little villages, rape all of the women, steal what they could. They were an embarrassment to the French with whom they fought. They left behind the *Marocchini,* or bastard children, in the hundreds. There are still many lawsuits pending against them."

He stopped and looked at me. "This is the sort of thing that happens in a war and has always happened in a war."

"The Americans did not behave that way," I said. "We had strict laws for our soldiers, codes. I was an American soldier, we were told to obey the law. We would have never tolerated that sort of behavior."

"You are right," said Luigi, "the Americans did not behave that way. But they did drop bombs on our cities. And the Moroccans were fighting on the same side with the Americans."

"We had no choice," I argued, "the Germans were here and they had come at the invitation and with the cooperation of your government."

Luigi smiled. "So," he asked, "if you had lived in a village during the war, which death would you have preferred, an English shell, American bomb, a German mine, or a Moroccan bullet?"

He let the question settle in.

"Why should we be mad at the Germans?" he continued. "This has been going on here for thousands of years. It's not just the Germans or the Europeans, it's people. I don't think we can live long enough to wipe this out of the human race, this need for war. There will be more like Yugoslavia, like parts of what used to be the Soviet Union, and in Asia. It is unavoidable. We can't really live with one another."

"You're so pessimistic," I argued. "The Europeans can have such a dark view of things. There has been peace now since the end of the Second World War here, isn't that something to celebrate? Isn't that proof we *can* live with one another in peace?"

"And you Americans are so optimistic," he replied. "Yes, there has been a so-called peace here for a long time now, but has there been peace in the world? What about Vietnam and Cambodia and now all over Africa, the Balkans, where there has never really been a peace since the Roman Empire? You Americans can't stop it with your bombs any more than we Europeans can stop it with our philosophers."

It was completely dark now. We had reached the Autostrada. Lights from the other motorists pierced the black sky and flooded the gray river of road.

We were following the same roads with our Volkswagen that the Roman legions had traveled on foot and horseback, descending the same passes, accelerating on the same flats. We were headed, once again toward the Eternal City, and found ourselves lost, once again, in eternal questions.

6

The Road Widens

Musical Roots . . .

"Once a musician, always a musician," John said. It was more dare than comment. John, another American ex-pat living in Rome, conducted an amateur jazz group. He needed a trumpet player. He had learned from Luigi that I had studied music; he was convinced I was the answer to his search. Luigi and I had bumped into John and his friend Enrico one evening in the Centro district.

"It's been twenty years since I played a horn in front of anyone or thing besides my stereo," I argued. "I haven't played for real people—not sober at least—since playing with a jazz combo in the army in Germany. That was a lot of years ago."

"*Beh,* you don't forget. Have you listened to music since the army?"

"Of course I have."

"Then your ear has continued to develop."

"Besides," his companion Enrico added, "you have a musical name."

"Yes, I know. All Italian names are musical."

"Maybe so, but yours is famous for music."

"What?"

"Francesco Paolo Paolicelli."

"That's my grandfather's name."

"Does your grandfather live in the South of Italy?"

"No. My grandfather is dead. He went to America before my father was born. How do you know the name?"

"Because Franceso Paolo Paolicelli is one of the most famous composers of band music in Italy today."

I'm sure my mouth gaped open as I stood there, feet glued to the cement of the Via del Corso, blinking and trying to comprehend the words I'd just heard.

I looked at Luigi. He shrugged. Obviously he didn't know any more than I about this composer with my grandfather's name.

"He what? Who? Where . . . ?"

"He is from somewhere near Matera. There's a famous music conservatory there."

"Matera!" I shouted to Luigi, "that's the town the clerks in Miglionico talked about. This could be my father's family."

"If you studied music you must be related," Enrico said calmly. "Music, like freckles, is inherited." He seemed sure of his assumption.

"Do you have a horn?" John was all business and wasn't much interested in searching for lost relatives.

"Not with me."

"Did I hear Luigi say you're going to Prague?"

I had recently returned to Rome from doing some television news consulting work in Slovenia. I had been asked to volunteer consults from time to time in the new countries that had been formed from the regions of what had been Yugoslavia, and had planned to drive to Lubijana with a stop in Prague. That changed when my travel had been arranged via rail. I returned to Italy committed to visit Prague in the near future. I had heard so much about the transition taking place there, I wanted very much to see it firsthand.

"I hope to visit Prague," I said. "Why?"

"They make good horns in Prague. Not very expensive. You should buy one and start practicing. We start rehearsing again in the fall."

Prague...

A few weeks later I found myself accepting the dare. I was sitting in the closet of my *pensione* in Prague playing scales on a new horn into my hanging clothing to muffle the sound.

In Prague, in the home of Franz Kafka, I underwent my own reverse metamorphosis. I did not, thankfully, turn into a huge bug, but, and for a second time in my life, a hopeful musician. In the years since I had abandoned music, I had often dreamed about taking the perfect solo. I still heard the chromatics and chords sing in my sleep; I hummed a thousand remembered tunes.

Now I felt like I had awakened from a Kafkaesque sleep in his city. A city where the smell of burning coal wafted over the morning chill, an odor reminiscent of the winters of my childhood in Pittsburgh. And, once again like the young music student I had been, I was hearing tonal transitions in the trolley bells, minor modulations in subway chimes, jazz sevenths in the baritone barking of vendors.

I marveled at how quickly the years had passed. The man whose reflection I saw in the opposing subway window as I rode about Prague was balding and paunchy. Young girls wouldn't even consider glancing his way. The virile twenty-three-year-old, however, was still running around in my brain wondering why the paunchy guy was looking back from the glass.

And now, the balding, chubby guy was carrying a trumpet again, as though the instrument had never left his hand. A trumpet that represented my life's savings when I was sixteen. Now it was a dalliance, a return to something long lost, yet somehow no less important.

I was in Prague carrying a trumpet. There was something surreal about the geography. Wenceslas square is there, a main junction point for the city, the convergence of subway and highway. The Square lies in front of the State Museum, which overlooks the hill sloping toward the old city. A gigantic bronze statue of a mounted medieval King Wenceslas overlooks the downward slope.

The first tune I ever learned on the horn was the Christmas carol "Good King Wenceslas." I must have been ten or eleven years old and had absolutely no idea of just who the Good King might be, but it was a fairly easy tune to play. Like all beginners, I desperately wanted to play something that sounded like actual music.

I practiced my lessons in my parents' bedroom, the only room in our small house where I could have a modicum of privacy, along with enough space for a chair and a music stand. Probably the second or third time I played the tune, my mother came into the room singing. She knew the tune, could sing the lyrics.

> *Good King Wenceslas looked out,*
> *on the feast of Steven,*
> *when the snow lay round about,*
> *deep and crisp and even . . .*

I passed King Wenceslas with my brand-new trumpet and remembered his hymn and my mother's voice singing in the still afternoon as I practiced on my first old secondhand horn. I've never forgotten the carol. How desperately I would love to hear my mother sing it once more.

In the evening, in the rain, on the day I returned to trumpeting, I walked about the bottom of the hill in Prague where the good king sat. I passed a nightclub, a place that would have been called a "honky-tonk" in my mother's day. The disco spilled its noise into the damp night.

I listened to another tune I hadn't heard for a long time, "My Happiness." It is an old song and was my mother's favorite. The version I heard that night was instrumental; saxophones played the melody. *"Evening shadows make me blue . . ."* they intoned in harmony. On the *blue* they "bent" the note. If the note was a word it would have sounded like Blu-ooh-ooh.

I was in college in Southern California, writing an arrangement of the same song when my mother died. It was to be a present for her. I worked on it whenever she left the house and I could be alone at the old pink Ivers and Pond piano. I bought the ancient upright for one hundred dollars and stored it in the dining room of our house in Costa Mesa, where we had moved from Pittsburgh during my junior year in high school.

I never finished the arrangement, but I do remember I wasn't bending the note on blu-ooh, I was changing the rhythm. Before too long the only thing I was arranging was my army foot locker. "My Happiness" became a part of a remembered past; it certainly didn't describe my state of being.

The tune persisted. The song and the memory floated above the din in the damp Prague night, a sound filled with music and the voices and energy of foreign youths on distant adventures. My mother would have liked that, I think, in a melancholy way.

Rome . . .
Mendicanti—The Beggars

We could see them everywhere, no matter where we walked in Rome. Some sat on old, faded blankets and reached up with a cup or small box to those passing by, never making eye contact, their clothing tattered, hair unkempt. Others stood at strategic intersections, modestly dressed, coats and dresses clean and pressed and held out a desperate hand, giving direct, ardent, pleading looks. Still others, gray and stooped by age, women wearing the widow's black of an older generation, offered inexpensive flowers or holy cards in return for "donations." They were a class of professional beggars ranging in age from young adult to very senior citizen and well beyond anything I'd ever experienced in the States.

"This is part of our heritage, especially in Rome," Luigi explained. "Beggars here can make two hundred or three hundred thousand lire a day, or nearly three hundred dollars. It has always been this way."

"They aren't resented or feared?"

"No." Luigi scoffed. "Why should they be? They aren't criminals. These poor *gente* generally aren't Italian, and there is not enough employment for everyone, anyway. These people come from wherever there is trouble."

"What amazes me is how generous your countrymen are." I had often seen Italians handing money to beggars, and some of the donors didn't seem much better off than those they gave to. The Romans appeared to be a giving lot.

"Don't forget that Rome is the head of the church, it's a Christian act to give to the poor. And it's good for the soul." Luigi grinned. "You burn less."

"Burn?"

"Yes, purgatory. You know, the church used to offer plenary indulgences for the giving of alms. Do you know what I mean?"

"Oh, yes," I replied. "You can't go to Catholic schools and not know about plenary indulgence."

"So then you know you got time off from purgatory if you give to the needy."

"But what if they aren't needy? What if they're just lazy?"

"Ah, that's the beauty of the system. It's what is in your heart that counts. So a man has nothing to gain by begging if he only wants money and a donor has everything to gain, since he is trying to help those less fortunate. He gets less time in purgatory and feels better about himself. The system works very well and has worked well for a long time. We are a naturally generous people anyway. Most of the world's Christian beggars can only dream of Rome."

142

I thought about Luigi's comments as we strolled up the main boulevard toward the Vatican. There had been a great discussion lately in the media about heroin addiction. The Italian solution to the problem was to sell sterile needles to anyone asking for one. Jail sentences were handed out to those convicted of dealing drugs, but users were treated in hospitals. Luigi argued this was more humane than locking people up in jails for an addiction. Health care was free and for anyone in need. The system did have its points and did, I thought, reflect the general attitude of the Italians I knew.

Like the way they treated beggars. Luigi and his contemporaries never dreamed that anyone would beg or become addicted to drugs without serious misfortune or mental illness, and they looked at these people with compassionate eyes.

In front of us on our walk that evening was one of the most photographed and revered buildings in all the world, the Vatican, with its instantly recognizable dome designed by Micalangelo, and Bernini's crowning achievement, the design of the grand piazza.

"I guess pilgrims and beggars have been coming to Rome and walking these same streets since there was a Pope," I mused.

"Yes, but not this street," Luigi said. "We are on the Via della Conciliazione—the Street of Conciliation. Mussolini had this street built as a gift to the Pope for recognizing the nation of Italy, and so visitors could have a good view of the Vatican as they approached. Do you know the story of the American braggart and the Vatican?"

"Please, tell me."

"A man from New York came to Rome for the first time during the 1920s and paid a hansom cab driver to trot his horse around the city and show him the sites. The driver was well educated and pointed out all the main buildings and churches, telling the American with great pride the period during which they had been constructed and how long it had taken to build them.

"Each time, his fare would reply, 'Oh, that's nothing. We built one twice as big in New York and it only took us a couple of months.'

"The driver was irritated, but said nothing. He continued the tour until he turned onto the little street that led to the Vatican, before Mussolini built the *strada* we're on right now. 'Say, what's that up ahead?' the American asked—"

I interrupted. "And the cabby said, 'Gee, I don't know. It wasn't there last week.' "

He gave me the Luigi-eye. "You know that joke?" he asked incredulously.

"My grandfather used to tell it all the time."

"I don't believe it." He laughed.

We saw several more beggars that evening as we strolled through the Vatican and environs. "They are God's children," Luigi said at one point. "And it could be you or me if things were just slightly different in our lives."

Luigi's comments captured my thoughts. I wondered about the generosity I'd seen on the part of the Italians. I was never comfortable sitting in traffic and having Algerians or Albanians approach the car and ask to wash the windshield. The cleaners were always men, always foreigners, and a polite group who would not touch the car if waved off. I noticed most Italians gave freely and seemed to appreciate the service.

That evening by the Vatican with Luigi I began studying the street people more closely. Over time, and as I walked about the many other neighborhoods in the Centro, the notion came to me to make a photo-essay depicting the rich contrasts of the acts of begging I saw each day; the extended hands and the giving of alms; the faces of those in need and of those not; some beggars' eyes direct and piercing, their posture and stance a story in themselves. Ultimately, I abandoned the project because I felt it would be exploiting these all too real people, obviously in distress. But their images burned into my memory.

There was an old woman beggar near my favorite Roman site, the Pantheon, who could have been a model for a Grimm's fairy tale. She was nearly doubled over from an apparent backbone malady. She had to lift her head with great effort in order to make eye contact with the passing crowds. I never saw her wear anything other than a long black dress. Her brilliant white hair was partially covered by a heavy black scarf. Her old and lined face was very pale and pink, the cheeks naturally rouged as if she were living in a cold climate. Her nose was prominent and hooked and her mouth was perpetually drawn into a grimace.

The old woman carried a bouquet of brilliant, scarlet roses in a woven basket. She offered them with a shaky, extended arm, holding them out for passersby to see. She had no set fee for the flowers; she'd take whatever was offered. I never saw her in the evening, only during the day, and always standing in the shade of a building overhang or portico.

When I first spotted her, my natural cynicism wondered if her appearance wasn't just a little too "central casting" for the old woman beggar. I'd visit the beautiful Piazza della Rotonda often and, as time went by, I'd seen the old woman in a variety of weather. I'd watched her difficult, and probably painful, movement about the narrow streets and broad plazas in and around the Pantheon. I came to respect her work ethic. I often gave her a few thousand lire without taking a flower. She was impassive as she took the money and chanted a monotone *grazie*. I hoped, just maybe, I would burn a little less.

Then there was Stewart.

I met Stewart one day as he took a coffee break at a local bar. I had seen him just a few minutes earlier begging from the steps of a nearby church. He ordered his espresso with a decided English accent. I offered to pay for his coffee and we struck up a conversation.

Stewart was from Australia. He was a beggar. It was his way of life. He'd practiced his craft in his native country, England, Germany, and now Italy.

"Italy's the best," he said. "People here don't look down their nose at you. I was always being hassled in England. One night in Germany a policeman broke my arm with his club because I didn't move fast enough. I was drunk and couldn't move very fast, so the bastard hit me. The Italian police leave you alone or take you to a hospital."

I estimated Stewart's age at about forty. He had a scruffy beard and was skeleton thin. His clothing seemed adequate and basically clean, except his pants were about six inches too short for his long legs. His socks came only partly up his ankles, and didn't quite make up for the lack of trouser—about two inches of shin was exposed when Stewart stood. He wore a knitted cap that, when removed, revealed a full head of completely undisciplined and uncombed brown-gray hair, matted every which way about his head.

"You really a journalist?" he asked, as he noisily sucked down his coffee in a single slurp.

I nodded.

"You know," he knitted his eyebrows and took on a serious expression, "I'm really concerned about this situation in Chad. Have you done any stories on that? I mean, the world should pay more attention to these sorts of things. Sub-Saharan Africa never gets the attention it deserves."

I didn't know how to reply. I didn't really know anything about sub-Saharan Africa, either. I asked Stewart for details.

I would bump into Stewart from time to time over the nearly three years I lived in Rome. It was always the same; Stewart was just sobering up from a drunk and accepted his recovery as a natural part of things. He'd been in and out of the hospital in San Giovanni several times, but he seemed to have no interest in making any behavioral changes. He made enough money begging to support his lifestyle and seemed content with that.

Stewart never wanted to talk about begging with me. He always brought up some article in the newspaper about distant wars or upheaval. He was distraught over the situation in Bosnia and felt the Europeans should be doing more to help the Albanians get established in the new world economy. He seemed completely oblivious to the fact that he made these comments while wearing pants that didn't cover all of his legs and old, cast-off shirts with holes in them. He felt that since I was a journalist, I could fix what was wrong in the world with a well-placed story or two.

The last I heard, Stewart had moved to Africa.

My old college friend and Amendolara doctor lookalike, Mike Gibb, was visiting from California. One beautiful spring afternoon we rode a bus to Centro and walked over to the Pantheon, erected on what had been the ancient Campus

Martius—the Field of Mars—where the Roman Legions had trained during Republican times. I was conducting my special tour for sojourning dignitaries.

I led Mike through a through a warren of ancient, narrow streets as we approached the Piazza della Rotonda from the northeast. In that way, the piazza appeared as it was intended, a great open space contrasting with the narrow streets, and welcoming the visitor with its size, fountain, and activity.

I loved the piazza. I had learned to time my visits carefully and to arrive in late afternoon to catch the setting sun bracket the Pantheon's perfect dome. There was a majesty to the building's proportions, an echo in its dramatic portico, especially at sunset.

Of the many ancient buildings and sites in Rome, for me the Pantheon is the most evocative. It is the only building to have remained essentially intact from Roman Imperial times. Originally built during Caesar Augustus's reign, the vaulted ceiling was an amazing feat. The dome's dimensions are perfect; the diameter is precisely the same as the interior height: 142 feet.

The Pantheon's architecture couldn't be duplicated or copied for over a thousand years—not until Brunelleschi's work at the Florence Cathedral of 1420–36. Brunelleschi spent much time in Rome studying the Pantheon's structure in order to build his own dome in Florence. It was his greatest achievement and marked the official beginning of the Italian Renaissance.

The size and weight of the Pantheon's dome wasn't surpassed until the Astrodome was built in Houston in 1968. There was no corresponding Renaissance to accompany that particular construction.

Mike's reaction was like most who first entered the piazza

and walked into the cool of the shadow of the ancient building. He stood silently and studied the place, then sighed an appreciative sigh.

Entering the plaza is like walking back through time. No one can visit and not contemplate how many eyes have rested on this building during the past eighteen centuries. The original structure built by Augustus was struck by lightning and destroyed by fire, the current building was rebuilt and slightly reconfigured from A.D. 118 to 126. It is truly a place that ties us firmly to the past and the transcendence of history.

Often, as Mike and I did on this gentle evening, I'd enjoy a slice of pizza from a nearby stand that featured the Neapolitan style—thick crust in big, square pieces and topped with thin slices of zucchini or eggplant or fresh Gorgonzola. I enjoyed my snack and watching the passing and constant crowd.

Mike and I sat for a long while that evening on the steps of the fountain in the middle of the plaza, and enjoyed the pizza, cool shade, and lengthening shadows. The Pantheon's fountain is one of the many erected by the Popes during the Renaissance to take credit for local sites the Romans had actually built.

Pope Boniface IV "reconsacrated"—removed any pagan references from—the Pantheon and blessed it as a church on March 6, 609. It was renamed St. Mary of the Martyrs. Raphael, the prince of Renaissance painters, is buried in the building's wall, along with several other state dignitaries.

I told Mike my favorite story about the portico we faced; it seems that during the late Middle Ages, a group of fishermen decided to set up their stalls on the building's porch and vend their smelly wares. Everyone from priest to bishop to cardinal to Pope tried to evict them, but the big portico offered shade, relief from the sun in the summer, and protection from the rain and wind in winter. The fishermen weren't going anywhere. No matter what the religious authorities tried, the fishermen returned. For me, it seemed an amusing irony that a group of humble fish hawkers could thwart the will of what was then the most powerful institution on earth.

Another favorite story deals with the interior of the dome; stepped rings of solid concrete and originally decorated with gold—which was stripped and taken away by the Catholic Church during one of the many building campaigns of the Renaissance. There had been much criticism of the church for this "theft" of antique Rome. As it turns out, engineers now say had the gold remained in its original place, the dome would have been pulled down by its sheer weight. By removing it, the church inadvertently saved the building for our times.

As Mike and I enjoyed the sights and sounds of the plaza, we were approached by the regular Pantheon beggar—or, in the more current politically correct argot, a "non-domiciled" man. I had seen the man several times in the plaza dozing on the drainage grates or panhandling. As opposed to the old lady with the roses—who was never in the piazza after sunset and never actually begged—this fellow's main interest was in panhandling at any hour and, judging by the smell of him, drinking.

He was a man of indiscernible years—he could have been thirty or sixty—the harsh exposure he endured made both his skin and his motions seem aged. His clothes were filthy and ragged and everything about him, from his hair to his matted beard and his torn clothing, was gray and faded.

As he approached us, Mike and I reacted in the manner I had seen most Americans display when confronted by street people; we shifted about uneasily and looked the other way.

We would have been far more comfortable had he not come our way at all. We were saved from confrontation by a tourist who offered a paper note, distracting the man's approach.

Later that evening, the beggar approached a group of German tourists as they sat on the steps of the fountain facing the main portico. They ridiculed the man and laughed rudely. They spoke only in German—probably assuming he couldn't understand—and poked fun, but offered no money, nor food.

Mike and I sat there and silently witnessed this scene.

Some time later—it was now fully dark—a well-dressed trio of Italians, two men and a woman, occupied the same seat on the steps where the German group had been. It was easy to see by the way they were dressed the Italians were quite afflu-ent. They spoke softly among themselves until our disheveled friend reappeared and approached them.

They greeted him gently. I could hear their accents, they were from the North and spoke a clear and lilting Italian. One of the gentleman stood and offered the beggar (*mendicante* in Italian—a mendicant—a much kinder term) a cigarette, which he quickly accepted. The group invited him to sit. The woman slipped a shawl over his shoulders. The other gentleman went to a nearby café and returned with coffee in a paper cup. The beggar seemed to greatly enjoy the smoke and the chat. The few snippets of conversation I heard concerned Vittorio Eman-uele II, the Italian king also buried in the Pantheon, and the current state of the Italian government.

Mike and I exchanged looks.

"They're talking about politics," I said. "They're discussing politics and the former king of Italy and talking with the beggar as if he were a visiting head of state." I was fascinated.

"You know," said Mike, equally taken by the scene, "I think

I just learned an important lesson. Only the Italians realized that fellow's humanity. We tried to ignore him and the Germans poked fun." He shook his head slowly. "I like these people. I'm a little ashamed we didn't think to buy the man a coffee."

It was a typical evening in the shadow of the ancient and magnificent building and one of the many reasons I came to feel so drawn to the place.

A Song of the South . . .

Luigi and I attacked the phone books for Matera. There were over two hundred Paolicelli households listed. I had no idea of where to start. I listed all of the Francesco Paolos and copied them all onto a big yellow pad.

That night I began the first of what was to become hundreds of phone calls looking for the correct family. I got nowhere. Some people heard my accent, asked where I was from, and hung up. Others said they didn't know any relatives who had gone to America. Still others made it clear I was annoying them.

"You have to understand something about the Southerners," explained Luigi. "They are very suspicious. Business is still conducted face-to-face. We Italians don't like doing business on the telephone, especially in the South."

"But what are they suspicious of? I merely want information about a man who died seventy years ago."

Luigi tugged on his goatee. "Do you have any idea of how many Americans come back to Italy and claim inheritance? The people who stayed here feel they have to protect themselves against someone who now thinks their dead grandfather was entitled to property in the old country."

"You mean this has been a problem?"

"Yes, especially since we have become a wealthy country once again. Look—" He gestured to all of the notes and papers littering the dining room table. "This isn't going to do you much good. You need to have a personal introduction to someone in Matera."

The search was becoming frustrating. Since first going to Miglionico and hearing of the Matera connection I had written the consulate office back in Houston, the records office in Matera, and the national records office in Rome. The consulate had written to Rome as well. I had received letters from Rome and Matera in return saying my grandfather was a mystery, no records could be found. Now, apparently, I had to deal with a Southern psychology as well.

I lamented my situation to Sebash over lunch later that week.

"Think of it from their point of view," he said as our *Polpette* were served—finely chopped veal and seasonings rolled into what Americans call "meatballs."

"What is their point of view?"

"First the Greeks came, then the Romans, then the Saracens, then the Normans, then Longobards, roving brigands, Spaniards. Southern Italy has always had strangers coming in and dominating. Mistrust is genetic. They trust no one and believe no one at first, or even second sight."

"So what do I need to do?"

"You're going to have to know someone in the area who can help. Maybe your family in Miglionico? They won't be comfortable talking with strangers."

I tasted the savory veal, lightly basted in a delicate tomato sauce. There was no such thing as "spaghetti and meatballs" in

Italy. One ordered pasta as either entrée or antipasti and meat as an entrée only. The American tradition was an obvious hybrid of this form of dining.

"But the records . . ."

"The records mean nothing," Sebash said as he sipped his red wine cut with mineral water. The Italians seldom drank wine straight and I had never seen anyone take more than one glass per meal. "As you've seen in Gamberale, wars happen in this country on a frequent basis. Records are destroyed. But we know your grandfather lived. After all, you're here to look for him."

Over the next few months I continued to strike out in Basilicata in my search for Francesco, despite taking Sebash's advice and driving the six-hour journey several times.

My only real accomplishment during this time was making photographs. Francesco and Caterina's first child, my uncle Bill, had been born on the "Street of the Second Fountain," a place that no longer existed. After asking several people, I finally found an old woman who remembered where the street had been. She said there had been an earthquake many years ago and that part of the village had been reconstructed. I took a photo of what was left of the area.

Aunt Mamie had been born on the Via Forno Castello— "the Street of the Castle Oven." The building still stood and was a grand-looking white house with an arched plaster entryway. The photo that I made became a prize possession for my aunt. She had no recollection of her first three years of life in Italy and was happy to see she had been born in such pleasant circumstances.

The street's name, the Oven of the Castle, reminded me of one of the very few stories my grandmother told of Italy; she remembered that no one had ovens or stoves in their own homes; because of the heat and expense, they were used communally—just as they had been in Roman times. The building where the big oven had been in Miglionico was still at the end of the street where my aunt had been born. It must have been the place Grandma recalled.

In olden times, the women of the village took their bread dough and other foods to the public oven, where they did all their baking for a small fee. My grandmother said the tradition continued in New York when she first arrived, and claimed the custom was what made pizza such a popular food.

The castle the street name referred to was the Castle Poderoso, an ancient and run-down place. Laundry hung in the courtyard on the day I poked my head through the huge and ill-repaired gate. A single family lives in part of the structure today, the apparent heirs of the ancient fortress. The only reference I could find for the place was for 1481, when local barons met there in an unsuccessful plot to overthrow the Spanish king, Ferdinand of Aragon. The texts I found didn't say what happened to the plotters.

The few people I saw as I moved about the village did not acknowledge me in any way. Only one man approached me on the day I stood some distance from the *casa* on Via Forno Castello to make a wide-angle picture. He asked why I was so interested in the house. He was pleased to hear my family had lived there. He gave me his card; he was a musician and advertised his band for hire. He was polite, but in a hurry. I had wanted to pursue the tenuous musical connection.

My search for Francesco was complicated. I had drawn a circle on the map around the village of Miglionico, where he probably lived at one point and had definitely been married.

Grandma had certainly lived there after he had gone off to America, and I had the photographic proof.

I went to all the villages in the circle I had drawn and searched for Francesco's birth records. There was nothing. I checked all the documents available in the small surrounding hamlets for the entire decade in which Francesco had been born, but still to no avail. I made several appointments at the cathedral. All of them were canceled for one reason or another.

I was determined, Italian passport or not, to find *official* proof of my grandfather's Italian birth.

The search had become a matter of principle for me. Francesco's life had been taken so quickly; there *had* to be some definitive proof of his existence.

But the pace of Southern Italy and my haste were not synchronized. I was learning, like all things in Italy, my quest was going to take much more time and effort than I had anticipated.

Portuense . . .

I was settling into some basic routines in Rome in between my forays into Basilicata and the Abruzzi, and I was learning a great deal more about the place. And as my knowledge of the city increased, so did my fascination and love.

Luigi introduced me to a little lunch-only trattoria just off the Via Vittorio Emanuele, a place only the locals and a few chosen visitors knew about. Much of Rome was like that; the city was described by several writers as a beautiful and intriguing woman who reveals very little of herself to a stranger. You had to take time and make an effort to truly know her.

Meanwhile, I had become known in my neighborhood. Certainly, at least, at the *alimentari* (basic grocery store) and the *frutteria* (fruit and vegetable stand) where I'd been shopping for well over a year by now. The husband-and-wife team at the grocery were very friendly and always spoke a simplistic Italian as I asked my childlike questions.

One day I inquired in the *alimentari* about popcorn, an addiction I couldn't manage to rid myself of, even in Italy. I didn't know quite how to say the word, so I literally translated, "dried corn which was fried." In response I got the now common, *"Cosa?"* accompanied with wrinkled nose and brow.

Some moments later I found exactly what I was looking for hidden away on a lower shelf. I held it up with pride to show the proprietor. "This is the fried corn," I said.

"Oh," he replied, "You wanted *pop-a-corn.*"

I should have known.

At the *frutteria,* I was always greeted very formally by the red-haired proprietess. I quickly learned that a single, middle-aged man was a rarity at the shops in my quarter, just as it seemed to be in all of Italy. The aproned, slightly heavyset woman always addressed me as *Signore,* and made a point of carefully studying her fruit and vegetables for the best selections.

In Italy the customer never touches the produce; this is considered unsanitary. Instead, there is an elaborate game of pointing and gesturing. All customers are made to feel that only the best selections are made on their behalf.

The fruit stand was always filled with children bustling about, most of whom were carrot-topped and obviously belonged to the proprietess. The selection and purchasing took time, but the show was entertaining. In Rome, there was no such thing as that peculiar American invention, the "quick stop."

I was also learning to shop in the Italian version of the supermarket. Sounds mundane to the average American, but going to the supermarket in Italy is like going to a matinee.

In the States, as a journalist, I have been in markets or other public places in the aftermath of earthquakes, hurricanes, and other forms of natural disaster. There was always a palpable energy in the air at those times, an aura of joy juxtaposed with tragedy. People were unusually active and talkative—there was a sense of celebration. They had survived a dramatic event and now felt a strong connection to their community, their fellow man.

This, I found, is the *normal* experience in an Italian supermarket. The Italians had survived another day and celebrated the fact by shopping.

They pushed their shopping carts in the exact manner they drove their cars. There was madness in the aisles. Women, looking in the opposite direction, plowed into unattended carts. Friends and acquaintances gathered in the middle of aisles, carts in a cluster, to discuss in great detail a label, evaluate a new product. Some simply abandoned their purchases and wandered off on solitary expeditions as the derelict carts caused huge pileups in the aisles and extending around the corners.

Just as I was ready to call the experience total lunacy, some sort of incident would occur. One day, as I pushed my cart by the frozen foods, a distracted young man pushed in front of me and reached into the freezer case, cutting off an elderly lady from her frozen zucchini. He saw the expression on the woman's face and realized his rudeness. He apologized very formally. He explained to the woman that he was in a hurry to pick up frozen peas for that evening's meal and he'd be on his way.

"What," demanded the well-dressed lady, "do you plan on doing with those?"

The man explained the special recipe his wife was preparing.

The elderly lady told him, just this side of disdain and with the eloquence women reserve for speaking to younger men who just aren't ready for complete membership in civilization, that he had the totally wrong peas for such a concoction. The ones he had chosen would not work properly for that particular dish. She directed him to another aisle, for what I think were canned peas.

The young man was grateful; he thanked her profusely. *La Signora* sighed wearily and continued to inspect the freezer case.

There were always very long lines at the registers, the kind of queues I'd found in America only on the big holidays. In Rome, the crowd occurred daily. As we customers awaited our turns, carts parked angled sideways so others could pass in the crowded aisle. I'd use the time in the checkout line to study my companions.

On one memorable afternoon the mental snapshot remains vivid: a young mother two carts ahead of me kibitzed with her husband as he teased their five-or-so-year-old daughter. The mother noticed something in the basket of the older woman directly ahead of me.

"Say," she asked, "how do you prepare your *melanzane*?"

They were, to my knowledge, complete strangers, but it was older woman to younger woman, an important bond in Italy, and they discussed this recipe for the next several minutes, going into great detail about food preparation.

In the meantime, the little girl was helping everyone in line unload their carts. No one objected; the child was completely involved in the task.

One line over, a woman massaged the middle back of her husband as he leaned over the groceries. There was strength in her touch, her husband was thin and muscular, wore an Izod shirt and designer-frame sunglasses.

There was a young man across the way tossing a toddler up in the air, the child squealing with delight and laughter, as the man kissed the child after each descent.

Two lines over a middle-aged couple leaned against one another. At one point, the woman looked up into her husband's eyes and smiled, then moved her forehead upward in an obviously habitual gesture to receive a kiss. I felt jealous of the embrace. It was very public, very sweet, and went completely unnoticed by the others in line. There seemed to be a continual tenderness among the Italians that went to my *straniero,* or stranger's heart.

To an American, much of this shopping madness would seem dysfunctional. But I was learning to read the subtleties and coming to understand it was really a very polite process. Like everything Italian, these activities were filled with noise and energy and, like all important events, took place around food. They were survivors shopping in the supermarket. It was another completed day, there was food to be prepared, meals to be served, love to be made.

I wanted this life, or some form of it. I wanted to take it with me wherever I went. I hoped the Italians appreciated what they had.

7

Andata e Ritorno (Round-trip)

I had returned to the States for the holidays. I made a quick stop in Houston to clear up some financial matters, then made my annual Christmas trek to Pittsburgh.

This year, I was armed with partially filled genealogy pages that I gave to every member of my family for their completion. I was collecting birth dates, places, names, children, anniversaries—all of the data—in one place. I passed out the forms like homework assignments as my father and I made holiday visits around the city.

Dad was fascinated with my stories of the search for his father's family. We talked constantly as we drove about the icy, potholed roads.

I had forgotten how drab Pittsburgh could be in winter. The steel mills had long since stopped belching their black clouds into the sky, and the pollution levels when they had operated were always greatly exaggerated by outsiders. But I still felt a darkness to the place.

There had been many changes in Pittsburgh in the past few years. The local economy had undergone a sweeping transformation as the industrial and financial bases evolved into the new global economy. It was a new glass and steel and shining city, but to me, Pittsburgh would always be the home we left—with mixed emotions—for sunny Southern California. We had missed the extended family—more than any of us had ever suspected we would—but we never missed the climate.

On one of our first holiday visits that year, Dad, my sister, brother, and I drove out of the city and down the Monongahela Valley—Pennsylvania's industrial heart. Our destination was Clairton, the mill town where Dad had been raised.

The place now struck me as absolutely bleak. The coke mill still operated, but the huge steel works that once filled this valley with smoke and employment had been shut down. The downtown shopping area had stopped developing and changing sometime in the 1950s. The streets, buildings—even some of the people—looked run-down, like a set for a Hollywood movie about the Great Depression.

Our clan gathered at my uncle Jim's small home. Uncle Jim, like his father and uncle before him, spent his entire working life in the mills. His son, my cousin Frankie, still worked there.

The mills had been a lure for the Italian, Croatian, Serbian, and Polish migrations two generations earlier. Steel mills didn't require higher education or language skills, only strong backs and the desire to work. When my father was a child, the entire valley had been filled with first-generation immigrants working in the mills. The babble of languages must have sounded like a United Nations session.

Uncle Jim and Frankie were the last in our family to remain tied to both the valley and the legacy.

My clan was, of course, curious about my adventures into our family's past.

"Everyone in our family could play a musical instrument," my aunt Mamie said casually, as we discussed the Italian composer with my grandfather's name.

"I thought I was the only musician," I replied.

"Of your generation. But my father and all his brothers all sang and played instruments. Your godfather, George Manicone, was also from our village. He was so talented he became a professional—he played the guitar, mandolin, and clarinet. He gave it up to raise his family, but when we were young all the women loved George. He always had a mandolin or ukulele, and he knew how to play all of the songs. When George was around everybody sang."

We sat at the kitchen table and passed around the photos I had taken in Italy. The afternoon went by like a fast-paced talk show; there were nonstop questions and answers. I had obviously struck a nerve.

"Grandma used to say someone had put the 'evil eye' on her husband's family," Aunt Mamie said, when asked about her father and his two brothers. We laughed at the old-fashioned saying.

"Why did she say that?" I asked.

"My father—your grandfather Francesco—and his two brothers, Raphael and Antonio, came to America as young men. I came here as a little girl with your grandma in 1911.

My father had been back and forth between Italy and New York at least three or four times. He and his brothers set up a business in Manhattan. They collected old newspapers, bundled them, and resold them as packaging material."

"See that," said my brother, "you're not the first journalist in the family. Sounds like our grandfather was in the newspaper business."

"He had to work with a horse, too. And I thought anchormen could be trouble."

"So why the 'evil eye'?" my brother persisted.

"Well, poor Uncle Ralph, he was killed not too long after we came to America. He was run over by the wagon they used in their business. It was horrible."

I looked around the table at our surviving clan. There were a dozen or so of us, each obviously fascinated by Aunt Mamie's story.

"Then, Uncle Antonio died in the terrible flu that broke out after the First World War. I remember your grandfather coming back to our apartment on Cornelia Street after his brother died. He really took it hard. He cried and cried." She paused and carefully rearranged the photographs on the table in front of her, as if searching for some magic combination or juxtaposition of the images.

"Daddy was a big man, he loved to play with us children, loved to sing. He and his brothers had been always together; now he was alone. Then Daddy was killed in a mill accident less than a year after leaving New York. We had come here, to 'the country,' where Grandma didn't have to worry about losing her children in the busy city streets. All three boys dead. All three died young, two of them violently. It seemed like a curse."

"Were there any children from the brothers, any cousins?"

"Daddy had a sister who married and stayed in New York. We kept in touch for a while, but eventually lost contact. No one wrote much in those days and long-distance telephone calls were a luxury beyond our means.

"Uncle Antonio had a family, I think one or two kids, but his widow was young. She remarried—those kids knew her second husband as their father. It was really very sad; those boys had such ambition."

"So Grandma blamed all that misfortune on the *'maloc-chio'*—the 'evil eye'?"

"It seemed to Grandma to be the only logical explanation." She blinked back a tear.

"My question," I said, after having answered an endless stream of interrogatories, "is why we don't know Vito Buono. Everything checks out, it's the same family in Miglionico, it's definitely Grandma's family, but who is Vito?"

I studied the faces of our group over the trays of cookies, carafes of wine, and cups of coffee. My father looked as puzzled as me as to Vito's identity.

"It has to be Uncle Charlie," I said, "but how come no one ever knew him by his right name?"

Aunt Theresa exchanged a telling smile with Uncle Jim. She let out a long sigh. She and Uncle Jim had lived with, and taken care of, Uncle Charlie until his death.

Grandma had lived there as well. Then one day, after over forty years of widowhood, she finally took off her black dresses and married a suitor who had been after her for decades.

If anyone knew of any "bones in the cupboard," it would be Uncle Jim or Aunt Theresa.

"You tell them, Jim," she said.

Uncle Jim looked at me and smiled. "Uncle Charlie was Vito," he said softly.

"So why all the mystery?" I asked. There was a general murmur about the table.

"Uncle Charlie was a foreman at the mills. Maybe he thought 'Vito' was too ethic sounding?" my sister suggested.

"He changed his name from Vito Buono to Charlie Span. He wanted to be American," Aunt Gloria said.

"Right." My brother laughed. "And he spoke with an Italian accent, used Italian phrases, and always had a flask of home-made 'Dago Red.' No one would have ever guessed he was Italian. He must have really had 'em fooled." We all laughed at the absurd notion.

"It was about his son and his wife," Aunt Theresa said quietly. We all turned and looked at her as she dipped a cookie into her coffee and slowly savored the mixture of anisette, coffee, sugar, and cream.

"What wife and son?" asked my father. "He and Aunt Mary didn't have any children."

"His wife and son in Italy."

It was as if a small bomb had gone off in the room. We all sat silent in the shock waves for several moments. Then everyone started talking at once.

"You knew about that? . . ."

"Wife and son where? . . ."

"You mean the Angelo whose name I found in Miglionico? The wife who went back because she didn't like America?" I asked.

"Yes," said Aunt Theresa in a tone suitable for confession. "The boy came to the house right here once," she said. "Came in the middle of the night, it seemed, everyone was in bed. I answered the door. He only spoke Italian and wanted to see 'Vito Buono.' I didn't know who he was talking about so I called Uncle Charlie."

Our entire clan hung on her every word. All eating and drinking had stopped.

"So what happened?" asked Uncle Chuck—who had been named after Uncle Charlie, whose real name, it turned out, wasn't Charlie.

"Uncle didn't want anything to do with him. He threw him out into the street, said to never come back."

"Holy cow!" There was a collective exclamation.

"But why?"

"There was obviously bad blood."

"Angelo Buono in Miglionico said Vito's wife didn't like America. Maybe that's what it was all about. I asked about the mystery wife in Basilicata. They thought she had remarried and moved away. No one seemed to know very much."

"But that's just it," said Uncle Jim. "There was no 'remarry' for them. They were married in the church. You couldn't get a divorce. Especially not in those days."

"Do you mean Uncle Charlie and Aunt Mary were never married?" My father sounded astonished.

"Yes," said Uncle Jim. "And Uncle didn't want anything to do with his son or the Old World. They had rejected him, I guess, and he changed his name and became somebody else. I don't think he wanted any connection with Italy or Miglionico or any of it. That's probably why no one stayed in touch."

"How long were Uncle Charlie and Aunt Mary together?" Cousin Laura asked.

"It had to have been thirty years or so," Aunt Mamie answered.

"Living in sin, all that time."

"What a scoundrel," joked my brother.

"You know," I said, "after digging around for a couple of years, if this is the worst 'bone' I can find in the 'cupboard,' we're really a pretty innocent bunch."

"What are you talking about, bones where?"

I explained Luigi's metaphor.

Later that afternoon as I was leaving Uncle Jim's home, my cousin Frankie escorted me to the car. He threw his arm around my shoulders as we walked, the way we used to do as boys.

"You know," he said, "ever since you moved to California, when we were in high school, we haven't gotten together as a family. This is the first time in a lot of years we could sit and talk—no one died or got married or baptized, or anything. This was fun."

"Yeah," I agreed. "Funny. You dig around looking for ancestors and the living show up to hear the story. It's a real benefit I hadn't anticipated."

It was good having the sense of a big family again.

The next stop for my brother and me was to visit my mother's brother, Uncle Al. Uncle Al and Aunt Ange had been married over fifty years and still lived in the Oakland apartment building my grandfather had bought at the end of the Second World War.

The apartment was only the second place Uncle Al had ever lived in his entire life. He had moved there from the house my grandfather had built and where he, Uncle Eugene, Uncle Robert, and my mother had all been raised.

Uncle Robert now lived in the apartment above Uncle Al, and Uncle Eugene in the house behind the apartment building.

My mother had been the big adventurer, moving to a suburb six miles away. When my mother announced our move to California, her brothers found the notion incomprehensible.

The Oakland section of the city was now known for the big University of Pittsburgh, which had grown remarkably larger in recent years. The area had been an Italian ghetto of sorts when my mother and Uncle Al were children. The Italian quarter had been called "The Hollow" and was at the bottom of a hill near Shadyside—the place where big Pittsburgh industrialists like Andrew Mellon had lived. It was close enough so the women could work as maids and household help in the big mansions, but they were conveniently out of sight when they returned home.

My grandfather built his house on an opposing hill. Not only an architectural statement, but an obvious social one as well.

As children, we all rode the streetcars to town or to Oakland. We'd visit my mother's extensive family. In the summer we'd go to baseball games in old Forbes Field, where most of the family men worked as ushers, bookkeepers, or maintenance workers. Forbes Field had been, in a sense, the family business.

The ballpark had been torn down in the early seventies. The University of Pittsburgh Law School now stands on the site where, as a wide-eyed boy, I saw Mickey Mantle, Willie Mays, and the great Pittsburgh Pirate, Roberto Clemente, play.

We had driven to Oakland—the streetcars were now also a distant memory—to clear up some of the questions about the Abruzzi side of the family with Uncle Al. We sat in what had been my grandfather's office and smoking room; the dank odor of ancient cigars still clung to the walls. Popa's huge wooden desk sat in the corner, his blotters and his long-dry silver-encased inkwells still placed carefully on top, though slightly dusty—a condition that would have never occurred in my grandfather's day.

Uncle Al was clearly ill. He sat uncomfortably in an over-sized cushioned chair, a blanket draped over his shoulders. I shared with him all I had learned about my grandfather's village of Gamberale and its terrible, bloody struggle during World War Two.

Uncle Al seemed dispassionate, almost disinterested.

"You mean you knew about the massacre?" I asked.

"Not all the details, but we knew most."

"Why didn't anyone tell us?" my brother, Ralph, wondered.

"It all happened before you were born in what could have been another planet. Why should we have talked about a town my father couldn't get away from fast enough?"

As a young man, Uncle Al had lost the hearing in one ear from a childhood bout of scarlet fever. Now that ear had a constant ringing the doctors couldn't silence. The agony showed on his round and once-happy face.

"But he went back. He visited the place at least a couple of times. His name is still known there. He must have cared."

"He was recruited. They paid for his trip."

"Who paid?"

"Mussolini."

It seemed to me that, since I'd been delving into this family history, every time I thought I had the right question I'd come up with a totally unexpected answer. Once again, I felt like the village idiot.

"Mussolini? Why would Mussolini send Popa a ticket to visit Italy?"

"Did you ever hear the term *'uomo di rispetto'*?"

"Yes, I think."

"It referred to immigrants like your grandfather and meant a 'man of respect,' or a man who was a leader in his community. Your grandfather came to this country with nothing but a third-grade education and a smart mind. He wound up a major road-builder in this city."

Uncle Al shifted in his chair with obvious discomfort. He had relished telling stories when I was younger. His letters to me in college were greeted with absolute joy, not only by me, but my friends as well. We loved his references to Shakespeare and classical poetry.

He seemed so tired now. His enthusiasm and energy had seemed limitless when I was young. His sense of excitement about life and passion for all his interests now seemed a pale reflection of what they'd been in the past.

"What's that got to do with Mussolini?" I asked.

"Mussolini was a lot of things. Stupid wasn't one. He had his people find out where all the successful Italian emigrants had gone and brought them back to Italy to show them the joys of fascism.

"His little scheme worked very well. Most of the men, Popa included, thought Il Duce was doing a great job of modernizing a country they left behind as pathetic. Of course, he only showed them what he wanted them to see. Then he sent these men back to their original villages, where they all had relatives, to spread the word."

"So that's why . . ."

"That's the main reason he went back to Gamberale. At least once. The other trips I don't know about, but Mussolini was a sly old fox."

"That's why Popa never spoke about Italy," I said, finally understanding. "He felt betrayed. Used. That's why we never

171

heard the stories of Popa's meetings with one of the most powerful men in the world."

Aunt Ange shuffled into the room. She needed a cane to get around. It seemed like just yesterday she was a vibrant and energetic redhead, filled with laughter, always on the phone talking with her numerous sisters. If in my mind's eye I was always twenty-three, Aunt Ange was always thirty-something. It was hard to adjust to the old woman with the cane.

"Can I get you boys something?" she asked, stooped in my direction. "How about some coffee?" There wasn't a "boy" within sight, but it was her habit to use the term. My brother and I smiled.

We declined her offer and watched as she slowly and achingly shuffled away. We sat in the old office with its tile floor, full wall of windows, and huge plants. Since I was a boy, the room had been reserved for male conversations and cigars. Now, no one smoked and we would have welcomed Aunt Ange's company, but the years of tradition must have led her back to her telephone and television.

Uncle Al, with his seemingly unending curiosity, had also been an amateur botanist. I remembered orange trees growing in this very room.

"So Mussolini found out that Popa had been the first to leave his little village and come to America where . . ."

"Who said he had been the first?"

"But I thought . . ."

"Gaetano Diulius was the first, my mother's father, your great-grandfather, and Popa's eventual father-in-law."

"Wait," I said. "Before you go any further. I've seen about twenty spellings for that name. What is the name?"

"Diulius." He spelled it. "In America we pronounced it, *die-ulus.'* There's no 'J' in Italian, it means 'of Julius.' Some say it relates back to Julius Caesar."

I laughed. "He left no sons," I pointed out. "Couldn't be true even if we wanted it to be."

"None that we *know* of," My uncle smiled. "But 'there is a tide in the affairs of men . . .' "

"Julius Caesar. Fourth act," I said.

Uncle Al had spent his life editing and annotating Shakespeare's plays. The Bard of Avon was his greatest passion, just slightly ahead of Beethoven symphonies or Verdi operas. When I was a boy, Uncle Al never said 'hello,' in the traditional way. Instead, I'd get a Shakespearean quote that I'd be expected to identify by both play and act. I loved the game. We hadn't played it in a long time.

"So Popa wasn't the first to come here?" my brother asked.

"No. Gaetano. Then all of his brothers. Nine in all. Don't you remember the story about Guy Diulius at the tavern?"

I didn't.

"One day, before he was married and my mother was born, my grandfather—your great-grandfather—walked into a local tavern, right here in Oakland, where the University of Pittsburgh dorms are now. He ordered a beer.

" 'We don't serve your kind here,' the bartender said.

" 'I beg your pardon?,' my grandfather asked. He had never been refused a drink before.

" 'You heard me. We don't serve your kind here.'

"So, without a word, my grandfather left the bar. About an hour later he came back, along with his nine brothers. All ten of them formed a long line as they walked up to the bar. 'Say,' he said to the bartender, 'I'll take that beer now. And while you're at it, you might pour one for my brothers as well.'

"My grandfather got his beer."

My uncle smiled for the first time that afternoon. The story seemed to strengthen him.

"You know," he continued, now obviously interested in the subject, "Guy Diulius couldn't read or write. When my father started to court my mother, Guy wasn't very happy about the relationship; he thought my mother was too young. My father would give Guy newspapers to bring home to his daughter."

He shifted himself in the chair and took time to catch his breath before continuing.

"Guy never thought to look *inside* the newspapers. He couldn't read. If he had, he'd have seen my father's love letters to my mother scrawled about the margins of the *Pittsburgh Sun*. Popa got a big laugh out of that. They were all a bunch of characters—Falstaff had nothing on them."

Uncle Al was tiring. It was time for us to go. I had to ask one last question, however.

"The films." I said. "The movies Popa had made in Italy. There's nothing left? Nothing we can salvage, send to a restoration lab?"

"Gone." The pain was now obvious on my uncle's face. "Gone for years. They were merely a 'brief candle, a walking shadow . . .' " He stood up shakily.

"*Macbeth*. Act Five." We smiled and embraced and said our good-byes.

"I'll see you again," he said, waving his finger. He sounded determined.

I clung to his words, hoping they were true.

174

• • •

I wasn't satisfied with either the amount of information or the speed at which I was learning about my grandfathers. While a few "bones" had turned up—we now knew for sure who Vito was, and Uncle Al had at least explained the "Why" of the Mussolini meetings, there was still so much more I wanted to know.

Why couldn't anyone find a record for Francesco? Why was this man's short and painful life so obscure? What did Pietro do when he returned to his native village? And why did he feel such an attraction to a place he had left at fourteen?

It seemed for every answer I found I had twice the amount of questions. I still had enough in the bank for at least another year in Italy. If it meant spending every penny, I was going to find some official paper, some document that verified and confirmed Francesco's name and family—my family. And I was going to return to Gamberale as often as I could to fill in the blanks in Pietro's partial story.

8

La Bella Italia

The Shadow of Mussolini ...

Luigi, his mother, and I took a long Sunday afternoon walk in their hometown of Foligna. Luigi's daughter was off on a skiing trip in the North; she would train to Foligna that evening, and the three of us would then drive home to Rome. As we walked about the neatly kept town, I could see the foothills of the Apennines as they loomed in the bright late-afternoon sun on the Umbrian plain to the east.

"I'm surprised you came back," said Luigi. "I thought once you returned to the States, you'd stay there."

"Why would you think that?" I asked.

"Because most Americans are happy with America, they really *do* believe in their sense of nationality."

La Signora said hello to several friends and acquaintances as

176

we strolled. We made frequent stops—hellos were exchanged and brief introductions made.

"I still want to know more about Italy. I still don't have answers to my questions." I told Luigi and his mother about my conversation with Uncle Al and my surprise that my grandfather had apparently been duped by *Il Duce*.

"At least, with Mussolini, we knew who was in charge," *La Signora* said. I found it interesting that Luigi's mother would defend *Il Duce*. I had been hearing more and more native Italians justify the "good times" under the former Fascist leader. It was hard to believe, especially from survivors of the Second World War like *La Signora*.

"There are thirteen political parties in Italy today," *La Signora* argued. "*Tredici*—thirteen! Who can keep track of which one stands for what?"

I pointed out the obvious. "But Mussolini was a Fascist. He represented an authoritarian state. He was a thug."

"Only when he decided to be friends with Hitler," said Luigi. "When Mussolini was an Italian, leading Italians, we made progress. When we tried to become Germans, it was a disaster."

I studied the mountains in the east. The Italian countryside was filled with the most brilliant colors I had ever seen. As the afternoon wore on, the mountains turned deep purple, contrasting sharply with the bright yellow plains leading to the foothills.

It occurred to me, as I gazed eastward, that the myth of Mussolini still floated over Italy like the purple mountain haze. Only, unlike the haze, it didn't disappear as night fell.

On a trip to the north to hear a jazz concert, my musician

friend Enrico and I had visited Mussolini's tomb in the dictator's hometown of Predappio. I stood behind the huge stone sarcophagus trying to make a photograph, attempting to be as inconspicuous as possible. As I waited for the room to clear of people, I witnessed two young men—in black shirts—stand at the foot of the huge stone tomb and throw their right arms into the air in the Fascist salute. I had never seen the gesture done in earnest before. *Vi Saluto,* each man wrote in the visitors' book—I salute you.

And, in Rome, I had seen swastikas in the graffiti along the walls of the San Giovanni quarter, the local headquarters for the Neo-Fascist political group. *Swastikas* on the walls in Europe, again. It was shocking to see the Nazi symbol.

When I had been a soldier stationed in Germany, political graffiti were never tolerated. If symbols or slogans had been painted, some earnest citizen would have come along with bucket and paint and, in mere moments, covered over the obscene logo of the Third Reich.

I described what I had seen to Luigi and *La Signora.* "This is the work of complete illiterates," I said. "People who make Fascist salutes or paint these signs can't read history books."

"They have a different interpretation than you," said Luigi.

"You think these people can actually read, that they understand what happened here over fifty years ago?" I asked, incredulously.

"I think it just proves the myth of a multiracial society," he replied.

I felt my face getting red. "There are people, real human beings, throwing their arms in the air, drawing swastikas and writing *'Juden Raus'* on the walls of San Giovanni. I don't think they're practicing German."

I looked off to the hills again. Somewhere up there lay Assisi, the hometown of another famous and far more illustrative Italian, St. Francis. His gentle ways and loving demeanor are still depicted in all his statues; he is universally represented with forest animals perched on his arm or sitting peacefully at his side. I was an American, yet I yearned for an Italian symbol more graceful and benign than that of Mussolini.

Luigi interrupted my thoughts. "Why would anyone be threatened by anything that happens in Italian politics?" We entered the immaculate rail station to await his daughter's train. "Look," he continued, "in America you are taught to believe that everyone can change what they don't like. You can't, really, but you *think* you can. We know we can't change much. In this country, our politicians spend most of their time just trying to form a government—no one party ever has a clear majority. The government never has time to actually govern."

We walked directly to the coffee bar, of course, and ordered a round of espresso, and mineral water for Luigi's bad stomach. *La Signora* felt guilty she wasn't entertaining us in her home. She insisted we were wasting our money, she would have been happy to make coffee. "It is silly to pay for things you needn't buy," she argued.

"But, Mama, then we would miss the train. Drink your coffee."

"It doesn't taste as good as mine," she said.

"See what I mean?" Luigi smiled at me. *"Tosca!* Even coffee is an aria."

La Signora ignored the comment and looked askance at her little coffee cup.

"Maybe you're better off?" I suggested, getting back to the

subject. "Your lack of government hasn't seemed to hurt your economic development. This is a very wealthy country."

"Maybe," agreed Luigi, "but it would be nice, just once in my lifetime, to actually know who was in charge and where we were headed. Our wealth today comes from the Communist Party."

As always, with Luigi, I knew he was headed somewhere with this outlandish statement, as most Italians I knew had a completely different insight into politics as art form.

"Boy," I said, "I can't wait to hear this one. Why are the Communists responsible for your wealth?"

"Because they frightened the Pope. And the United States. Do you know about our Communists?"

"Yes," I said. "I was here in 1968. I actually covered the election when the Communists polled nearly a third of your parliament. It was one of my first major assignments as an army reporter."

"Then you know the secret." He smiled.

"I must have missed it." I studied Luigi's big, smug grin. "Okay, I'm ready. What was the secret?"

"The Communists almost took over in 1968. It scared the pants off the CIA and the miter off the Pope. How could the United States and the Catholic Church allow Communists to control a central, key European country?" He glared at me in mock anger.

I shrugged.

A whistle shrieked, announcing the arrival of the evening train from Austria.

"They couldn't. So they pooled their money and made sure the Italian Christian Democratic Party maintained control. That was the true secret to our economic miracle."

"Ah," sighed *La Signora, "L'anno."* The Italians still referred to 1968 as "the year." It marked the clear turning point in the postwar economy and began the period of incredible affluence and wealth Italy still enjoys.

"Let's say that's true. Mussolini was better?" I wondered.

"Not better, maybe, but easier to understand. Today nothing is as it appears to be."

We spotted Laura struggling with her skis and bag on the ramp alongside the train. Luigi and I went to help. Laura was tanned and energized from her weekend in the mountains. She rushed through a description of the fresh snow and her adventures with her many friends.

We returned to the bar where *La Signora* waited. I offered more coffee.

"No," *La Signora* said quickly and firmly. "We will go home. It is a waste of money to stay in a train station when we have a perfectly good house for eating and drinking."

We walked the mile or so back to *La Signora*'s apartment, chatting away in the dark and sharing the toting of the skis and baggage.

Like all discussion of politics in Italy, ours was inconclusive and troubling. The idea of a former dictator who plunged the country into war and devastation—yet still made sense because his policies weren't confusing—didn't sit well with me. It was an issue as dark as the Umbrian night.

A few weeks later, in Rome, I went with a friend studying for the priesthood to a lecture on Julius Caesar. The talk was given by Father Reggie Foster, a Vatican priest, considered the foremost living expert on the Latin language. His instruction occasionally consisted of walks about Rome to the actual sites of events described in ancient Roman history and texts. His talks, like all of his documents, were in Latin.

Through an elaborate word-of-mouth publicity, the walking lectures had become very popular, and very crowded. The babble from students translating for friends became so incessant Father Foster now did the walks in both English and Latin. On this day, even the BBC came along to tape some of the atmosphere and produce a radio special on Father Foster's unique approach to Roman history.

On the Ides of March in our year, we stood on the site of Caesar's assassination over two thousand years before. Flowers marked the site. I had also seen flowers on the pedestal of Julius Caesar's statue in the Foro Romano area as well. Romans were still commemorating a man who was dead before the birth of Christ. What I thought of as ancient history was a contemporary memorial day to whomever left those flowers.

Reggie explained Cicero's misunderstanding of the event. The assassins and their conspirators—Cicero among them— had expected popular support, but the average Roman was incensed by the murder. We walked the same route the assassins had taken immediately following the bloody deed in 44 B.C. Reggie passionately detailed the sights and sounds they would have seen and the geography they would have traversed. I was truly sorry I hadn't studied history in any depth. Reggie made it so exciting I could visualize real people in real situations instead of white marble statues. He was a terrific teacher, no wonder his Latin classes overflowed.

Father Foster talked about the Romans' yearning for clear leadership. Caesar, he said, despite dictatorial leanings, provided clear answers.

"Just like Mussolini," I whispered to my friend. "Clear answers from a very confusing character."

"Ah-ha," a voice from behind me piped up. "Your contrast of Caesar and Mussolini isn't far off the mark." We struck up a discussion.

The visitor was an American writer researching Mussolini's treatment of the Jews during the Second World War. Alexander Stille's book, *Benevolence and Betrayal,* was eventually published and is a fascinating look at the period.

Stille believed the Italians had never really accepted any of Hitler's outlandish racist theories. Early on, Mussolini himself had criticized the concept of Aryan superiority, Stille pointed out.

"Look at the Italians," Mussolini said as Hitler was rising to power. "They are a mixture of everything and proof that there is no such thing as pure blood." It was only when Il Duce's political power was threatened that Mussolini went along with his German comrade.

"It is a befuddling history," Stille added after our walk. "The Italians didn't really believe much of the Nazi policies. Mussolini seems to have known how crackpot Hitler's ideas were. The deportation of Jews in Italy occurred only *after* Mussolini was thrown out of power and the Germans occupied the country. And, at that, the Nazis were greatly frustrated by both the government's and private citizens' refusal to cooperate. Still, Il Duce was a dictator, and had some very dangerous friends."

I had spent the afternoon contemplating Cicero, Caesar, and Mussolini, not so odd a combination after all. The only thing I knew for sure was that debates still swirl over the effectiveness and ability of both men. And in a country where the verbs have a continuing meaning, I shouldn't have been surprised.

I Sassi di Matera...
The First Link to Francesco

I'd now invested nearly two years into the search, yet officially there was no Francesco Paolo Paolicelli. According to the record keepers in Rome, Basilicata, and Potenza, my grandfather's family just didn't exist. There didn't appear to be a single notation anywhere to prove Francesco's or his siblings' birth and early life in Italy.

My phone calls to like-named, potential relatives in Matera were no help—they only added to my frustration. Most hung up before I completed my appeal, probably thinking I was a phone solicitor or American-accented bandit. Other phonebook names I contacted sounded interested, promised a return call or some other piece of information, but no one ever called, nothing arrived in the mail.

Surprisingly, the amateur music was keeping me very busy. Enrico was right, my ear *had* continued to develop over the years my horn lay fallow. I was amazed at how quickly—almost like riding the proverbial bicycle—the basic technique of trumpet playing had returned. And now, much to my amazement, I actually performed jazz solos better than I remembered from my younger years.

I felt this newfound soloing skill was undoubtedly due to attitude—as a student I had been terrified of making mistakes and played only in areas and ranges where I had complete confidence. As an adult, my middle-aged goal was simply to have fun and enjoy the ride. I wasn't afraid any longer to take risks and go exploring. I'd never had so much fun playing the horn.

Rome's professional musicians weren't exactly quaking in

fear that I would cause massive unemployment among trumpet players, but I was getting hot on the amateur circuit. Before too long, I was involved with four different amateur groups ranging from conservatory big bands to combo work. I had turned down invitations to play with other groups.

With the music came a vastly increased social life. In almost no time, I was spending most of my evenings either rehearsing or performing. It was just short of a miracle as far as I was concerned; a totally unexpected and completely joyful turn of events.

Luigi said I knew more people in Rome than he, and enjoyed coming to the clubs and hearing the groups. Especially if he thought single women would be in the audience.

I even had an inquiry from a percussionist who occasionally worked with Romano Mussolini, the accomplished and famous jazz pianist son of the former dictator. I wasn't that accomplished and couldn't make that level of committment—it would have meant complete dedication to rehearsal and performance. I was content with the part-time amateur diversion. But I couldn't help thinking that, in Rome, anything was possible and even probable, if I stayed there long enough. My grandfather had been invited to meet with Il Duce during the height of his dictatorship; now the grandson had an opportunity to play jazz with his son. Don't tell me the world was not making progress.

Finally, one cold winter night in the Club Metteranneao, where John Heinemann's group, Works in Progress, did occasional performances, a major break occurred in the Francesco file. I was introduced to a substitute bassist, filling in for our regular bass player, who was off at a family wedding. As we shook hands in the smoky jazz cellar, he recognized my name.

"You must be related to Professor Nunzio Paolicelli at the Conservatory in Matera?"

"I didn't even know there was such a person."

"Oh, yes. He and the conservatory are quite famous."

That was all I needed to hear. The next day I had the actual professor on the phone. He was the *Solfeggio* teacher at the school—he taught sight-reading and interpretation, which had been one of my hardest classes.

"What was the name of your grandfather?" he asked.

I told him.

"My father is Francesco Paolo. Perhaps we are related?"

For once, I was being taken seriously. Nunzio wasn't suspicious of my motives, especially since I had the names of Roman musicians to verify my identity. We made a date to meet and within a week Luigi and I made the six-hour drive to the heart of Basilicata and the amazing city of the Sassi.

Matera...

We arrived in the provincial capital on a crisp, cold Friday afternoon, having planned our trip to allow ourselves enough time for a leisurely tour of the city.

What we found was astounding.

The instant we got out of the Volkswagen, we were set upon by young local men offering services as tour "guides." None of them had the required badges the Italian government issues for such work. I was leery.

"Let's hear what he has to say," Luigi insisted, when one rather hungry-looking fellow offered his "special tour of the Sassi."

Luigi had read aloud from his guidebooks and histories during the long drive down the peninsula. We had learned the basic facts of the place, but hadn't fully understood the nature of the Sassi or the town of Matera—we still couldn't completely grasp the concept of the Sassi, despite the reference material.

Our guide led us to a lookout point in the plaza of a pre-Renaissance church. From the plaza, we had a panoramic perspective of the ancient hillsides.

"How many homes and churches are there in the Sassi?" I asked our "guide." He shrugged.

"Thousands," said Luigi. "Just look at this. Amazing." We stood silently, taking in the view for several minutes. "If Matera were in any place in Europe other than Southern Italy, it would be a major tourist attraction." Luigi seemed truly impressed. "I'd heard of the Sassi di Matera all of my life, but never imagined how incredible this place would be."

The Sassi do all but defy description. The word *sassi* itself refers to the area of stone homes built in the ancient town on two steep cliffs. They are intricately woven and engineered. From Luigi's books we had learned that each home is the result of forty thousand years of continuous inhabitation. What were originally cave dwellings before recorded time have come down to this day as a complex, crowded stone grouping of houses and churches dug into the hillside and filling the valley.

Our guide explained, in heavily accented Italian, the original valley was formed by a river that cut through a very soft rock called "tuffa." It was the tuffa, and its malleability, that led to early forms of sculpture in Italy—which wasn't Italy then—or even Greece.

"Just think," said Luigi as we stood on a observation deck studying the detailed series of houses, "these people were an ancient civilization *before* the Greeks got here."

I looked at our young companion. "No one lives here now?"

"No one has lived here for a long time," he said.

"How long?" I asked.

He shrugged.

"It was just after the Second World War," said Luigi. "I just read about this. The Italian government was re-formed in 1945. The new Minister of Health of the Christian-Democrats declared the Sassi a health hazard."

Luigi explained the apparent lack of adequate sewage and an infestation of mosquitoes that had led to serious illness. All of the residents had been ordered to move. The government built massive housing projects in the areas surrounding the old quarter. The Sassi themselves had remained abandoned and eerily deserted for nearly fifty years.

"There's a new government program now," our guide explained. "They want people to move back."

Luigi added he had learned from his reading that, for those with an urban-pioneering spirit, the Italian government was issuing financial grants for people willing to rebuild the ancient dwellings and bring them up to modern safety and sanitary standards.

"Not many people are moving back," our guide offered.

"Why is that?"

"Not many young people stay here now," he said. "The old people are settled and the young move on."

We spent an hour walking about the cliffs and poking around the abandoned buildings. It felt odd looking into rooms once filled with furniture and people, now filled with musty odors, trash and dust. There were occasional pieces of abandoned furniture, all charred. We saw the remains of small fires everywhere, along with occasional graffiti. The Sassi had become a playground for local teenagers.

Walking about the place on that cold afternoon, I had the eerie feeling of being surrounded by the ghosts of time forever.

An ancient chapel lay in the valley between the two hills and was built into a huge rock that dominated the center of the antique city. An old man stood by a doorway at the back of the cave, chopping firewood. He welcomed us gutturally and, for a small fee, showed us the interior of the building.

His prize possession, behind the altar surrounded by frescoes made in the fifteenth century, were two skulls and a collection of bones that had been found in a crypt at the back of the cave. He showed these relics proudly, he claimed the skulls were of a man and woman. The bones were the remains of three children. He didn't think the remains were old enough to have been early-Christian martyrs. The fact that the graves of these poor long-dead people had been defiled seemed of little interest to the old man and our guide. Tourists apparently like to see such things.

I couldn't leave the place fast enough. "What famous person came from here?" I asked our guide, as we walked away from the macabre reliquary. "Who is from these caves I would recognize, have read about or seen?"

He shrugged again.

I prodded. "Surely in forty thousand years there's someone I would have heard of,"

"Nessuno," he said. No one.

I found it hard to believe.

I thought about the eternal continuum that afternoon as we paced about. Countless generations were from this town, just as my family seemed to be. Almost all of them, but for a tiny fraction, are completely forgotten and gone to dust, dust that is also now ancient. A town that was here before any of the ancient civilizations ever appeared on the historical horizon.

"It's so old," I said. "I can't get over my amazement at knowing this town goes back to the Paleolithic era."

"Americans always think of their country as being so young," Luigi said. "You have such a short sense of things, but for how long has man lived in America? Not long for European men, but human beings have been there a very long time. And where did the Europeans come from? It is only the American part that is new, the form of government. You Americans tend to forget that with your sense of youth."

Luigi and I paid our guide handsomely for his complete lack of information and said good-bye. We checked into the lovely and modern Albergo Italia, had a quick coffee, and set off for the Cathedral of, not coincidentally, San Francesco. Nunzio was to conduct a concert there that evening and we were to meet with him afterward.

The walk from our hotel to the church took all of about thirty seconds. The man we asked directions from looked at us as if we were drunk or demented. We were standing on the edge of the piazza of the very church we were searching for.

There was a large audience already seated in the cold building as we entered. We had to stand along the side aisle. The concert—a series of choral works called *Omaggio a S. Rachmaninov,* or an "homage" to the Russian composer, had already started. A man, obviously Nunzio, stood to the side of the altar in the way professors do during student performances. He watched intently as each vocalist faced the large crowd, which I assumed was mostly parents and friends.

It was a long evening. Each number was separately performed with different vocalists and accompanists entering and exiting the altar area of the church.

There was one truly gifted *tenore* voice, Francesco Zingariello. His power and range brought the house down. He, like all the others, sang in the composer's native Russian. The Italians never translated from the original score—a reverence for the total composition we didn't share in the States.

I was excited by the prospect of meeting my possible family. A long operatic concert, in Russian, only added to my impatience. It was hard to focus.

Finally the performances ended, the students had taken their bows and the crowds filed out. Luigi and I stood in the cold piazza until the final few trickled away from the church and then there was no one.

"Perhaps he forgot," I said.

"He's *Il Professore*. He must be the last to leave. He will be here."

What seemed like an hour went by before a final grouping exited the church, an elderly couple, two youngsters, a middle-aged woman, and Nunzio. The others walked ahead toward Luigi and me as Nunzio stopped and locked the huge cathedral doors.

Nunzio had brought his entire family with him. We shook hands. He introduced his father, Francesco Paolo—the first son of another Francesco Paolo.

Papa Francesco broke the ice by kidding about our "family reunion." We stood in the frigid night exchanging introductions and asking rapid questions.

Nunzio introduced his wife and two sons, the eldest boy another Francesco Paolo.

Francesco Paolo the elder asked about my grandfather. I told him quickly of my search. Luigi complimented Nunzio on the concert. Papa told us he was a band musician, a clarinetist, and his father had been the same. For generations his family had been musicians.

"We must be related," he said, echoing Enrico. "You studied music and play jazz. Music is in the genes."

I explained my dilemma, how my grandfather seemed to have disappeared. They suggested we meet the next afternoon to compare notes.

Papa talked about how many boys from this area had emigrated in the old days. "You know nothing of your grandfather's family here?"

"Only that they were living in Miglionico. Three boys and a girl went to America. I don't know if their parents survived them here or not. I only have the names."

Francesco suggested photographs might help.

I had some family photos in my briefcase. Francesco asked to see them. All talk of tomorrow disappeared; Francesco Paolo wanted to settle this now. We were invited to his home, a welcome relief from the freezing night. We walked for several blocks.

Along the way Fracesco Paolo stopped by a poster to point out the famous "F. Paolicelli" I had heard about from my musician friends in Rome and whose music was to be performed in one of a series of public concerts advertised on the placard. This was another distant cousin "of ours," he said.

Francesco lived in a well-appointed apartment at the top of a very steep staircase. There seemed to be little room for infirmities or weak joints in modern-day Italy, I thought. There were still many apartments in Rome, too, with several floors and no elevators. Yet the spry and very lean Signore and Signora Paolicelli seemed to have no trouble scaling the small mountain.

We entered the apartment and went into an enclosed study. Francesco scurried about the room collecting photographs from old books while his wife went for coffee and sweets.

Nunzio, his family, Luigi and I sat in the comfortable room around a small, elegant table. Soon we were exchanging family pictures and talking like family about them.

"This is a picture of my band," Francesco said proudly. Everyone in the photo wore a crisp, white uniform and sat holding an instrument on the right knee. "And here is my father's band many years ago." The photo was almost identical, only the handlebar mustaches indicated the change of time. There were dozens of pictures of musical groups and both Francesco Paolos at the clarinet.

"We must be related," Francesco kept saying, as I showed him pictures from my various musical groups. He was clearly excited with the prospect of discovering a long-lost *americano*.

Since I'd started my research, I'd assembled a fairly large folder complete with documents and photographs. Francesco eagerly searched the likenesses for similarities and the papers for any missing links.

We could find no relationship. The more we looked at pictures, the more we realized we shared a name, but no relatives or commonalty beyond our mutual love and instinct for music.

While showing Francesco and Nunzio the single, shabby copy of the picture of my grandfather, it suddenly dawned on me how much I looked like this man. In that instant I realized I had his face, cheeks, mustache. His eyes, from beyond the fading sepia tone, had my glance, my stare. How much I wanted to know him. I had never seen the resemblance until this chilly evening.

Francesco Paolo joked maybe we were all from the Sassi. Not a bad guess, given how long man has been living in this region. While examining the genealogical charts I had assembled, Francesco immediately spotted my great-grandfather's name.

"Ah!" he exclaimed excitedly, "Emmanuele. That is not our family, that is another branch of the Paolicellis. You must see Don Emmanuele. That is his family." Franceso, like all firstborn sons, knew the lineage of firstborn names, and my great-grandfather's was important information in that family grouping.

"Don Emmanuele is a priest at the Church of Addolorata. He has a brother who is a doctor," Nunzio said.

"These men are known for their tallness," Francesco added. "You are tall, they must be relatives." Francesco wasn't going to give up until he had me placed firmly in the right family. He also eliminated the possibility of a relationship with the famous composer, F. Paolicelli. "That's another branch entirely," he explained, based on the family names I'd shown him. I was disappointed.

The Paolicellis offered to make some phone calls the next day and check around for me. Over cake and coffee they asked the predictable questions about my marital status and where in the United States I had been born and where I had lived.

I asked if they had ever done any research on the name and they had not. Nunzio shrugged when I suggested that someone might have conducted research. There didn't seem to be much interest in the subject.

Luigi and I thanked our hosts for a fascinating evening. We hurried back through the cold night to the warmth of our hotel.

My window looked out on the abandoned Sassi. A full moon glinted off the countless empty stone houses. Luigi had read that afternoon of wild dogs still roaming the Sassi hills at night. I could hear their howls as I studied the eerie moonscape. I found sleep difficult.

A local bakery was next to our hotel. The aroma of bread and baked goods wafted into my room before dawn, awakening me and causing ravenous hunger. When I couldn't take it any longer, I rang Luigi and roused him for an early breakfast. We feasted on fresh warm rolls and delicious coffee.

The Italians didn't believe in big breakfasts—my friends thought the English custom of meat, fish, and eggs was a hideous departure from balanced cuisine. Breakfast in Italy meant a sweet roll and coffee. Only the morning coffee had milk—*cappuccino*—to line the stomach. The rest of the day, coffee was drunk straight and in short bursts.

Luigi said most Italian housewives made a point of rising early and getting the family bread each day while it was still warm. Italy refused to support any effort at large, centralized bakeries like those in the States.

"Local bakeries, fruit stands, coffee bars, and markets mean local employment," Luigi explained. "We'd rather have full employment and fresh food than cheaper costs. I am unable to eat what you call 'white bread' in the United States."

"I mostly eat out," I said. "I can't picture myself or any wife I know in America getting up at dawn to fetch bread. In Italy you have a separate word for women who work at home, *la casalinga*. In the States, housekeeping's a chore. Here it's a profession."

"Yes." Luigi sighed. "But not for much longer. I'm afraid if

I want warm bread in the morning, I'm the one up early. My daughter, like American girls her age, is off each day to the university and her colleagues, not the marketplace."

"It's called progress, my friend."

"Ah, yes. Another favorite American disease."

Our appointment with Don Emmanuele wasn't until mid-morning; we had time to continue our tour of Matera. We strolled about the huge piazza in the newer quarter above the Sassi, half of which was roped off with red tape. Behind the tape, an excavation was in progress and, next to the huge pit, stood a large marble pedestal. An indistinguishable statue on top of the pedestal had been covered over, apparently being refurbished.

I had a camera with a telephoto lens and focused in on the bronze lettering on the sides of the pedestal. The streaking and bleeding letters listed veterans of "The Great War." I squinted to read the names. There were half a dozen Paolicellis, including a Francesco Paolo. It was the first time I'd ever seen our family named on a war memorial. It felt odd.

"At least we were on the same side in *that* war," Luigi added. "How would you feel if it were the Second World War?"

I couldn't help notice throughout my travels in Italy, there were few memorials listing veterans' names for the Second World War. Most monuments were like the little neighborhood altars in Rome; they listed events like Rome's liberation, not the names of combatants.

On the city hall in Matera, adjacent to the piazza, a plaque commemorating a "tragic day" in 1943 when the Nazis swept through the town and apparently took "innocent hostages" was the only memento we could find from the most recent war. Again, no specific names were mentioned.

I asked a workman about the excavation.

"It is a Greek temple," he replied. "Some old burial chambers from long ago."

"And the statue over there?"

He shrugged.

After a stop at a couple of local churches and another coffee, it was time for our appointment. As we walked through the modern section of the city, I spotted two clothing stores in separate locations—one for women, the other men, named "Buono." I wondered if there was any link between them and my seamstress grandmother of the same name.

Don Emmanuele is very busy," said the old man who answered the door at the Church of Addolorata. "I will take you to him, but we have a holy day coming and poor Don Emmanuele has very little help. He is such a good priest." The elderly guide shuffled his way down an unlit corridor, leading us to the rectory of the Roman Catholic church. "Everyone loves the Don," he said, smiling through his many wrinkles as we neared the priest's office.

Don Emmanuele was a big, jowly, middle-aged fellow with dark, sad eyes. He looked tired, as if he had seen all the sorrow in the world, but his eyes still held an ironic twinkle. He welcomed Luigi and me with warm handshakes and showed us to a couple of stiff-backed, wooden office chairs. He sat opposite us behind a completely covered desk—papers and folders strewn about. It looked a mess.

Our guide remained standing in the doorway, apparently watching over his pastor. He gave me a thumbs-up sign when I glanced his way.

"I understand we might be cousins." The priest laughed as he studied Luigi, obviously mistaking my friend for me.

"Yes," I said, and returned the smile as Don Emmanuele's gaze rotated to meet mine. "I've been trying to find any family of my grandfather. I need his birth certificate for a passport, but it's become more than that, now. I can't find a trace of him or his family."

"And he was a Francesco Paolo."

"Sì, vero," I replied. "He was the son of Emmanuele and Filomena, if that helps."

"Emmanuele with one 'm' or two?"

"Due."

"Aha." The priest's eyes brightened. *"Con due emme!"*

"The number of 'm's makes a difference?" I asked.

"Yes, our family is the Emmanuele with two 'm's. There is another Paolicelli family in town, but their Emanueles have only one."

The priest's face seemed jollier now. His big hands were folded on the desk, as he looked directly at me with a bemused expression. There was an aura, a genuine warmth about this man, which filled the room. I liked him immediately.

"So, if my great-grandfather had two 'm's, we're from the same family?"

"Probably, but who knows?"

Don Emmanuele must have seen a look of concern on my face. "I can't say for sure because there is no one left for me to ask. My father was Francesco Paolo. I know he had family and his father had family that went to America. My father died during the war, I was just a little boy. I never had time to learn about his people." The sadness returned to his eyes.

"You have no other family?" It was almost a plea.

"No. My father had relatives in America, but that's all I know."

The telephone rang. Don Emmanuele reached for the phone but, in a move surprisingly quick for his years, our elderly escort dashed across the room and lifted the receiver before the priest could take it.

"Pronto, chi parla?" he answered in the abrupt manner of the Italians—it literally means "I'm ready, who's talking?" It was a phone etiquette I found difficult to adjust to in a society that was generally overly polite.

Don Emmanuele looked up at his helper and smiled. "Giuseppe's trying to make sure I don't work too hard." He shook his head with amusement.

Giuseppe informed the caller of the hours of the holy day services scheduled for the next day and hung up the phone with an exaggerated nod toward the priest. "You don't need to be taking such unimportant calls," he scolded gently as he returned to his leaning position in the doorway.

The next day was Ash Wednesday, the start of Lent. I'd forgotten. I was embarrassed. I now realized the obviously busy schedule any priest would have during the Lenten season.

"I'm sorry, Don Emmanuele, I forgot about the calendar. Perhaps I could come back another time?"

"There is no good time of year," the priest joked. "With helpers like Giuseppe, I have all the time I need. Unfortunately, I don't have any information. I'd like to share what *you* learn about this family."

Luigi spoke up. "Don Emmanuele, my friend has contacted the *municipio* here and in Miglionico, has written to all the surrounding counties and to Rome. Where else might there be a record?"

"Have you been to the cathedral here in Matera? They have records that go back hundreds of years."

I had called the cathedral several times, but had not succeeded in getting anyone on the phone who could answer my questions and request for access to the archives. I explained this to Don Emmanuele, and my frustrations with the difficulty of accomplishing anything by telephone, especially in this region of the country.

He opened his arms wide. "I can help you," he said, as if the thought of helping me greatly pleased him. "I can call the cathedral and make sure they will take your call. Let's see, I have the number here . . ."

Giuseppe jumped back into the room and lifted the receiver before Don Emmanuele could find his phone book. "Do you want to speak to Don Doneti?"

The priest grinned and gestured to Giuseppe with a sweep of his hand. "You tell me, *Peppi*. You are *il capo*."

Giuseppe winked at us. "Of course I am. I will get Don Doneti on the phone for you."

"What kind of documents can I find in the church?" I asked.

"Everything regarding the basics; getting baptized, confirmed, married, buried. If your grandfather or his family ever belonged to this parish, there's a paper somewhere."

Luigi added that we had been to Miglionico and the records clerks had been helpful with marriage documents and birth certificates for my uncle and aunt.

"Here is Don Doneti," Giuseppe interrupted.

The priest took the receiver and spoke for several minutes with his cathedral colleague. He gently and unhesitatingly explained my situation. He told the other priest I would be calling to make an appointment and not to forget the name. "If you forget his name, Don Doneti, that means you've forgotten me." He laughed and ended the call.

"Don Doneti says to phone for an appointment, but not this week. He, too, is busy."

"Yes, I know." I felt guilty, again, for being such a poor Catholic—but then reminded myself that one of the main reasons I was a lapsed Catholic was to avoid feeling guilty.

"We are here to serve. He will make some time for you." Don Emmanuele laid his hand on top of mine. His touch felt healing. If I had known priests like this at home, I'd have probably been a lot more involved with the church. I doubt I would have forgotten Lent.

We stood to leave. Don Emmanuele came around his desk and stood next to Giuseppe. "Did you talk to the priest in the village where your grandparents were married?"

"No, only the records clerks and my grandmother's family."

"The parish priest is always the best place for information," he said. "You know, for two thousand years we have had many governments here in the *Mezzogiorno*. But there has only been one church."

"What about the Baptists?" asked Giuseppe.

"Well, *mostly* one church," he said sheepishly. "The Baptists haven't been here very long."

"It's a good idea," said Luigi. "We should go back to Miglionico." We shook hands with the priest. "Especially since we can't go to the cathedral. Maybe we can stop and take another father away from his busy Ash Wednesday."

"I'll say a prayer for you," Don Emmanuele said as we started down the dark hallway.

"Thank you, Father." I waved to him as Giuseppe guided us into the shadow of the corridor. The priest's big hand waved back. I was disappointed we didn't have more time with my possible cousin. He was someone I wanted to know and whose prayers were appreciated. The way things were going, it didn't hurt to have an in with Don Emmanuele's Boss.

Miglionico . . .
The Olive Trees

A service was in progress at Santa Maria Maggiore in Miglionico when we entered the church. The first two rows of pews were filled with women, all wearing head coverings in the traditional, old-fashioned way. Like all of the services I had observed in these little villages, there were no men except for the priest, who stood on the altar accompanied by a single altar boy. We didn't want to disturb the Mass; we waited for it to end in the coffee bar on the opposite side of the plaza. A few minutes later, the ladies—all of them quite elderly—exited the church.

We found the priest in the sacristy and introduced ourselves. Don Mario seemed pleased by our visit. "We don't want to take you from your Ash Wednesday preparations," I said.

"Nonsense. I was ready two weeks ago." The elderly priest was small, lean, and slightly stooped. He nonetheless seemed very energetic.

Don Mario insisted we see the restoration work being done on the beautiful big church. The side altars were being repaired and repainted from water damage that had occurred over the centuries.

I studied the main altar, its marble steps immaculate and gleaming. I realized my grandparents had stood in this very place when they married. I doubted the church had changed much since then.

Don Mario explained this was another "new" church, dedicated by the Pope in 1500. The "new" building had been built on top of the "old" church. He pointed out its columns and arches now incorporated into the construction.

"Who was the Pope in fifteen hundred?" I asked.

"Alexander the Sixth," he replied as if surprised by the question.

"Wasn't that the Borgia Pope?" asked Luigi. "The one who many say caused the Protestant Reformation?"

"Yes." Don Mario stood more erect. "One of the most powerful Popes in history, and certainly one of the most powerful Italians. And he came to our little village to consecrate our beautiful church." The Borgia political corruption didn't seem to bother our elderly friend.

"You know," said Luigi, "this church is built on the ruins of another church. That church was probably built on top of still another temple or church, presumably built when the Greeks were here."

"And certainly here when my grandfather got married," I said, trying to steer our tour to the subject I was most interested in.

"Ah, your grandfather," said the priest. "Let us see what we can find. . . ."

Tommaso Buono, my second cousin, lived in a huge stone house directly across from Santa Maria Maggiore. His wife, Margherita, ran the card shop on the corner that was part of the same building. I spotted Tommaso as he was leaving the shop and waved hello. He insisted we come into the shop and greet his wife. My cousins were disappointed I hadn't called before visiting. Margherita said she wanted to prepare a big meal.

"I didn't want to impose and wasn't sure what I'd find in Matera," I explained. I asked about the clothing stores bearing the Buono name in Matera. "Any relation?"

"No, same name, but different family."

"I hear that a lot lately," I said.

"How goes the search for your grandfather's documents?" asked Tommaso.

"He's still a mystery man. I can't find a single, legal trace."

My cousin seemed concerned. "Did the priest know anything?"

"No. We found several Paolicellis from this village in the marriage records, but no Francesco Paolo other than my grandfather. In the birth records there were very few and, again, only ones I already knew about."

"Ah." My cousin sighed. "You must eat something. Come."

I knew it would be useless and perhaps even insulting to protest another meal. We followed my cousin up the wide staircase to his very big and well-appointed apartment. The building was in the same style of architecture as the church across the piazza. The construction was obviously done at the same time, meaning my cousin owned and lived in a building nearly three hundred years older than my native country.

Tommaso and Margherita have four mostly grown and good-looking children whom they proudly introduced—Maurizio, Angelo, Maria, and Valeria. They ranged in age from their twenties to mid-teens.

"Is Maurizio your firstborn?" I asked.

"Yes."

"Then you have done away with the custom of the firstborn being named for the father's father."

"Yes, three of the children have names we liked; there are no family members with the same names. My second son, however, is still an Angelo."

"But it will definitely affect the way someone like me in the future can find which son belongs to which father. As boring as the system might seem now, it sure makes it easy to know which family is which."

"Did you hear that, Maurizio?" asked his mother. "You must distinguish yourself so no one can mistake your identity."

We sat and had coffee and an assortment of prosciutto, bread, olives, and fruit at a large circular dining table made from beautifully grained wood. I told my newfound relatives of the searches in Rome, Gamberale, Matera, Potenza, Lanciano, and of the few family papers.

"One thing that saddens me," I said. "There are no tombstones from before the 1920s and the cemeteries don't keep records. I made a brief stop at the graveyard here on my last trip—it was the same as Gamberale, nothing from the last century or before. The idea of putting all the bones in a single pit every thirty years seems really eerie to me."

Tommaso's children sat quietly as we talked. They all had their father's dark eyes and their mother's bright smile. They appeared interested in my story, though I was sure they had more exciting things to do with their time.

Luigi sighed heavily. "These are your olives, no? I remember how delicious they are."

"Yes." Tommaso smiled as he offered the tray to Luigi for another serving of the plump, green-black fruit. "From *la mia terra*—from my land."

"There are no words to describe this," moaned Luigi, who stopped trying to describe them and continued to eat.

"You are thinking like an American." Tommaso turned back to me. "Someone with more land than people. You know, if the professors are correct, man has been in this area since we had nothing but sticks and stones to protect ourselves. Can you imagine," he continued, "if we buried everyone since that time? All of Italy would be nothing but a cemetery. There would be no room to grow olives, or anything else."

"Why not cremation? Then you wouldn't have to desecrate the bones of your ancestors," I suggested.

"For a long time the church was opposed to cremation," Margherita said.

"Yes," Luigi added, "that's how the catacombs were started over two thousand years ago. It was illegal in ancient Rome to be buried within the city limits. Most Romans were cremated. If a family chose burial, they had to find a place outside the city walls—where the catacombs are today. It didn't start with the Christians, but they used the same chambers for their early Masses. The Romans had superstitions about burials, but the Catholic Church considered the bones of dead Christians, especially the martyrs, to be relics and holy objects."

"We never liked the Romans very much here," Tommaso said. "We always considered ourselves more Greek than Roman."

It was amusing—my cousin was talking about a preference for a civilization that had been in this area five hundred years before the birth of Christ. I had to laugh. "You're right," I agreed. "I am thinking like an American."

"Where is your land, Tommaso?" Luigi asked while still munching olives.

"Not far. About fifteen minutes by car. In the old days it would have been more than an hour's walk."

"Is the land from your family?" No one had ever mentioned the family owning farms.

"No, we bought the acreage when Maurizio was born. We want the children to know how it was in olden times here in our province."

Maurizio smiled and his sisters and brother all squirmed slightly. I could tell it was a subject of much discussion.

"How's that?" I asked.

"People forget that Southern Italy was virtually a feudal state until this century. Big landowners, mostly foreigners, controlled all the property. The local people worked like peasants or slaves on the land." Tommaso grinned at his children. He seemed pleased with what he saw, then continued. "They got up at dawn and walked from their village to the acreage they were responsible for. Many walked hours to work still many more hours before trudging back home, exhausted, and in the dark."

"Yes," said Maria teasingly, "Papa always tells us how hard life was."

"It is important for you to know. Life was very difficult here for most people for a very long time. It's no wonder so many boys went off to America as soon as they had the chance."

Margherita offered the olive tray to Luigi, who, patting his stomach to indicate his fullness, waved it off. "Our beautiful church," she said placing the glass tray gently in the center of the table, "was the only thing of beauty in the people's lives here for a long time. The Church offered the only hope, a better life with God. There was little pleasure except for an olive, a fresh fruit, something sweet to eat. Life was hard and sad—*la vita era dura e triste.*"

Tommaso winked at his children. "That's why it's important to have *la mia terra*," he said. "It reminds us of how things once were and keeps us rooted."

The afternoon was nearly gone. It was time for the long drive back to Rome. We thanked our hosts. I promised to call before coming to the area again.

"Only optimists plant olives," said Luigi as he winked and shook Tommaso's hand.

"Yes, I know," agreed Tommaso with a laugh.

As we got into the car and pulled away I asked Luigi what he meant by his remark.

"We used to say 'a man plants a vineyard for his son and an olive orchard for his grandson.' It takes many years for an olive tree to fully produce its fruit," he explained. "That's why we say only optimists plant the trees."

"I didn't know that."

"Yes, but the good part is, once the tree is planted and has survived, the rest of us get to enjoy the fruit. The olive tree ties us directly to our ancestors. Maybe that's why your cousin believes it's important for his children to know something about farming."

"This is a country with a long memory, that's for sure."

We stopped briefly by the village's only war memorial— again the First World War—on our way to the Via Appia. Two men with my surname were listed. Still no link.

Instead of starting our drive on the superhighway, we followed the Via Appia Antica for the next couple of hours of remaining daylight. An occasional ancient milestone stood at the side of the road, stones I'm sure marching Roman legions, moving to and from the south, noted as key distance markers.

The Romans were great engineers and builders; most of the roads they built are still in use throughout what had been their empire.

The Via Appia Antica curved gently through the beautiful winter countryside. The surrounding fields were brown-yellow in the late-winter sun. The highway was lined on both sides with trees; a beautiful amenity that offered shade to travelers in olden days, but a terrible menace for modern automobile drivers. Serious accidents occurred throughout Italy from the meetings of cars and trees as the result of speeding drivers or foggy roads.

But despite the danger, the tree-lined highway did offer a rare ambiance. The vegetation in this region of the *Mezzogiorno,* even in late winter, was much more lush than that farther west.

Luigi, my Volkswagen, and I were virtually the only traffic on the ancient roadway. We passed through half-a-dozen small villages, all marked by stone construction and all with some form of ancient city wall or guardian castle. In Roman days there would have been an inn-like structure every eleven miles where couriers changed horses on fast rides to and from assignments. It was the equivalent of satellite communications for the times.

"But how much more lovely to travel this road than simply aim a dish into space," I said to Luigi, as we discussed the timelessness of the highway. "So much wonderful countryside to see."

"Now, yes. But remember, after the revolution started by Spartacus? Six thousand slaves were crucified as a result of the revolt. They were hung on the west side of this very road at an interval of about one every thirty yards. Their bodies rotted all along this highway from just north of Naples nearly all the way to Rome."

Luigi studied the impact of his words on me. I shook my head in amazement.

"It wouldn't have been lovely then." He chuckled.

Luigi and his fellow Italians' instant recall of the ancient past always amazed me. Once I asked Luigi for the name of the shrub that lined the dividing strip of the highway leading from Rome to Ostia.

"You know it's the ... er ...," he said, trying to think of the name, "oh, yes, oleander. It's related to the plant whose roots Socrates used to make poison to kill himself."

9

Holy Water, Heartbreak, and Blue Jeans

Rome...

One evening I met a priest in a coffee bar. He was dressed in European fashion; a black cape drawn about his shoulders, a black beret covering his graying hair. I was surprised to learn he was a fellow American from Chicago, Father Bill Myers. We struck up a casual conversation. I learned Father Myers had been in Rome for several years. He worked as an instructor and taught fellow priests at an American Theological Seminary.

"Have you been to many Masses here?" he asked, somewhat connivingly—I felt he suspected my lapsed state of Catholicism.

"Father, I'll be truthful," I said, "I haven't really been to church, except for weddings or funerals, since the Mass was in Latin. I miss the Latin; I liked the repetition and tradition of it."

Father Myers laughed. "You're not kidding. You haven't been to Mass in a long time." He was a handsome man, his chin was broad and firm, his full set of white teeth gleamed when he smiled. He smiled often. He seemed quite happy. We talked pleasantly for almost an hour on a variety of subjects.

I escorted the priest to his bus stop. We walked in the European fashion; he took my arm as we strolled. We talked amiably as we maneuvered through the busy street. We traded cards and I filed the experience away as another pleasant exchange in a Roman coffee bar. I was surprised, on Holy Saturday, when the priest rang up on the telephone.

"This is Bill Myers. How are you?"

It took me a few seconds to remember him.

"Listen, do you have plans for this evening?" he asked.

"Not really," I replied. The musical groups were taking time off for the Easter observances.

"Do you know the Piazza San Silvestro, off the Via del Corso?"

I did.

"Good. Meet me there at the bus stop at six-thirty. I have something to show you."

Father Myers stood regally at the assigned rendezvous point when I arrived, his black cape and beret cutting a distinctive figure.

"Hello, Father," I said.

"Call me Bill," he said. We embraced in the Italian way and he took my arm, leading me across the piazza in the direction of a small church.

"Do you know the Church of San Claudio?" he asked.

I didn't.

"I think you'll be pleased," he said mysteriously. "Do you remember the ceremony of Holy Saturday night?"

I didn't.

"In ancient times, it was the only day of the year to conduct the formal sacrament of baptism. The main baptistery for the entire Faith was at St. John Laterano. Are you familiar with that church?"

"Yes." I almost gushed, grateful to finally have an affirmative to offer. I had passed the basilica many times by both bus and car as I traveled to and from the San Giovanni quarter—named for the same saint.

"That was the place where all of what was then Christianity was baptized."

Father Bill moved his arm in a wide arc. "Think of it. On Holy Saturday night, newly converted Christians from all over the European world would come to Rome. They'd wait in line, in candlelight, probably from the Colosseum all the way up the hill to the baptistery at San Giovanni, for their brief moment in St. John's cleansing water."

He sighed as if he could visualize the winding, candlelit queue. "It must have been a marvelous experience; the sounds, the light, the musical conversing of all the world's known languages at one time, all here in Rome."

The priest steered me into the main doorway of San Claudio as he finished his story.

"I thought of you when I heard of the ceremony this church was planning for tonight," he said. We stood behind the last pew, joining other latecomers in the crowded church.

"This is the evening when all the holy water the church will use in the coming year is sanctified," he explained. "In the old days only water blessed in Rome on Holy Saturday evening could be used throughout the Catholic world."

The service was in progress. The blessing of the Holy Water and the entire service, including the singing of the choir, was in Latin.

"*Sanctus, sanctus, sanctus, Dominus Deus sabaoth,*" went the ancient Gregorian chant. I was instantly transported back to the religion of my childhood, the countless hours spent memorizing the "universal tongue" of the church, the timeless and beautiful rituals of an ancient faith.

"Now maybe you won't feel like such a stranger," Father Bill said, poking me gently in the ribs.

I had now been in Italy two full years; the time had passed quickly. My days and evenings had been delightfully filled with music, visitors, and travel. I had also done more volunteer television consulting work in the newly formed republics of Bulgaria and Macedonia and filed long reports to the International Media Fund on those visits, each journey an education into the arcane world of failed economies.

There was a constant flow of much-welcomed guests from home; family visits always included trips to both the villages of my grandparents. If my visitors were friends, we'd speed along the Autostrada to Florence or Naples and spend wonderful, long hours in Il Duomo and the digs at Pompeii and Hurculaneum. The musical groups continued to perform on a regular basis. Life was full and fascinating.

Luigi and I continued our visits to Zanussi's dance hall, where Luigi would cha-cha and rumba like a Cuban, and I would study the beautiful rhythm and motion of the elegant, swirling couples. As the weather warmed, we also included outings to the beach on weekend afternoons.

Luigi knew all the shortcuts to Ostia—the southern public beach, and Fregene—a series of private beaches north of the ancient Roman seaport and modern airport. As we drove to the beach one day, I turned onto a farm road, a shortcut to the beaches, which led to the far end of "Fiumicino"—no one called Rome's main airport by its designated name, Leonardo da Vinci.

"You see those tower-like things there?" Luigi pointed out a pair of cement structures built into the hillside.

"I see them," I responded. "What am I looking at?"

"The were the German bunkers from the last war. They were here to keep the Allies from advancing inland and liberating Rome. Of course there was never any invasion on this part of the coast. That came at Anzio. The men stationed here were on a permanent vacation."

"What are they used for now?"

"Local youngsters make love, not war."

"That's an improvement," I joked.

Luigi agreed.

The beaches were, in the more liberated Northern regions of Italy, topless. I confess to an unregenerate and hopelessly American fascination with the place. I'd sit contentedly behind my Ray-Bans, my San Francisco baseball cap pulled down about my eyes, and silently celebrate the parade of beautiful Italian womanhood.

European men, Luigi included, seemed accustomed to this feminine display. Luigi acted blasé. He, and his European colleagues, would carry on conversations with half-naked women as if it were a completely normal and comfortable circumstance. I lacked their sophistication.

Luigi and I continued our long talks about the nature of life, our differences and our similarities. Once, as we sped off down a country lane toward the beach, Luigi became nostalgic.

"I remember the many times when I had a family and we would go to the beach on Sundays," he said. "Those were the happiest times of my life."

"You still have a family," I said. "Have you forgotten your daughter?"

"Of course not. But I haven't told you about my son. His name was Luca—which means light—he was two years younger than Laura. And he was the light of my life."

"My God," I said. "What happened?"

"A brain tumor. There were two operations, but they didn't help. I lost my son, then my wife. She went back to America. Now those days are long ago. But how much I still think of them. How much I miss my boy. My family."

So that was it.

Now I understood the nature of Luigi's heartbreak. Now I understood his constant movement and ceaseless attempts at connecting with someone, something. Now I understood the sadness in his eyes.

I was invited to a choral concert at the Church of San Clemente in the central district near the Colosseum. I loved the ancient church and especially the Renaissance courtyard, where I had seen several musical productions ranging from piano recitals to Mozart's opera *The Magic Flute*.

San Clemente was run by the Irish Dominicans and was a

major archaeological dig as well as an ancient place of worship. As the priests conducted renovations late in the nineteenth century, they discovered, as at the beautiful church in Miglionico, the remains of an older, forgotten edifice upon which the modern structure was built.

The original church, built in the fourth century and destroyed by the Normans in 1084, had been completely lost to history. While the excavations of the ancient church were under way, the remains of still more and still older buildings were found beneath the fourth-century church. A Roman apartment building and villa of the Roman consul, Titus Flavius Clemens, had been destroyed in the great fire of Rome—the one Nero was supposed to have fiddled over in 64 A.D.

By walking down the equivalent of three floors, the tourist could enter ancient Rome. Titus Flavius Clemens was an early Christian who gave over his building for the clandestine practice of the Mass. He was martyred by the Roman government for his actions. The Colosseum, the site of other Christian martyrs, is a short couple of blocks from the church.

One of the prize possessions of the Dominicans is the white marble choir enclosure that was built into the "new" church in 1108. It is still used and the acoustics under the dome are marvelous.

Luigi and I heard a choir sing several Gregorian chants, some Italian Renaissance religious music, and a segment from a Bach Mass. I could only imagine the grand sweep of history the site had witnessed. It was thrilling to attend a ceremony where they had been going on for so very long.

The church was, obviously, in the Centro, or central district, and parking was impossible. Luigi and I had taken a bus to the concert. Afterward, we walked a few blocks through the balmy spring evening to our stop directly next to the Colosseum.

Three young German women waited for a bus as traffic passed by in the roadway. In an eye-blink a car carrying three Italian youths climbed the curb, screeched to a halt, and parked halfway into the bus stop. The young men popped out of the Fiat like circus clowns. They approached the women with exaggerated greetings.

In a great gabble of pidgin German, elementary Italian, and British English, the young men managed to quickly convince all three young women to accompany them to a local dance club, where, they promised, the cover charge wouldn't be expensive and they could all have a great time.

I was flabbergasted when the women piled into the Fiat with the Italian boys and sped off. I shook my head in disbelief.

Luigi chuckled. "They didn't even offer to pay," I said, as if that were an element in what I found to be a startling notion: young women running off with strangers from a bus stop. My sisters, at the German women's age, would have been threatened with their very existence for behaving in that manner, had my parents ever learned of it.

"You know, of course," Luigi started in his full-macho posture, his chest puffed out, a slight swagger of his head as he spoke, "many of the Northern European women come to Italy just to meet Italian men."

"That's what the Italian men think," I said. "I lived in Germany for nearly three years. I never heard a German woman talk about coming to Italy to meet a man."

"Why would they tell you? Besides, it's true. I know it for a fact. We know how to treat women with respect."

I laughed. It had been a topic I had heard much about in

Rome. A middle-aged woman friend of mine from Houston had told me Italian men were the most courteous and gentlemanly, no matter the lady's age. "It's genetic," she said. "I know what I'm speaking about, I'm Italian."

Another friend of mine, a young, pretty blond American woman who lived in Rome with her Italian husband and spoke fluent Italian, had another view on the issue. "I hate to be thought of as a piece of meat," she said. "I'll hear the conversation between a couple of men about my physical attributes, or worse, they'll propose something directly to me. When I respond in their language, they always apologize profusely and say they didn't know I was Italian. 'It would be okay to say these things if I didn't know what you were saying?' I ask. It embarrasses them, but there's no stopping the comments."

"That's the crude youngsters from the city," snapped Luigi. "All cities have such inhabitants. She's not talking about educated and mature men."

The only thing I knew for sure was that I never saw Luigi in the company of women when he wasn't completely attentive and filled with enthusiasm. Women seemed to supply him with an energy nothing else quite matched.

As far as Luigi was concerned, the greatest invention of modern times was blue jeans for women. Luigi loved to watch women from the south side as they advanced to the north.

"You see that?" he would ask, eyebrows raised, and in a worshipful whisper, indicating some passing presentation of pulchritude. "It reminds me of a peach," he'd say, referring to that certain portion of the feminine anatomy most conspicuous from behind.

Luigi was fanatic about the subject, yet I never heard him utter a word to a woman that was impolite or risqué.

"You American men are overrun by your women," he would say. "The American women have lost some of their femininity with their militant feminism. The Italian women are feminists, too, but have remained feminine as well."

Like their contemporaries in the rest of the developed world, Italian women enjoy an increasing equality in the professions, the workplace, and in politics. Yet Italian feminism is not without its peculiarities. There are two national festival days dedicated to women in Italy. There is the conventional mother's day for those women opting for the more traditional role of *casalinga* or homemaker. And the Italians set apart another Sunday, a separate day, for *La Festa delle Donne*—the feast of *all* women, whether they exercise reproductive options or not.

"You see," Luigi explained, "we celebrate *every one* of our women, not just our mothers. We love our women. And they have been liberated much longer than those of other countries, even though many have remained in traditional roles."

As usual, I asked for him to explain that one.

"Have you heard of the *vedove bianchi*? The White Widows."

I knew he was referring to the period in Italy when many of the young men had gone off to the new world to find work. They left behind wives who were, in a sense widows, but did not have to wear the traditional black clothing of grieving widows. Their husbands were still very much alive but not with them. Thus, the term "white widows" described their circumstance.

"Yes," I said. "I know about the women without their men."

"Well," Luigi continued, happy to once again inform this uninformed American about things Italian, "what most people overlook is the economic impact that had on our country. For the first time in modern Europe, the Italian men sending their paychecks across the ocean to their wives meant Italian women *controlled* the economy. They were the first truly liberated women in the modern world because they controlled the paycheck, not the men. And they've understood the difference ever since."

I mulled over what he said.

"Let me ask you," he continued to make his point, "did you consider your mother equal with your father?"

"Most definitely," I replied. "An 'Italian mother' in my neighborhood meant someone who took charge."

"And were your grandmothers equal to your grandfathers?"

"They had their own lives, if that's what you mean."

"Ecco," said Luigi triumphantly. "My point is made. Italian women were the first to be what you Americans call 'liberated.' Only we can still celebrate the differences. We can still celebrate romance and the female figure. Especially in blue jeans, which you Americans *did* give us and for which I am grateful."

10

~

Gamberale, Ancora

Pietro's Parties and the Pirates

Claudio DiUlius owned the La Fonte Hotel in Gamberale. I met him as I paid my lunch bill with a credit card. He asked about my name and instantly knew our relationship. Claudio was a distant cousin to my grandmother and shared her dark brooding eyes and gentle smile.

I had come to know Claudio over the previous year and some, during which I had made several quick trips to the village of my grandfather. Claudio was Stefano's father—the young man whom I had encountered on my first solitary visit to the mountaintop town.

I made a point of staying at the lodge-style hotel whenever possible—for a now discounted rate thanks to Claudio—and found my cousin curious about, and interested in, my search for the past. He told me the names of people I should contact who had any recollections of my grandfather's family, and he served as both host and adviser when I visited.

One evening we ate in the spacious, aerie-like dining room overlooking the rugged mountainside. Claudio's chef had prepared homemade gnocchi—pasta-like potato dumplings—in a light tomato sauce, seasoned with fresh basil and a fabulous goat cheese.

"This cheese is the freshest I've ever tasted," I raved.

Claudio looked at me curiously. "It comes from our local farms," he said, as if I should have known the source.

I was becoming like Luigi; fresh food could nearly bring me to tears.

Later that evening, Claudio and I had coffee outside on a bench in front of the hotel and enjoyed the cool, fresh mountain air.

"That's the road your grandfather took to leave this village." Claudio pointed to the asphalt ribbon that ran by the hotel. "It is a famous story here. Your grandfather left this village *in piedi*—on foot, and walked all the way to the train station in the valley below. I can see him walking away in my imagination."

"He told me he was hungry," I said.

Claudio laughed. "I think that was a story. The DePasquale family he comes from has always been one of the most successful and wealthy families in our town. I think he left because there was nothing for him to do. His challenge was in America. He went to find my great-grandfather, the first from our home to get to Pittsburgh."

"My great-grandfather, too," I said, finally understanding our linkage. "Do you know the story about Gaetano DiUlius being refused a drink in a Pittsburgh bar?" Claudio hadn't heard the tale, we shared a big laugh together over Guy and his brothers demanding their drink.

I mentioned I had been researching the history of the area, and wondered what Claudio had learned in school about the ancient times of his native region.

"The people who lived here during Rome were very tough," he started. "They were a tribe called the 'Samnites' and they were the only Italian people from those times to actually defeat the Roman legions in battle. The Romans had to ask them to become allies and respect them. Many people believe the Romans fled to hills like these when the barbarians came."

"You mean here, in this village?" I couldn't find any historical reference for the village during the ancient empire.

"I suppose so." Claudio shrugged. "I really don't know. But the records show that nearly a million people lived in Rome at its height and, after the final sack in the fifth century, only a couple of thousand remained. Those people had to go somewhere. Why not here?"

"I read where this place was founded later," I said.

Claudio shrugged again. "I don't know. I'm not sure they ever taught us that, but then between the war and what happened after the war, history lessons weren't the most important things on our minds." He laughed quietly, just like my grandmother had.

I went back to my room, retrieved my laptop, and returned to the fresh air. I shared my notes with Claudio. It was especially difficult for me, since Claudio spoke no English. I had to use all my translation skills—first from Italian to English in the formal histories I had found, then back into what was becoming my peculiar brand of Italian—in order to communicate with Claudio at nine thousand feet. At any altitude, this whole language thing could be dizzying.

As I organized my notes, Claudio offered a bowl of what looked like candy but I knew to be candy-coated pecans.

"I haven't seen those in years," I said. "I remember the brides at all the Italian weddings gave a little sack of these to each guest. They were wrapped in a cheesecloth and tied off with colored ribbons. I can't remember its name."

"*Confetti.* It is one of our traditions. This candy was invented in Sulmona, one of the oldest towns in this region. It was the Roman town where Ovid was born. They say *Confetti* is about as old as Rome. It was a very special treat."

"So, we'd been celebrating a local tradition all those years and I never knew it."

"There are probably many more traditions we all have shared," Claudio said. "But tell me about this history you've been reading."

I went into my notes and read from a combination of computer pages and handwritten scribbling on legal tablets. According to the histories I'd paged through, sometime after the fall of Rome the Longobards—literally the long-axes, named for the weapons they fought with—arrived and began to fortify defense positions on innumerable hilltops throughout the mountain ranges. These people, it was claimed, originated in Scandinavia. Some histories claimed the word "Longobard" meant "long beard," but Sebastiano said that was a misinterpretation.

From the far north, the short- or long-bearded long-ax wielders began a long migration, first moving into the area of the eastern Alps in what is now Slovenia, Austria, and Hungary. Then, in the fifth century after Christ, the tribes were forced southward into Italy, where they snaked along the central Apennine spine of the country.

In the Abruzzi, this was apparently a peaceful incursion. The Italians who greeted them had taken many clues from the Romans; a system of laws were already in place. They had the habit of bathing—the most important habit of civilization according to the Romans and the custom that separated the barbarians from the nonbarbarians. The Christian religion was widely practiced and the Latin language was the official form of communication. The Longobards seemed to have embraced these customs and blended in.

Gamberale was named for a Longobard chieftain, Gambara. The first mention of the town in any literature historians could find was in a register of the baronies from the twelfth century, and the best guess was the town had already been there for at least three to four centuries.

Claudio listened attentively as I droned out the information. "Ah," he said when I finished my review, "I didn't know any of that. I always thought the town's name had something to do with *gamberi,* or shrimp."

I chuckled. "The Italians can relate anything to food. Of that, I'm sure."

A Sculli couple from Pittsburgh was visiting the village for the summer months. Claudio told me where to find them and said I should talk with them. "They are elderly. They remember the old times here."

I arrived at the Sculli's door in midmorning. The couple stayed in a reconstructed home—what would be called a "townhouse" by American standards—which they kept in their birthplace village for a summer retreat.

Carmen, a full head of brilliant white hair gracing his scalp, greeted me warmly—as if he knew me. The couple welcomed me into their neat home and Mrs. Sculli had cookies and coffee on the table. They had obviously been waiting for my visit.

Carmen asked me to guess his age, then quickly told me he was eighty. Teresa, his wife, looked to be in her seventies.

This branch of the Scullis had been living in Pittsburgh since shortly after World War II. Though they lived in an American city, watched American television, and navigated the American system, they refused to speak English while staying in their hometown. I was back to lingual disadvantage.

Carmen moved slowly and deliberately. He seemed to have some trouble hearing. His responses, however, were clear and direct. He was obviously pleased to talk about the history of the village and share his stories with a *paisano.*

"I was a soldier during the war," he said.

"American?"

"No, Italian. We were taken prisoner when Mussolini was thrown out. Do you know Nuremberg?"

"Very well. I was stationed near there for almost three years."

"Well, do you know the *Bahnhof*—or main train station?"

"Yes, the army radio station I reported for was directly across the street."

"Well, I was forced to work in a factory four blocks from that station. The Americans bombed us every day. One day they blew a hole in the wall of the camp where I was living. I walked out through that hole and came home. That was the end of the war for me."

Mrs. Sculli smiled as she listened to the story she had undoubtedly heard many times. She poured more coffee as I concentrated on Carmen's wording and double-checked my translation.

"How did you get home?"

"I walked."

"You *walked*? From Germany? Through Austria, across the Alps and down the Apennines?"

Carmen grinned and nodded.

"My God. How long did that take?"

"A couple of months. I could have done it faster, but I had to hide from both the Italian partisans and the Germans." The old man had a guttural laugh.

"Everyone walked in those times," added Teresa. "When the Germans came to this village, we had to walk away. There was no other way to move about."

"You were here when the Germans came?" I asked.

"Yes, I was a young girl." Teresa moved about the kitchen as she talked, straightening things on the sink and watering the beautiful bright red geraniums she kept in a window box. "They made us all go live with the nuns. We had to walk for days. I remember how cold it was and I had no boots, but we had to walk through the snow. We were all very young and very frightened."

"Where did you go?"

"To the Castel del Sangro in the valley. We didn't know if we would ever see our families again. But the worst part for me was the salt."

"The salt?"

Teresa stopped her movement and stood by the table.

"Yes." She giggled like a little girl. "The nuns didn't have any salt. It was wartime and there was none. Their food was

terrible, no seasoning at all. That was the worst part for me."
She laughed again.

"Come," Carmen said, "let's walk now and see our little
hometown. Would you like to see the house of your grandfather's family?"

"Very much so," I said.

Carmen donned a jacket to protect against the cool mountain air. We left the little house and slowly climbed the steep
hill that ran by the Scullis' place up to the ancient castle, *"Il
nostro castello"*—our castle, as Carmen put it. I had never
thought of myself as claimant of a castle before. I took Carmen's arm as he struggled with the incline. He continued his
narrative as we inched along.

"I remember your grandfather very well." Carmen gasped
for breath. "He came back to our village in, must have been
1928, and made the greatest *festa* we'd ever had in these mountains." He paused for breath as we neared the crest. "Oh, how
well I remember! I was fifteen or sixteen, so I can still see it
very clearly. There was food, so much food—lamb, chicken,
sausage, all kinds of sweets and pastries. Some food I'd never
seen before."

We reached the top of the climb and stood on the observation deck. The old man looked off into the endless valley
below. A light mist hung in the morning air. Carmen paused
and caught his breath.

"Then there was the *fuochi artificiali*—the fireworks. Your
grandfather, Pietro, had professional men from Rome come to
our village to make a wonderful fireworks display. No one from
these hills had ever seen such a thing before. It was something
no one could forget."

He continued to scan the misty valley as he recalled that long-ago party. "Your grandfather also had a cameraman with him. A professional from a movie company in Rome. He made films of your grandfather's activities. Those movies became very famous for us. They were shown in America. They made us feel important."

"I know," I said. "I think I saw those same films once, but they are all gone now, turned to dust."

Carmen turned as if it were time to go. He motioned toward the castle with a slightly shaky hand. "The Germans burned the old castle. This one has been rebuilt since the war," he said, dismissing the subject. He obviously didn't care for the current construction. He motioned for me to follow.

As we started down a narrow alley away from the castle, a tall, elderly man with another full head of gray hair and a bright pink complexion climbed the walkway and approached us. The lanky stranger held up his hand in a greeting.

"Ah," exclaimed Carmen, "here is my brother-in-law."

Signore Paterra smiled broadly as we were introduced. "I know who you are," he said, as we shook hands. "I knew your grandfather, he was a great man from our little town. Do you know, your grandfather came back to this village in, oh, what year was it, Carmen?"

"It was 1928."

"No, it was later than that."

"No, it was 1928."

"Carmen, it couldn't have been 1928 because I didn't go off to the army until . . ."

"It was 1928."

"I know he made several trips," I offered, hoping to stem the argument.

"He made a magnificent festival. I met him for the first time that year." Signor Paterra smiled broadly, stretching his bright pink cheeks, his gray hair tousled by the wind, his gray eyes clear and alert. "He showed me his pen," he added, as if I'd understand the reference. He cupped his fingers as if holding an imaginary writing implement.

"His pen?"

"Yes!" he said excitedly. "Pietro took a *penna stilografica*—a fountain pen—from his pocket and told me it had been a gift to him from Benito Mussolini. I will never forget that. I was holding a pen, a gift, that Il Duce himself had given to your grandfather. Things like that didn't happen in this village every day."

"It did in 1928," Carmen insisted.

I studied Signor Paterra's full head of gray. I wondered if there was some secret to this altitude and keeping one's hair. Mr. Paterra seemed to be enjoying his reminiscences and was obviously not in any hurry.

"I'm not really from here," he explained. His father, like Sebastiano's grandfather, had been a trader who walked these ancient hills for many years. The father decided to resettle his family in this village, apparently unusual for that time. It had been over seventy years before our meeting, but Signor Paterra still described himself as being "from" another place.

"Have you seen your family's home?" Signor Paterra was now officially part of our tour.

"We were just walking that way," said Carmen. "It is a famous house," he continued as the three of us strolled down the incline.

"Here." Carmen pointed to a row of homes hugging the top of cliff. "The big stone house. It is one of our finest buildings."

Carmen pointed to the largest townhouse in the row. Its facade was made from gray fieldstones and trimmed with a light-colored wood. It was a handsome edifice and confirmed the wealthy status of the family that Claudio had described.

I remembered my grandfather's comment when I related how beautiful I had found Italy after my first brief visit. "*You saw it with a full stomach*" always meant to me that *he* hadn't. It was fairly obvious now that poverty wasn't what drove him to America; it had to have been ambition. By all accounts, my grandfather had not missed many meals.

"That is the house where your grandfather was born and where his brother, Bartolemeo, your great-uncle, lived when he came back from the Americas. He was caught here during the war."

"Does anyone still live there?" I asked.

"A lawyer from Naples owns it now. But he doesn't come here very often, it is a summer home to escape the Mezzogiorno heat. Most of the time the house is empty. Like almost all of the other places in this village."

"You don't worry about crime?"

"There have been thieves on occasion, but they are easy to spot now that so few people live here. And we know how to make good locks. These houses have been here for a long, long time and thieves have been around even longer."

"You don't know the story of the *briganti*?" Signor Pattera asked?

"Brigands?"

"Yes. Thieves. Pirates. They used to live in bands through-out the hills in this area and further south. Your grandfather never told you the story of his famous ancestor, Bartolemeo?"

"The only Pirates I've ever heard of wore uniforms and played in Pittsburgh."

"Ah," sighed Carmen, "that is why your grandfather's house is famous." He smiled and took my arm. We continued down the cobblestone alley.

"Many years ago *briganti* came to the village to steal and plunder," Carmen explained in his gruff voice. "Your great ancestor, Bartolomeo, and his three brothers were home and saw what was happening. They were only boys—Bartolomeo was seventeen years or so, his brothers were younger. The four of them ran into the street with swords and knives. They fought the brigands by themselves, while calling out to alert the rest of the village."

Carmen chopped the air with his hands as if wielding a sword. "They drove the thieves away, though Bartolomeo was wounded and died. Here on these very steps. His brothers survived." Carmen pointed to a long stone stairway leading from the side of the house to what looked like a small fountain and plaza below. He studied the steps carefully as if to search for traces of the ancient conflict.

"I'd never heard any such story," I said. "When did this happen?"

"That was in the 1750s," Signor Pattera said.

"No," said Carmen. "It was in the 1850s."

"The brigands weren't here then. It was the 1750s," insisted Signor Pattera, "there were no brigands after Garibaldi."

"That's right," said Carmen, shaking his fist. "And Garibaldi cleared out the bands from the south in the 1870s. You have your dates all confused."

"Well, I know it couldn't have been 1928."

My mind was still processing the information. An ancestor who had been killed in a sword battle with brigands while driving them away from his village. Why wouldn't my grandfather have told that story? Of course, he had never been much of a storyteller, but Uncle Al had been exactly that; the family's repository of what precious little lore we claimed. Yet here I stood on a chilly mountainside, hearing the story of a long-ago ancestor's bravery for the first time.

My grandfather named his last son Bartolomeo, our Marine and Iwo Jima hero. I didn't know of his formal birth name until I began my records collecting; to me he had always been simply, Uncle Eugene. His son, my cousin Alfred, was wounded in Vietnam. Maybe there was a link there? Maybe my uncle had been told the story about Bartolemeo? Maybe the war heroics in his line were, in some small part, the result of hearing of his namesake?

"Come," said Carmen, interrupting my thoughts. "I will show you the place where your last relative died. The De-Pasquales, like all of our families, have shed their share of blood in this little place."

Carmen kept hold of my arm as we descended the long stair-case where Bartolomeo had died, then a second staircase on the opposite side of the small landing, then still another set of stairs dug into the hillside. We finally reached a flat section of land at the crest of the valley below the town.

"Here," Carmen said. He panted from the long descent. He pointed to an old, dirt road that ran along an ancient wall. The road was now more of a path, strewn with tall weeds jutting through what was left of the gravel. Two wheel tracks were still faintly visible, but the path obviously wasn't used much any-more.

"Here is where your uncle was killed. He was walking along this road, right there, next to the cemetery." Carmen indicated the spot. "He stepped on a land mine. The explosion blew a hole in his back. He died quickly."

"Were you here?" I asked.

"Yes, it was early in 1945. It was almost the end of the war. The Germans didn't really care who they killed, they wanted to make it as difficult as possible for the Americans and English to catch up with them."

"So they killed my noncombatant great-uncle in the process."

Carmen shrugged. "It was wartime. Every one was an enemy. No one was ever really safe."

Later that evening I told Claudio of my experiences that day. I shared my wonder at having visited places where my ancestors, my own blood, had shed theirs.

"What happened to your family during the war?" I asked.

"We lived in the woods when the Germans came."

"Where in the woods?"

"Just in the woods. Anywhere we could find food, trap a rabbit, or whatever. My brother and mother died that winter, so did many others."

"How old were you?"

"Six or seven. I was old enough to be frightened but not old enough to care for myself. They tried to get all of the girls out of the village and to the nuns, but the sisters could only take so many. The men, boys, and older women mostly lived in the forest and hills. Many starved, some were shot, others killed in bombings."

"My God. What a horrible way to spend your youth."

"It was all of Europe." Claudio sighed deeply. "It was all of

Russia, too," he added. "In fact, it was everywhere in the world *except* the United States."

We sat on a couch in the high-ceilinged parlor, its centerpiece a large circular unlit fireplace made from local fieldstones. The hotel was empty, but for me and one other couple who had noisily made love the evening before—an intimacy I'd have preferred not to have shared.

Claudio and I sat alone, dwarfed by the huge room, and sipped coffee as my cousin recalled the past. We heard occasional kitchen noises off in the distance as the chef and his helper cleaned up after the evening meal, which only half a dozen had eaten.

"We all cursed ourselves for not having left here and gone to America with our other relatives, but what could we do? We survived." Claudio paused and offered me another coffee. While looking at his sad, dark eyes, I remembered my grandmother's face.

"Now we have our country back and the people are wealthy and healthy again." Claudio seemed comfortable with his memories. He didn't seem especially disturbed by the recollection of so much violence and death. "Things come and they go," he added. "It is all part of life."

I shook my head. I had lost my mother as a teenager, but to natural causes. I had lost friends in Vietnam to man's violence. I had lost two family members on American streets to drunk drivers. Perhaps Claudio's calm acceptance was correct. Loss certainly is a part of life. But the loss in this village seemed so stark.

"You must come back for our festival," Claudio said, changing the subject. "I will save a room and I have a surprise for you."

"A surprise?"

"Yes. Let's call my brother Gino in Milan."

We left the sitting area and Claudio motioned for me to follow him into the small office behind the reception desk at the end of the main foyer. He picked up the heavy black telephone and dialed long distance. He exchanged pleasantries with his brother for a few moments, then handed the receiver to me.

I had no idea what was going on. *"Pronto?"* I ventured.

"Ciao, cugino. This is Gino. My brother Claudio has told me all about your digging around for the history of our little village. Do you know your grandfather had movies made from his visits?"

"Yes," I replied with the now almost-cliché response, "but they no longer exist. They turned to dust in Pittsburgh."

Gino laughed. "I have a copy."

"What? You have the movies?"

"Yes, I had a copy made years ago and now have made a video from it."

"When can I see this?" I was half tempted to leave for Milano that evening.

"At the festival," Gino said. "At the festival next month for our little town of Gamberale."

11

Onoranze Funebri

Rome . . .

Federico Fellini was dead. The genius Italian filmmaker had died after a lingering illness that had been publicly reported in great detail. The entire country seemed to have hung on the deathbed developments. Fellini's death marked an important passing in Italian postwar culture. He had been, in many ways, far more important to the country's image than most of its ever-changing political leaders.

Now the Italians set about marking the end of his life in a dignified and memorable manner. The government announced that his body would lie in state at Cinecittà—the huge film studio on the outskirts of Rome. During the halcyon days of *La Dolce Vita* in the sixties, Fellini had made the studio the center of modern European cinema.

238

Luigi and I drove out to Cinecittà to view the lying in state. It was a Felliniesque day; gray, dark, heavy skies lay low and sodden above the city. A hint of fog hung in the air. The clouds cast a filtered, muted light over everyone and everything. The normal chaos of Rome seemed subdued, the highways calm.

At Cinecittà there was none of the usual pushing, shoving, and wheedling for position I had witnessed at other public events. On this day, people looked directly at one another, exchanged nods, offered directions. We walked through the enormous film lot, scattered with abandoned sets from long-forgotten spaghetti-westerns and cheap Roman epics, until we reached Studio 5, the largest indoor studio and the favorite of the Maestro's.

The scene inside the gigantic building was stunning. On the opposite wall a couple of hundred yards from the gigantic main doors, a huge mural artificially created a bright blue sky streaked with high clouds. Below the enormous backdrop was a small riser. A simple, closed, dark-wood casket lay at its center. The coffin was strewn with bright red flowers.

An honor guard of Carabinieri in Napoleonic-era uniforms and tricornered hats braced at attention on the corners of the flat. Many in the crowd stood before the coffin for long periods of time, silently staring at the last earthly reminder of the great director.

As we exited the studio, television crews stood by conducting interviews with visiting dignitaries and occasional members of the public. A nun directly in front of me talked with a reporter about Fellini's vision of religion. As I walked through the huge plaster-of-paris replicas of Roman monuments, reminding me of the many surreal visual sequences in the Maestro's films, I heard an old man say to an elderly couple that Fellini was a *"un uomo importante"*—a very important man. The comments sounded like the random sound bites Fellini sprinkled throughout his movies.

As we passed a huge pseudo-marble foot about the size of a garage, I watched a family feed a stray dog and her pups. The dog's teats were extended, swollen, and dragging the ground beneath her. She apparently had a very small litter; two puppies.

My mind raced; *the most sacred symbol of ancient Rome, orphans being suckled by the she-wolf.* Was it pure coincidence she would be here at this studio on this day? Dogs played a major role as Roman omens. Fellini played such a major role in modern symbolism.

As we drove home on the circular highway around the city, a bus passed us in the fast lane. A placard on its side read, *"Onoranze Funebri"*—honorable funerals. In one of its most ancient funeral customs, Roman patricians paraded through the streets carrying the death masks of their ancestors. It was considered a curse for a man not to have a son, for it was the son's responsibility to honor his father and his forebears with a huge funeral parade, followed by lavish games and dramas.

It was also the son's responsibility to tend to the upkeep of the grave or memorial. Without sons, a man was condemned to eternal indifference. There are shards of marble on almost every wall in the central district, relics from these ancient tombs proclaiming the existence and passage of so many still-not-forgotten ones, the sons apparently successful in their duties.

As a man without a son, I think of this often. I know Luigi does, too.

. . .

A few months before my visit to Cinecittà, the phone had rung very early one morning. It was my brother calling from Pennsylvania.

"I've got bad news," he said. "Uncle Al died last night."

It couldn't have been a surprise. He had been so frail the last time we had visited in Pittsburgh, so obviously ill. Yet the words were sudden, harsh, unwanted.

My brother and I talked for a short while. He gave me the details of a funeral I couldn't attend, a brief sketch of my uncle's last few weeks of decline.

I called my aunt as soon as my brother and I ended our call.

"Oh, Paul," she said. "He talked about you all the time. He told me he saw you last week, that you had been looking in his room. Of course, I told him you were in Italy, he was seeing things. But he was convinced he had seen you in the doorway."

"He was out of pain, I hope."

"Yes, and his mind seemed clear, except for his insistence that he had seen you. He asked me what date it was. He said he wanted to die on the anniversary of Shakespeare's death, April 23. He died on the anniversary of Shakespeare's funeral, April 25. That seemed to be important to him."

Her words stayed with me, hung in my psyche like a giant shadow. I imagined my uncle on his deathbed. I fantasized about our never-to-be-spoken last conversation.

Like Fellini, like Luigi, like me, Uncle Al had no sons. He spent his life insisting that we, his nephews and nieces, share his enthusiasm for grand opera, Shakespeare, baseball, cinema, and a host of other lesser interests. But he didn't insist through pressure or force; he let his own unlimited and joyous passion carry us into his excitement and energy.

My uncle's cat was named Rigoletto. His apartment was a shrine cluttered with copies of famous sculpture, prints of famous paintings, bookcases filled with old 78 and 33 rpm record albums. Over the mantelpiece was a placard with a simple quote:

> *Our doubts are traitors,*
> *and make us lose the good we oft might win*
> *by fearing to attempt.*

I'd never spent more than ten minutes in that apartment without my uncle retrieving some precious composition from his collection and excitedly playing the disk. Our shared love of music was a special bond between us. His musical understanding and insights were uneducated and nontechnical, yet I never had a college professor who could touch his exacting sense of the composition and his inner compass for quality and beauty.

We had spent many hours at the old Victrola. Many evenings at the local movie house. Many dinners going over the improbability of the "Murderers Row" of the 1927 New York Yankees or the sheer poetry of Roberto Clemente's natural stance.

Even Fellini, with his unlimited imagination, couldn't have invented a character like Uncle Al. He was an original. He could not have been duplicated.

As a surrogate son, I could not let him pass into oblivion. Like the ancients, I yearned for some marking of the man's passing.

Fellini left no son, but left his films.

Luigi lost his son.

I have no sons, nor any prospects of sons.

But Luigi keeps on dancing.

Maybe the Romans had it backward. Maybe it's the life that counts, not the funeral.

Why else would we dance or listen to Beethoven?

Bambini Malamati . . .

The picture-perfect summer in Rome was ending. I was into my third, and what had to be final, year in Italy. I still hadn't found anything positive about Francesco, but not from lack of trying. So far all of my phone calls to Matera, my letters to various local and state officials, rummaging through record halls throughout Basilicata and talking with priests had been fruitless. As soon as the festival in Pietro's hometown of Gamberale was over, my remaining available time would be spent completely devoted to the search for Francesco.

Meanwhile, I had learned much about Pietro's life and village. And would undoubtedly learn more at the festival, now just two weeks ahead. It was hard to focus knowing the films I thought disintegrated still existed. They would be icing on a fairly complete cake, or so I thought.

Luigi knew how excited I was about seeing Pietro's movies. He, too, seemed anxious. "Are you sure they are the same ones?" he asked, for at least the tenth time, as we strolled about the Pantheon's Piazza della Rotondo one perfect evening.

"No. I know he made at least three trips and, from the sounds of things, he made more than one home movie of his travels. The people in the village talk about a visit and party in 1928—they distinctly remember a photographer on that trip.

My mother came with him in 1933, and there was a photographer and visit with Mussolini in that year as well."

"But are they the same films your grandfather had made?"

"My cousin claims they are the same movies my grandfather had commissioned. He says he made a copy from the originals in Pittsburgh several years ago. It seems no one on our side of the ocean had the interest to preserve the films."

We stopped for a gelato at Della Palma, a huge, modern, stainless steel and glass parlor facing the ancient cobblestone way just beyond the famous Piazza della Rotunda. Tourists and young people crowded the narrow street. Dusk settled on the ancient walkway.

Luigi reminisced about *La Dolce Vita.* "How wonderful it was to visit this section of Centro in the sixties. Here and at the Piazza Navona, there was music and adventure every night. You could feel the youth in the air, everything seemed new. It was the best entertainment in town and it didn't cost a single lire."

We savored our gelato as we walked the few blocks to Navona. The modern-day piazza was built on the ruins of Domatian's Circus Agonalis. Some historians claim it was this arena, and *not* the Colosseum, that was flooded for the mock naval battles during the Roman games that have been written about.

We sauntered to the center of the piazza and stood by the famous Bernini Fountain of the Four Rivers, just in front of the equally famous facade of the St. Agnese Church by Borromini. We listened to a modern-day folk singer sing and strum his guitar. A group of young girls thrilled to his bohemian aura.

Luigi laughed. "Nothing ever changes. The musicians are always the favorite of the young women."

"You mean folk singers are," I said. "We jazz players are a lonely lot."

"That's because no one can understand what you're doing."

It was a typical conversation with Luigi.

We sauntered through the many artists' easels scattered about the center of the plaza. They contained paintings and sketches of everything from clowns to ancient Roman cityscapes.

My walks with Luigi had covered every quarter of the city. On Sundays Luigi religiously went to the open-air market at Porta Portese, the Italian equivalent of the world's largest flea market. Vendors from all over the world assembled there each week. Russians sold cameras and painted lacquer boxes; Africans hawked big and small wooden sculptures, bright scarves, and flowing gowns; Chinese offered trinkets and puzzles; Peruvians played lutes and guitars and entertained at intersections, passing the hat at each performance; there was clothing and luggage of every type, timepieces, music CDs and cassettes—both bootlegged and legal—jewelry, coins, all kinds of collectibles, art reproductions, furniture, books, videotapes and, of course, food. A shopper could find just about any object one ate, constructed, collected, wore, viewed, listened to, played, or admired.

It was overwhelming. The market spread over several city blocks, and was always completely packed with both Romans and tourists. It must have been what the marketplaces in ancient Rome were like. It was both exciting and confusing at the same time.

Once, on one of our many Sunday outings, Luigi laughed after I paid full price for an inexpensive wristwatch that had caught my fancy.

"You'd make a terrible Italian," he said, shaking his head and clicking his tongue in mock disgust.

"I hate all this haggling," I said. "Why can't they just post a price? It's simple that way. You either want it or you don't. You can either afford it or you can't."

"You are like my daughter," he scoffed. "It is old-fashioned to discuss the goods and prices. She wants nothing to do with this place. She wants designer names on her clothing. She is so very American about this, she thinks I'm hopeless."

"This haggling over how much to pay is crazy."

"You'd eliminate the art from the marketplace," he said. "You Americans consume to consume. *Consumption* is your national pastime, not *baseball*. Here, we shop to see what's going on in the world, discover the availability of things, determine the value. It's a different way of looking at the world and at goods."

"Still," I persisted, "what's so difficult about setting a firm price?"

"Because a firm price would indicate a firm value. We don't value goods, we value ideas. Look at our money. Look at the 100,000 lire note."

He took a note from his billfold and held it up.

"Who's picture do you see? A politician? No. An artist. It is the picture of Caravaggio. Look at our basic note, the 1,000 lire."

He held the paper extended to arm's length.

"You see Maria Montessori," he said, slapping his hand against the note. "She's the most familiar face in our society. Not a general. An educator. She symbolizes a value, the way we want to be thought of. Not a price."

246

"I didn't even realize that was Maria Montessori, I'm sorry to say. What does she represent?"

"The future," Luigi said simply. "She invented a method of teaching that the entire world is now using. She invented the future."

I thought about the many hours I had spent riding Rome's buses. I invariably enjoyed the journey, despite the insufficient seating and the lack of air-conditioning. I loved studying my fellow passengers and was touched, every single time, by the tender and loving moments I witnessed between parents and children. There was always a great deal of smiling and touching, smoothing of hair, conversation. I told Luigi about my experiences.

"There is one thing I do believe the Italians do best," he said. "Though there are many things we could do better," he quickly added, punctuated with a jab of his finger.

"But the thing you do best?"

"Children. Despite the fact we aren't having any. We make beautiful children. And we generally care for them well. I talked with an associate of Mrs. Montessori once. She said she thought the world's biggest problems were caused by what she called, *'i bambini malamati.'* Do you know what that means?

"Sick babies?"

"No, not exactly. *Badly loved* babies. My friend claimed children who aren't properly loved when they are babies bear grudges, hold harm inside them. Well-loved children care about other people. I think it makes a great deal of sense. If you love the children well the future will take care of itself."

"And who said Europeans are such pessimists?"

I brought up the subject again on the evening we strolled

about the Piazza Navona. I mentioned an article I had recently read. An AP story cited a child psychologist as saying the German culture, during the period of the Nazis and before, had included severe beatings of children, especially of sons by fathers. The expert called this practice national child abuse and said it could, in part, explain the brutality of the Nazi era.

"*Ecco,*" said Luigi. "We Italians might have been stupid during the Second War, but we were not brutes."

Later that same evening we spotted Sebastiano with a group of male friends. He saw us at the same time. We hugged and embraced. By now, Sebash had stopped speaking English with me. He insisted I should be speaking only in Italian.

"Did I tell you about Natasha and the *Carabinieri?*" Sebash asked us. He nearly giggled at the thought.

Natasha was Sebastiano's American girlfriend. The *Carabinieri,* of course, were the elite Italian national police force, formed to check on all the other police forces, both local and national. Funny thing about them; they were all young men over six feet tall, movie-star handsome, and well aware of their appeal to young women visitors from all over the world. In a word, they swaggered. They also walked beats.

Sebastiano launched into a story about his friend, a breakfast roll, and the police. Natasha had gone into a bar one recent morning for a croissant and coffee. She told the elderly woman cashier she wanted a roll, *senza*—without marmalade—and a cappuccino. Natasha was, she claimed, very specific about not wanting jelly.

The lady said nothing, collected the money, and served the American a roll *with* marmalade. Natasha had been living in Italy for several years and, despite her New York-accented Italian, considered herself a Roman. She had had enough.

"This is what gives our local shopkeepers a bad reputation," she insisted to the startled older woman. "This is why tourists are afraid to spend their money here. This is unfair." She demanded her money back.

The woman refused.

"But I said *no* marmalade," Natasha argued.

The cashier shrugged.

Natasha stormed out of the bar and found a pair of *Carabinieri* on the next corner.

"What do you want us to do?" they wondered, undoubtedly trying to keep straight faces.

"Arrest that woman," she insisted. "This is what can give all of Italy a bad name."

"It apparently did not occur to Natasha that the national police force might not think a jelly donut to be a matter of national policy," Sebash said. He, Luigi, and I all had tears in our eyes from laughter. We could readily visualize the look on the *Carabinieri*'s faces as Natasha articulated her complaint in her New York–accented Italian.

It was good to see the gentle Sebastiano again. "I often think of our festival in Amendolara," I said. I told him about the Gamberale festival and the movies.

"You should come with us," urged Luigi.

"I am teaching this summer." He sounded disappointed. "I want a full report when you return from the mountains."

"I will take careful notes," I promised.

12
∼

Gamberale: La Festa

My Grandfather's Movies

Luigi and I went up to Gamberale for the annual festival. We arrived late one evening, two days before the events were scheduled to start. Gino DiUlius, my cousin from Milan, was due the following day. I wanted lots of time to visit and to view my grandfather's films.

On our way to the village, we passed shepherds in their fields at twilight—Luigi looked at peace. After settling into our hotel he retired early, presumably thinking of *sheps.*

I was awakened early the next morning with what sounded like screaming directly below my window. I opened the shutters to my second-floor room and watched as a lamb, bleating for its life, was carted off by a young man pushing a wheelbarrow past the hotel. I watched as the shepherd made his way to the small butcher shop just down the street.

It was the first time in my life I'd ever seen what would soon be dinner still on the hoof. I felt sorry for the lamb, but knew I would forget the emotion when the meal was served.

My room had the combination water closet–shower that I'd only seen in Italy. The entire room became a shower stall when the water was turned on. I found it awkward to bathe like that, it was so unlike anything else I'd ever experienced. But then I remembered my Army days in the field, when I'd have given anything for hot water and the chance to get clean. I completed my ablutions as quickly as possible, grateful for at least the soap and warm water. I was not about to become a barbarian, no matter how difficult the bathing process.

I rushed down to breakfast and found Luigi sitting in the spacious dining room, enjoying his mineral water along with the scenery.

"You're missing half of life if you can't have the fabulous Italian coffee early in the morning," I joked.

"I'm missing half of life just being alive. My stomach hurts just thinking of coffee," he scoffed. "But isn't this a magnificent view? Look how clear and feel how cool the air is. This is the place to spend the *le ferie di Agosto,* not the hot, crowded beach."

My coffee and croissants arrived. I eagerly devoured my roll *without* marmalade. I shared the joke with Luigi. It was going to be a terrific day. It had already started with laughter.

My cousin, Gino DiUlius, pulled up to the Hotel LaFonte in a big black Fiat. I recognized him immediately; he was a bald version of Claudio with eyes not quite as sad. Gino was robust, in his early fifties, and accompanied by his attractive wife, Gabriella. He threw his arms around me and embraced me—a quick buss on each cheek—eschewing the formal handshake. He was an energetic man, obviously friendly, with a bright and engaging smile.

"*Ciao, cugino.* I am happy to meet you," he said warmly. "Let my brother and I get a coffee and say hello. Then you and I will go and view my tape of your grandfather's famous films. I know you have been waiting a long time to see them again."

Gino was *simpatico.* Within a quarter-hour he, Claudio, Luigi, and I were in a small townhouse across the street from the hotel, owned by a relative to the brothers who made part-time residence in the village. We sat in a very modern-style wood-paneled living room. Gino fussed with a video player and television set.

"But you work in television," he said. "Perhaps you should make these adjustments."

I laughed. "I'll defer that honor to my cousin," I said. I've spent my entire career in the TV industry and still don't know how a picture appears on a screen; it's always magic to me— and this day was to be especially magical.

Gino closed the shades and pushed the play button. The present disappeared. We were transported, in black and white, to an age, place, and time that no longer exists.

The first frames showed a Pennsylvania Board of Censors Seal of Approval. Apparently the films had either been made for, or had been shown in, a commercial house.

The date was clear: 1922.

The film was, of course, silent. It had been subtitled in Italian and what looked like newer, brighter subtitles in English. Gino had added sound. He had gone to a commercial production house in Milan and added a music track. He, himself, wrote and voiced the narration.

The film showed brief panoramic shots of several small villages scattered throughout the mountaintops of the province of Chieti, in the Abruzzi region of Italy. The scenes were intercut with subtitles naming the towns and giving a brief word or two about a particular church or other landmark. It was a travelogue, more or less.

Scratchy scenes followed—farmers in their fields, shots of women from the villages carrying large water pots on their heads. One scene showed a hunting expedition—*la caccia,* the root term for *cacciatore,* ("from the hunter"), in search of game, complete with a cutaway of a slain rabbit lying inert, then a cutaway back to the hunters holding their catch. There were pictures and subtitles of famous bridges and buildings in the area, and scenes of local festivals.

Gino voiced-over the names and nicknames of those pictured wherever he had a positive identification.

The River Sangro—the Blood River—ran through the valley between my grandfather's village and St. Angelo del Pesco on the opposite mountain. It would serve, some twenty-plus years after the film was made, as the dividing line between the Nazis and the Allies. But on this bucolic, silent movie-perfect day, the river rolled along in peaceful, silver-white beauty.

A wedding was taking place in Gamberale. "That was my parents' wedding," Gino said, his only live narration during the video. The young bride, his mother, would starve to death in the woods in 1943, but I was sure no one in these frames could have imagined such a thing.

During another scene of the crowd in Gamberale, Gino's overdub gave nicknames of individuals and their families.

There was a general crowd scene with a group of obviously prominent local men.

I instantly spotted my grandfather, though Gino made no mention of him on the soundtrack. He was hatless and smiling. He looked self-assured, confident.

Another village scene of Gamberale, a festival in progress. The women wore babushkas called *fazzoletti* by Gino in the narration—I know the word to mean "handkerchief" from the street vendors in Rome. Everyone gathered together to pose for this scene, but the men walked and talked separately. There was even a scene of men-only dancing, the women, heads covered with babushkas, standing to the side.

A subtitle read, "Residents of Gamberale with relatives in America." Smiles abounded. Gino's narration gave their nicknames and surnames, I recognized the name of my grandfather's sister, Sabia.

The villagers seemed comfortable playing to what must have been a big movie camera. They looked directly into the lens, and into the future, with the slight nervous movement of their upper bodies every modern video camera can discern. Overall, the *cittadini* appeared remarkably poised, I thought, for a group of people who couldn't have seen professional filmmaking, or have been its object very often.

Another subtitle: "Pietro DePasquale thanks the people of Gamberale for their generosity."

My grandfather stood on a balcony with two other men. The camera angled upward as he spoke to a crowd gathered below. Actually, he gestured more than spoke.

I recognized his movements and facial expressions, though I had never seen him look that way. He was so young! He had a full head of hair I'd never seen. He was exquisitely groomed, wearing a three-piece suit, a gold watch chain dangling across his vest, his tie perfectly knotted in the fashion of the time, his collar perfectly starched. He was obviously *un uomo di rispetto.*

This was 1922, the year Mussolini came to power. It would have been far too soon in his administration for Il Duce to be working his public relation tricks on émigrés. No, this film was a testament to my grandfather's success. Apparently, he alone was responsible for this trip, this *festa,* this filmmaking.

As my grandfather stopped speaking, the man beside him on the balcony, identified as a Dr. Pollice by Gino's narration, made a Fascist salute. *A real, genuine, arm-thrusting-into-air Fascist salute.*

What could my grandfather have said?

I had no memories of these scenes. I recalled seeing films that had been made during my mother's visit eleven years after these pictures had been taken. This was a younger version of my grandfather than I had ever seen. I never realized how much my uncle Al resembled him until that moment.

Then the final scene ran through the machine, the subtitle read, "Pietro DePasquale at the foreign office in Rome."

My grandfather left a government building I recognized as being just off the Via del Corso in central Rome. He exited through the main door, still immaculately outfitted, only now wearing a boater—a straw hat. Until the day he died, the out-of-date hat was all he wore in summer; he alternated with a gray fedora in winter. How many times I held his hats, studied the brims, the labels, the leather headbands. He was the only man I ever knew to wear a straw hat.

In the movie, after he exited the foreign office, he walked

255

from camera left to camera right, and out of the frame. Just like an actor. Just as if the camera wasn't there.

The videotaped film was over.

I sat alone with my thoughts for a few moments in the dark while Gino opened the drapes and retrieved the tape, which he presented to me as a gift.

"I have several copies," he said, "I had this one made for you." I thanked him as my mind turned over the scenes I had just scene.

One notion was immediately clear; while the film described the common villagers as "peasants," and Gino went to great lengths to describe each person and family from the small towns, the elegantly dressed gentleman speaking from the balcony and walking out of the State Department was clearly an *American*. He was not an Italian or a peasant or a *contadino*. He was a businessman, obviously representative of his generation in America, and very different from the villagers with whom he was visiting, relatives or no relatives.

Gino smiled at me. "These films are always the highlight of our little festival," he said. "They are the only way we have of telling our children and grandchildren who we are and where we are from. This video will be watched by everyone coming to our festival during the next five days. They help mark our celebration as special."

I couldn't speak for several minutes. I was still mentally replaying the images I'd just seen.

Part of me felt let down. I had been hoping to see my family, more of my grandfather's family. I knew that there were many more films not included in this video, but these scenes seemed to be the only ones to have survived. I was sure there were none left in Pittsburgh.

Gino passed around a tray of coffee, Coca-Cola, mineral water, and *biscotti*.

"I didn't understand all of the dialect. And why did everyone have a nickname?" I wondered, as I munched the anise cookie.

Gino laughed. "I love the dialect. It is fun to be able to speak it now. As for the names, you know there are really only a dozen or so family names for our entire village. So we had our own way of referring to which branch of which family— your grandfather was always called *il francese,* or from France."

"Why was that?"

"I don't know. Maybe someone a couple of hundred years ago learned French or spoke with an accent that sounded French and they called him 'The Frenchman.' "

It was my turn to laugh. "Everyone in Oakland had some sort of nickname," I remembered. "My grandfather's brother was called 'Frenchy' or 'French.' "

"Ecco," said Gino, "that's exactly what I'm saying."

"There were so many nicknames," I recalled. "There was *Bully, Amers, Jeep, The Globe, Struggles, Elmer, Frizzie, Du, Bright Eyes, Shine,* everyone from my mother's generation and the generation before her had one. All had names I never understood as a boy."

"Frizzie means *frizzante,* or bubbly,' " said Luigi. I suddenly realized how my laughing and joyful aunt got her nickname. *Frizzie-frizzante.* Of course that's why they called her that, it was so fitting! It was an epiphany.

"They were from this village and the village life," Gino explained. "Nicknames described people with the same family names, but they picked up on the individual's habits, looks, or mannerisms. These *soprannomi* were useful for us in the old times. In the days of those movies, their only identity was their village and their particular branch of their family. They all intermarried, so the nicknames kept the lines straight."

"Yes," I said, "and then they moved from this little village to America, where they set up their own little village and continued to intermarry for the next generation. Do you have any idea how difficult it was to explain my relations to my American friends?" I laughed again. "They were still living in their village. I realize that now."

"What we have just seen is a country that no longer exists," Luigi said with a big sigh. "It started to disappear when I was still a *guy*. That is a place we Italians can only remember."

"But the villages are still very much here," I pointed out.

"Yes, but only the old have remained. Very few of the young have stayed and made a go of things," Gino said. "Even Claudio here, who has spent much money and time with the hotel, has been thinking of leaving for the big city. The money isn't to be made in these little, out-of-the-way places, only in the big cities like Rome and Naples."

"And almost none of the children stay," Claudio added. "It started with your great-grandfather's generation. My boys are here with me, but they work over in Pescara, the nearest city. They drive up and down this mountain every day to help me, but their lives aren't in this little village any longer. We exist for ski season and our summer festival. Last winter the snow was poor."

"Did you know," asked Luigi, "the government will give people money to come back to these little villages and fix up a house to modern standards? The Italy of those films ended with the war," he said, "It will never come back."

"The people looked happy," I said.

"And they were for their time," Gino agreed. "But Luigi is right, the war changed everything. Once it was over and we started to rebuild the country, the big cities took over. Radio and television have all but eliminated our regional accents, especially for the younger generation."

"They're going to miss out on a lot of the fun of our language," Gino added as he sipped a Coca-Cola. "And because they are all so highly educated and going to the cities, our unemployment rates are running well over ten percent. They'd be better off staying home with mama."

Claudio picked up the theme. "Our children are more educated now than they've ever been. They don't want to be simple farmers or shepherds. They are lawyers and doctors and psychologists. And they don't have the connections to the old places and old people, their connections are to television and Arnold Schwarzenegger movies."

"And the yearly festivals." Gino beamed his big smile. "And the festival, don't forget."

"Ah, yes," agreed Claudio. "We do have a festival and it is for everyone to remember the past, if only once a year."

La Festa . . .

The first official day of the festival began with a bang.

Literally.

Fireworks exploded first thing in the morning, startling me awake. I could hear booming noises coming from the town square. The church bell began to toll and continued to ring for several minutes. I opened my shutters and looked down the way as a brass band struck up a march, then paraded throughout the village, down every *vicolo*. None but the dead could have remained asleep.

I jumped into the awkward shower, hurriedly dressed, and skipped breakfast. I found Luigi in the lobby of the hotel, humming along with the tune of the distant band music. He wore a necktie.

"A little formal, aren't we?" I asked.

"This morning is the religious festival," he said. "It will be like going to church."

I ran back to my room and put on a tie and sport jacket. When we arrived in the town square, I felt slightly underdressed. Almost all of the adult men were wearing dark suits. I was grateful for Luigi's fashion tip. At least I was wearing a tie.

Overhead decorations had been constructed across the little alleyways leading to the piazza. They reminded me of Christmas decorations back home; swooping arches of white and green and outlined with as yet unlit electric lights.

We mingled in the town square, introducing ourselves to different families and being introduced by Claudio to others. The town was flooded with Pittsburghers back for the festivities. They were a group of mostly retired people with roots in the village and homes in the States.

Signor Caruso, the town historian whom I had met my first day in the village and the first man to tell me about the German occupation, came over to Luigi and me and made a very formal greeting. He wore a purple sash across his chest, marking him, obviously, as an official of some sort. I introduced him to Luigi.

"How are you enjoying our little festival?" he asked, somewhat nervously. His horn-rimmed glasses perched on the tip of his nose, his eyes were dark and penetrating as they stared over the rims.

"Fine," I replied, "though we really haven't seen much as yet. We've been busy watching a festival from seventy years ago."

"Ah, yes, I know of your grandfather's movies. In those days, you know, we had wealthy men like your grandfather to pay for things." His face looked pained, as if he were uncomfortable. "These days," he continued, "we have to rely on the donations from the members of the San Lorenzo Society and our visitors." His eyebrows raised as he finished speaking, his eyes round as they looked out over his horn-rims.

It took a second for his words to translate themselves and sink into my brain. Luigi smiled and winked at me. He rubbed his thumb back and forth against the first two fingers on his right hand.

"Oh, of course," I said, finally understanding. "I'd be happy to help. How much is the usual donation?"

Il Signore visibly relaxed. He slid his glasses higher on the bridge of his nose as his round face broke into a smile.

"Whatever you'd care to give," he said. "These things get more expensive every year."

I handed him some wadded up paper lire. Luigi did the same.

Signore Caruso put the money in his pocket without looking at it. *"Mille grazie,"* he said, quietly.

"Prego," Luigi and I said in unison.

We bought coffee, sweets, and soft drinks from a few of the several vendors who had hiked up the mountain with their carts

261

of goods. We spotted Don Riccardo, the parish priest we had met on our first record-search visit the previous year. He was in the middle of a group of schoolchildren, organizing and giving gentle orders. His surplice was a brilliant white in the morning sun.

The air was electric.

Just before noon, the religious procession officially started the Festival of San Lorenzo. A life-sized statue of the patron saint was paraded through the streets, followed by the brass band and all of the children from the town, dressed in their Sunday finest. The children sang and responded to the prayers of Don Riccardo, who marched directly in front of them. The priest smiled and nodded in our direction as he passed by. I was pleased he remembered our unscheduled session in his sacristy.

There was something primitive, old-fashioned about the ceremony. The blaring brass had the tinny, outdoor sound of slightly sharp trumpets and thin-sounding trombones as the bass drummer banged the tempo with exaggerated blows—*ka-boom, ka-boom, ka-boom*—nearly drowning out the melodic line.

And yet, the ceremony was very touching.

Standing there with Luigi as the musicians, priest, and children paraded by the facade of the ancient church, it occurred to me that my grandfather, his father, his father's father, and ancestors even before him had witnessed this same ceremony, in this same place, and over many, many years. I felt a strong sense of connection with the tiny, obscure village in the middle of the mountains in the middle of Italy.

The House with the Balcony

"You must go and see Signora Pollice," Claudio insisted later that same afternoon. "She is the oldest person in our village, she is ninety-one." His dark eyes twinkled. "*Ma, Lei è molto lucida*—she is very lucid. I have talked with her nephew, he said to go to the *casa* this evening at six." I could tell from the way Claudio said this he knew something I didn't.

I recognized the name from the States. The Pollice family had been doctors in the Pittsburgh area.

It wasn't hard to find the right house. The Pollices lived in the largest building in the village, which served as the backdrop for the town square. It sat opposite the beautifully rebuilt eighteenth-century church. I maneuvered around the temporary stage, empty of people for the moment, but filled with musical instruments, amplifiers, and microphones for the evening's entertainment soon to start.

The Pollice's balcony—the same one from which my grandfather and Dr. Pollice had delivered their photographed speech—sat directly over the stage, offering the family an exclusive box seat.

Roman eagles decorated the corners of the building. An inscription in the stones under the eaves dated the building from the year XI of the *Era fascista*—or eleven years after Mussolini had taken over the government in 1922. The edifice was obviously much older than this century . . . I assumed the eagles and Fascist reference were more recent additions, or perhaps a reconstruction.

I knocked on the huge wooden doors. I felt a premonition about this meeting. Perhaps it was the hint I had seen in Claudio's eyes, but something told me Signora Pollice was to be someone I should know or remember.

A woman of about sixty years answered the door.

"Ah, we have been expecting you," she said, and extended her hand. "I am Signora Pollice's daughter. My mother is upstairs. She is eager to talk with you." I started to ask her name, but she turned and motioned for me to follow. She walked surely and quickly.

I followed my hostess down a corridor. The walls were covered with dark, carved wood. We walked up a wide, creaking staircase, down another corridor, and into a large paneled and shelved sitting room in the front of the house. Two tall French doors hung partly opened on the opposite wall. Signora Pollice sat, framed by the doors, on a wooden rocking chair. She wore an elegant black dress with a light blue silk shawl draped about her shoulders.

Signora Pollice started to stand. I quickly took her hand and asked her to stay seated. I told her, in my best Italian, it was an honor to meet her, that I had heard about her family for a long time.

She smiled at me, her dark brown eyes clear and bright. She motioned for me to sit in a straight-back chair opposite her. As I sat, I saw that the French doors led to the balcony overlooking the square. From her seat, *La Signora* could privately monitor the town's comings and goings.

I started, by way of introduction, to tell her about my family and the reason for my visit. She waved me off.

"We have known your family all of our lives," she said. She lifted her hand from the folds of her dress and revealed what looked like a card. "Here," she said as she handed the object to me. "I wanted you to come. I wanted you to see this."

As I reached for her hand, I realized she was giving me an

old photograph. I righted the picture and, for a long moment, sat frozen, completely absorbed.

It was a photograph of my mother, obviously from her visit to the village in 1933. She was standing in front of the door of the very building I was now sitting in. She stood, fashionably dressed in high-heel saddles, a long dark dress, her hair beautifully cropped, with her arm about another young and beautiful woman: Signora Pollice.

Unexpected emotions flooded through me. Tears came to my eyes. I silently struggled for control. My mother, so young and vibrant, her smile so bright.

"She was a very special friend to me," Signora Pollice said finally.

"Me, too," was all I could add.

"She came to this village with her father the first time we met, but we saw one another often after that, in America. I had many letters from your mother. They were lost in the war."

The light coming through the huge windows was fading. Signora Pollice talked in the growing shadows—shadows she must have seen overtake her home on thousands of evenings in this village. Her soft eyes watched me as I studied her kind and aged face. She was a contact with my mother. It was our bond, and it was powerful.

"Tell me about her," I asked. "What was she like when she came here?"

"She was very gay," Signora Pollice recalled. "She was charming. She made friends with everyone in the town. We laughed and laughed. We were all young, and your mother brought the American sense of humor with her. It was a very long time ago." *La Signora* sighed and adjusted her orange-gold wedding band on her surprisingly youthful-looking hand.

A trumpet began playing "Cherry Pink and Apple Blossom White" very loudly from the stage directly below the Signora's balcony. The music broke the intensity of our conversation and announced the evening's festivities were under way. The younger Signora walked quickly to the French doors and pulled them shut, only slightly diminishing the sound.

"You never wanted to come to America?" I asked the elder Signora.

"My father and husband were the town doctors. They had responsibilities here." It was hard to hear her words now. Her soft voice was muffled by the beating of a bass drum and the trumpeter playing the American standard.

"So your family was in medicine here, as well as the States?" I asked more loudly.

"Yes, for as long as anyone knows. By the time I married, my husband had already established a practice. My father and my grandfather were also in practice from this very house. Here," she said as she got up from her chair, "I want to show you something."

I reached to help her rise, but she was spry and quick on her feet. She led me out of the room and down the creaking staircase at a normal speed, her many years obviously healthy ones. We entered a paneled study on the first floor, an elegant room away from the drumming and trumpeting—he was now playing "Blue Moon"—outside in the square. A rolltop desk sat against the opposing wall. The Signora briskly walked over and took a large, leather-bound volume from a shelf in the desk's open top.

She handed me the book. The leather looked half eaten away. It was an old medical text. I opened the cover and saw the copyright of 1805 in Roman numerals.

"It is one of the few books I have left from my father's library. It was once the best medical library in these mountains."

"What happened to it?"

She pointed to the nearly destroyed cover. "Fire," she said. "The Nazis burned this house when they left. Nearly all the books were destroyed."

"The Nazis occupied this house?"

"Yes, this house was their headquarters when the general was in this village. Do you know of a German general Kesserling?"

"Of course."

"He worked and stayed here when he was in this province."

"Kesserling? He was the Nazi commanding general for all of Italy. He was here, in this house, in this village?"

"Yes. You see, we are the highest point in this province. They wanted the greatest protection for him, so they brought him here and he used my father's office for his own. Another German general, Rommel, was also here. He met with Kesserling when it was decided for the Germans to leave Italy."

I silently accepted this information.

Kesserling. Kesserling *and* Rommel.

They weren't just German officers, they were *the* German officers. Kesserling was in charge of the entire Italian campaign. The most important generals of the German defense in Italy used my grandfather's tiny, never-heard-of village as their part-time headquarters. I struggled with information overload.

"But that is not what's important," Signora Pollice continued. She was only slightly stooped. I could see where she had once been a very erect and stately woman.

"Here, this is what I really wanted to show you. It is all I have left from your mother. Some of the few things to survive from that time."

She handed me several old and fading cards. The documents were a form of customs declarations listing items sent from America. They contained lists of goods including clothing, canned milk, canned food, diapers, and medical supplies.

Signora Pollice looked directly into my eyes, her gaze firm and clear. "Your mother and her family made sure we received these things at the end of the war. The packages went from America to Naples, then to a warehouse, then they were distributed to the villages. It took a long time. Many trains didn't run, gasoline was scarce, and mostly our mail came by horse or donkey. But your mother and her family made sure we had what we needed to get through those terrible days. It seemed as if everyone in Pittsburgh sent something we needed."

I studied the handwriting on the cards. It was unmistakably my mother's. It made me feel good to know she had helped these people, even though she'd never told me a thing about the terrible times this village had gone through.

"She never mentioned anything about this," I said.

"She was living her life. For us the war was very different. Your mother and father were having a family. We knew your mother was about to have a baby just after the war."

"I am that baby," I said. "I hope I'm not the reason she lost contact."

"We lost contact because we lived in two different worlds, even more so *after* the war than before. But your mother and her family were very helpful to us."

"Thank you for telling me this. It is important to me."

La Signora smiled kindly. She took my hand and clasped it with both of hers.

"We are family," she said.

I choked back my tears, again. There was something of a homecoming in this meeting at the former headquarters of a German general.

"Ob-La-Di . . ."

It was night when I exited the Pollice house through the over-sized doorway. I found myself walking out into bright stage lights and a great deal of noise. The drummer played directly above me on the platform, his cymbals clashing in contrasting beats with the bass drum. As I turned the corner from behind the stage I saw the plaza was completely filled with hundreds of people watching the performers. White electric lights twin-kled festively overhead and extended all the way down the street.

As I walked toward the crowd, I spotted Luigi off to the side standing next to a gelato wagon. He stood alone and stroked his goatee as he studied the entertainment. We ex-changed a silent greeting as I stood beside him and looked up at the stage.

A woman with bright bleached-blond hair, heavy pancake makeup, and bright red lipstick sang a Beatles tune. She was dressed in a skintight leopard outfit, her large breasts pushed together and flowing over a low-cut neckline. She was accom-panied by another woman, a redhead, made up and dressed in similar fashion, whose only job, as far as I could tell, was to wiggle in a sort of dance while the blond woman sang.

The huge blond and red hairdos made both of their heads seem five or six times larger than normal. It looked to me as if the little village had been invaded by big-haired aliens singing

"Ob-La-Di, Ob-La-Da, *la, la, la, la, life goes on.*" An ironically appropriate, if strangely delivered tune.

"This must be the warm-up act," I said, in an aside to Luigi. "They'd go over big in Vegas."

Luigi laughed. "This is village life," he said, obviously enjoying himself. "These people make their living in the summer going from hill town to hill town playing and singing. It's like living in a Fellini movie. It's marvelous, really. I like them because you would never see this on television or hear it on the radio." He motioned toward the plaza with a sweep of his hand. "This was what village life was like for centuries, little circus acts coming through and singing for pennies."

A few minutes later an emcee took center stage. He was dressed in a gold-lamé tuxedo jacket, had long and flowing blond hair—which I suspected was dyed—and a huge hooked nose. He made an elaborate introduction of what was obviously the headliner act.

Our "star" for the evening turned out to be a young teenage boy named Saverio. He was accompanied by a girl, about his same age, dressed in a scarlet miniskirt and sporting another of those very big hairdos. She escorted the young man to the microphone at center stage and exited. Saverio then overdramatized several songs, including "O Solo Mio," a favorite with the crowd, and another song in English, which I couldn't understand.

Saverio reminded me of the show-off kids from the May Club, the Italian-American organization my father belonged to when I was a young boy in Pittsburgh. There was always a stage mother at the Friday night fish-frys forcing her little genius to tap dance or play the clarinet. My mother thought this was cute. She asked me to bring my trumpet once. I threatened to leave home.

Saverio took bows that were sweeping, dramatic, and obviously well rehearsed.

During one tune I spotted Signora Pollice, her silk shawl still about her shoulders, standing by her open French doors on the balcony over the stage. What did she make of all this? I wondered. I could only imagine how many amusements and tragedies she had seen in this square over the near-century she had lived.

Someone tapped me on the shoulder. I turned to see the stunningly beautiful face of an older woman. Her hair was pure white, her eyes *azzurri*—the word for blue in Italian and the color of the heavens—her cheeks ruddy and healthy. Maybe there was something to this link between the Longobards and Scandinavia—all these blue eyes. The woman was nearly as tall as I and obviously self-assured. A young couple stood directly behind her.

"You are DePasquale?" she asked.

"My mother's family," I said.

"I am DePasquale, I am married to DiNardo." She extended her hand. "Your grandfather was a relative." She went on to explain that she was the daughter of a DePasquale and her husband's family was the family of my grandfather's mother. Somewhere in that complicated structure was a relationship. Signora DiNardo was born in Gamberale and now lived in a nearby village. She told me she was over eighty years old, then introduced the couple standing behind her as her youngest grandson and his strikingly beautiful wife.

My distant relative and I shouted over the music to be heard.

As I introduced Luigi, a man carrying a folding chair over his head made his way through the crowd. The people standing nearest us cleared a path for the makeshift seating and ensured the old woman had an unobstructed view of the bandstand. It was an obvious gesture of regard for her age. She was the only person seated in the entire crowd.

Luigi had bowed as he shook the old woman's hand. "You see how much they respect this lady," he said so that only I could hear. "We are losing this in the big city. Our reverence for our elders has always been a part of our society, but today the big-city youngsters are in a hurry."

"I think the kids I've seen are exceptionally polite," I replied. "I've seen them make sure the elderly are seated on the bus. In my own music group the younger men call me *Signor.* I don't think you've lost it."

"Come back when you're eighty." Luigi squinted back at the stage, where Saverio seemed to be finally ending his dramatics.

"I knew you had to be a DePasquale," Signora DiNardo's grandson said in clear English. "Look at the two of us, we are the tallest men here. It runs in our family."

Here we go again with the tall genes, I thought.

The younger couple invited me to visit their town in the nearby hills, one of the villages that had been featured in my grandfather's film. I told them I would love to visit their *paese,* and I meant it, but knew that I was running out of time in these mountains and the visit would not be made.

There was a giant picnic the next day. People were scattered throughout the entire lush hillside just beyond the main road leading into the village. The hill sloped gently up to the base of a very steep, rock-covered mountain peak. At the base was an elaborate and beautifully maintained chapel dedicated to the Virgin Mary. It was big enough, I thought, to be a small church.

Gino wanted to personally escort me through the picnic area and introduce me to those I hadn't met. At each stop families lay about on blankets or sat at picnic tables scattered throughout the woods. Gino hugged and kissed everyone he met. He was clearly enjoying himself.

Each little grouping had a grill or campfire. I saw the fate of the lamb I had heard bleating a few days before. Grilled lamb was the specialty of the day and we were offered food and drink at each family gathering.

Gino's wife, Gabriella, walked with us. She smiled and shook hands with several people, but this was clearly Gino's reunion.

"This is so important for him," Gabriella told me as Gino conversed with an old *paesano*. "I'm from Milano, it's sometimes hard for me to understand the appeal of these yearly visits. Our children don't share Gino's nostalgia. They hate to hurt his feelings, but I can tell they don't have the connection Gino and his brother feel about this place. But I guess if you were born in a village like this there is something very special about it."

"Especially after what they went through in the war," I said. "That has to be a strong bond."

Gino took me into the chapel at the top of the slope. The people of the village had built it themselves from the stones of the mountain into which its altar was anchored.

"In the old days," Gino explained, "there was always a holy procession to this chapel and a Mass in this field as part of our *festa*. This chapel was famous in this area many years ago. Some people say it was the Virgin who helped keep the many earthquakes away from here. But then, we did have an earthquake about ten years ago and some buildings were damaged, but nothing like there has been in other parts of the country."

Who needs earthquakes when there were wars, I thought. The lapsed Catholic in me wondered who was looking over the place in the winter of '43–'44.

Target Practice . . .

Later that afternoon, while standing in the town square enjoying the sights and a cold drink, I met a jeweler from Pittsburgh, Alfio Bucci. He asked about my impressions of the festival and if any other members of my family were there.

"I have heard of your grandfather," he said. "I have seen our old films many times."

Alfio Bucci spoke in flawless English, a welcomed relief. I had been struggling with so much information, and the constant translation problems were exhausting. I was happy to have a fellow Pittsburgher to converse with. I asked why he had come.

"I was born here," he said simply. "But I left right after the war."

"It seems a lot more people left after the war than I ever thought," I replied. "Of course, my mother never said much about when people came to the States. As kids we just made the division between those born there and those from the Old Country. I wish I'd have been more curious when my mother could have answered my questions."

"What did she tell you about our little town? Anything you can remember?"

"She had to ride a donkey up and down the mountain from and to the train station. She thought of the place as primitive, though I'm not sure she ever used those words. We always found her stories funny. Actually, I remember her speaking more about her visit to Paris in the same year. It made a lifelong impression on her. I can't remember her saying very much about Gamberale specifically, other than it was Old World and Old Country. She claimed she had to eat a roll with a bug baked in it, and she liked all the people."

Alfio smiled. "It would be primitive to an American. Especially fifty or sixty years ago."

"Oh," I suddenly remembered, "she did tell a story about the war but my memory is very hazy. It has to be at least thirty years since I talked with her about it. All I can recall is a story about a family, relatives of hers, I think, who were killed. It was a mother with her baby, her husband and father. Four of them in all."

Alfio seemed interested but said nothing. He looked directly at me as I spoke, his face indicating no emotion. I continued with my dim recollection.

"The way I remember the story, the Germans, for some unknown reason, shot the entire family. A bullet passed through the mother, killed her, and into the grandfather, killing him as well. I guess they shot the husband and baby separately after that." I shrugged. "I remember my mother sighing and shaking her head over the story, but I think she held back on some details since we were very young. Have you ever heard such a story?"

"It was not the entire family," Alfio said calmly, his eyes now dark and sad. "They were killed in their fields. They had been foraging for potatoes. They were living in the woods and starving to death."

"Then you know the story, it is true?"

"Quite well," he said softly. "The family you speak of was mine. My mother, father, and grandfather. The baby was my little brother."

I didn't know what to say.

I didn't know what I could say.

We were speaking in English. I knew I hadn't misunderstood, and not only was the horrible story true, I was speaking with a survivor of the same bloody incident. I glanced over at Luigi. His face showed the same astonishment I felt.

Finally, I managed to put my hand on Alfio's arm. "I am sorry." They were the only words I could find.

Alfio smiled sadly. "I was only a little boy," he said. "I don't remember much about that terrible winter, but I do remember . . ."

"It was target practice." Signore Caruso, the town historian and festival officer, interrupted Alfio's thought. Caruso's purple sash was still draped officially across his chest. He stood behind us, and had obviously been listening to our conversation. He must have understood the English, though he spoke in Italian.

"Pardon?" I said.

"Target practice. The Bucci family was there . . ." He took me by the arm and walked twenty or thirty paces to a cliff overlooking farmlands in the valley below. I estimated the fields to be about four hundred yards from the top of the cliff.

He pointed to the area. "The Buccis were in that field, their own farm, trying to find something to eat. The Germans stood here, a group of them. Three or four." He indicated the spot where we stood. "They took turns aiming and shooting. They acted as if they were betting on the results. They were making target practice and the target was the Bucci family. Hungry and defenseless people."

Luigi and I stood silent.

Signor Caruso shrugged. "What do you expect from people who put their animals in our church and used it for a stable? Men who would pose as Englishmen and machine-gun farmers because they spoke bad English?"

I could see the anger in his eyes, a completely different attitude than the one he showed me on my first visit to the records hall. It seemed I was now a *paesano*. He could show his true feelings to us.

"It wasn't the Germans," said Alfio. "You can't condemn an entire people. It was the *SS*. They had to protect Kesserling. It was their job."

"Shooting starving people—your parents—was that their job? Your baby brother, a threat to Rommel and Kesserling?" He threw both of his hands downward as if to say, *enough of this horror.* "The SS should burn in hell forever," he said, and walked away, leaving our conversation as quickly as he entered it.

Alfio smiled his sad smile. "I have no memory of the war, only the stories people have told me. I guess if you were here and actually saw these things you would feel more strongly."

I agreed with my friend from Pittsburgh and could not even imagine his loss.

Una Bomba—The Bomb

My search in Gamberale was done.

I had found Pietro's secrets, I believed. Many of my questions had been answered. I now knew why my grandfather hadn't wanted to talk about his associations with Il Duce. Also, I suspected a sense of shame and frustration of his entire generation. The shame for Fascism; the frustration in not being able to do anything about it once they realized their mistake, and the horrible consequences of the system they had helped create.

He *had* to have heard the stories about the war. He *had* to have known. And he *had* to have grieved over the deaths of people he knew—relatives, his own brother.

No wonder Popa didn't want to talk about Italy. How could you explain mass executions to your grandchildren? How would you find the words to tell of starvation and death from exposure? How could you find the proper adjectives for the defilement of churches and cemeteries? And all the result of a political system that had enticed him into supporting it with free tickets back to Italy and the promise of trains running on time. I wouldn't have talked about it either.

As Luigi and I drove out of town for the last time, we noticed a commotion on the road ahead, just as it curved beyond the highest mountain peak. Several people stood in the field off to the side of the asphalt. They pointed upward.

I pulled over. We got out of the Volkswagen.

High above, near the very peak of the mountain, several soldiers moved about. Ribbons of yellow police tape flapped in the wind.

"*Che sucessa*—what's going on?" I asked no one in particular.

"*Una bomba*—a bomb," an old man replied.

"A bomb? What kind of bomb?" I asked the stranger.

"A bomb from the war."

"From World War Two?"

"Yes, they have found another one. They are going to explode it," he said. Then he added, matter-of-factly, "This happens all the time. It is nothing new around here."

"Where did they find it?" asked Luigi.

"In a Girl Scout camp on the mountain."

"That could have been dangerous."

"You should have been here in '45 and '46," the old man said. "They were exploding these things all the time. It sounded like the war was still going on for years." He laughed.

We got back in the car and started the long descent back to Rome. The effect of that war still hadn't ended for this tiny, out-of-the-way spot sometimes not even on the map.

I wondered if it ever would.

13

~

The Last Waltz

Rome . . .

It finally happened. I had my one night as an amateur musician that I could remember forever.

I had been playing with a conservatory big band conducted by a bright, cheerful, dynamic young man, Stefano Rotundo. On a tip from Enrico, I had gone over to the school on the Via Nomentana, where Stefano taught. The group was in need of trumpet players. I thought I could still read well enough to play a third or fourth part.

After a couple of rehearsals, Stefano pulled me aside and asked me to play *lead*.

The lead trumpet is to a jazz big band what the first violinist is to a concert orchestra—the musician who interprets the phrasing and drives the main melodic line.

I was shocked. I'd never been a lead player. I'd always

played section in the big groups that had been my passion in high school and college many years before.

"You have the sound for a lead," explained Stefano. "It's not something you can teach. It's a sound that is there or it is not there. You have it."

I've always been able to play the horn at a certain level. If well rehearsed and relaxed, I'm completely comfortable in front of an audience. But, like most amateurs, I'm a nervous wreck if I don't know the material or have to sight-read.

Now, playing lead for a big band, was an entirely different category.

Our book—or the selection of tunes—were all American charts, many of them standards, which is not surprising, since jazz is the only original American art form. The Italian students at the conservatory wrote all the individual arrangements. They were delightful interpretations, many of which, like "When I Fall in Love" or Count Basie's, "Silk Stockings," I had played in school as well. I felt as if I were in a time capsule.

The Italian system of music education was much more rigid than I'd imagined. In Italy, in order to receive a degree from the university, the students study only formal music; composition, sight-reading, conducting, transposition, arranging, and the like. Contemporary music and, more important, performance is not emphasized.

Is it any wonder America dominates the world's popular music? Our kids start performing at a very early age, usually in marching bands and stage bands at the grade-school level. Contemporary music in the States is what we mostly learn. In Italy, performance belongs primarily to the professional. The majority of students at the school had completed their formal study and were now paying money they hadn't earned yet for

an additional tutoring in jazz performance. They were a dedicated and vigorous group. I was energized in their company.

My big moment came at a popular disco in the Testaccio
section of Rome, on a hot September night, not long after the
festival in Gamberale. The place was filled to overflowing with
the parents, relatives, and friends of those attending the conservatory. It was the final performance for the year and, though
I didn't know it at the time, it was one of the final concerts I
was to perform there.

That night we played the music we had been rehearsing and
performing since the previous fall. I was intimately familiar with
every page, had played it all before—knew all of the changes
to Miles Davis's "So What?" and had all of my transitional
phrasing down pat in tunes like "My Little Red Shoes." By the
time we finally got onstage—every other section of the school
from vocal to soloists performed ahead of us—I was completely
relaxed.

My lip was perfect. I soared into a place that night I'd never
been before, and I took the entire seventeen-piece band along
with me. I became both leader and wanderer in the magnificent, broad jazz chords. The phrasing was exactly where it
needed to be, exactly when it needed to be there. The few solos
I took were flawless, resonant, and sweet. The high notes vibrant, clear, and exciting.

That night reaffirmed to my soul my absolute, unconditional
love of jazz. It also reminded me of the pain and frustration of
understanding: This night was the exception. This night was
the unusual. This night was to be treasured, remembered, and
probably not repeated.

The clock was ticking.

I still had not found Francesco's records.

My musical dates were becoming harder and harder to make and I was, inevitably, running out of resources—my daughter's education account was going to need replenishing before too long. That meant going back to a real job, earning a real living, not doing volunteer consulting work and playing in amateur jazz groups. Journalism was my craft, music my avocation, family history had become my passion.

I had been asked by the U.S. State Department to spend some extended time in Zagreb, consulting with the Croatian National Television Network. The arrangements for that three-month stint were fairly involved. It meant going back to the States for a time, then a return to Europe after the new year and straight to the Balkans.

"Let me get this straight," I iterated for the woman from the State Department in Washington. She had tracked me down by telephone at my Rome apartment. "You're asking me to volunteer to go to a country at war, in the middle of winter, in a cold climate, to work with a government-controlled news agency, for no compensation?"

"That's about the size of it," she replied.

"Sounds like a job for a complete lunatic."

Naturally, I took on the project. It was, after all, my profession.

La Bella Figura...

Luigi and I went back to Zanussi's for a Saturday night dance, not long after I returned from the Balkans. I hadn't been in the San Giovanni dance hall for a long time. Things hadn't changed. It was still a grand room, the band still excellent, the people well dressed and scented.

On this night, though, I experienced a sense of melancholy

I hadn't felt before. Perhaps it was due to the knowledge that, finally, the bank account was running down. In just a few short weeks it would be time to return to the States and to income-earning work. Or perhaps it was just that I had changed since my last visit.

I still marveled at the precision of the dancing and the elegance of the dancers. I stood at the side of the elevated floor and took in the entire show. It was beautiful, and yet . . .

For Luigi and for the other single adults involved in *il ballo* there was, I sensed, something not completely centered. In the dance, in the midst of the well-perfumed and dressed-up crowd, there was an almost haunting aura—a touch of loneliness—something that caused the single women to dress a bit too formally, smile a bit too quickly. The men could also seem overanxious attending to a partner, a little too smooth and practiced with the complicated steps.

For Luigi, the movement was a way to maintain equilibrium. The dancing was formal, stylistic, and disciplined. He knew how to behave in this circumstance. He knew the steps.

I found myself feeling slightly uncomfortable—out of place—like an awkward teenager at his first dance. For the first time I wondered if I belonged there. I felt a lack of grace, like a clumsy American passing judgment on things that were none of my concern, on a society that didn't want or need my opinion.

The Italians have a system for the dance, a way to do things. And though I might find some of it forced, it was a method of interaction that they could relate to, enjoy, indulge in. It *was* beguiling, attractive. It worked for them. Now I felt much the outsider.

Luigi introduced me to a pretty woman named Francesca.

She had piercing steel-gray eyes and was about thirty years old. She spoke no English. I was abandoned by Luigi to swim in my self-conscious scanning for verbs and nouns not taught to me by my mother.

Francesca, like everyone I had met during the previous almost three years, asked the predictable questions. She was curious about my impressions, what I *thought* of Italy, why I was there, if I planned to stay.

I answered her as best I could in my endless uncertainty over exact verb form and tense.

It was not long before the question of family was raised, once again. I explained I was divorced, I had no children. She replied with the expression *Che peccato!*—"It's a sin," or "What a pity!"

No matter what else was said, no matter what the circumstances, I was constantly reminded of family being at the very center, the core. More and more in Italy, events had reminded me of my childhood, when and where I felt an enveloping sense of safety and identity within a group of people I called family.

And it pointed out my loss, over and over.

I was never very far away from the question of family, the conversation about social place. Italy was one of the few modern countries in which the family still comprised the basic political unit. Luigi said it was both a strength and weakness. And for those like Luigi entering the modern state of divorce, the question posed confusion and fear.

I could understand Luigi's restlessness. He missed his son. He missed his long-ago Sunday afternoons at the beach when they had been all together; husband, wife, son, and daughter; sunny days accompanied by the music of children's laughter.

It was, after all, family we were both in search of in our own ways. That perhaps we are *all* in search of, or struggling to maintain, in one way or another.

On that last night in Zanussi's, standing next to the raised wooden platform as the endless twirling and stepping passed by, I felt apart from, yet strongly drawn to these people who moved like a brilliant, sun-struck tidal pool, responding to the eternal movement of the sun, moon, sea, and the human soul. I was beginning to understand their motion, to know that many of them, like Luigi, were probably lonely too, and that loneliness is a basic part of the eternal human dance.

They seemed connected in a way I was not. And even if it was artifice, at least it was a *bella figura*—a beautiful attempt to connect.

14

$\sim$

Matera . . .

Finding Francesco

The old priest wore a white, gravy-stained smock. He smiled kindly, his eyes peering over ancient and bent gold-framed glasses, the left lens horizontally split in half like a homemade bifocal. A cowlick accented the back of his full head of gray hair.

It was ten A.M., the exact time of our appointment. I had been standing in front of the building for the previous ten minutes waiting for the designated hour.

This was my last chance. My final attempt to find my grandfather.

"Buon giorno, egregio Signore," the old priest said with exaggerated formality—good day, most honored sir. "I am Don Doneti." He escorted me into a big, sunlit conference room

just off the entryway. We met in the chancellery for the ancient Basilica of Santa Maria Bruno in Matera.

Don Doneti motioned for me to sit in a chair next to a cluttered desk opposite a full wall of windows. A conference table filled the center of the room. The terra-cotta floor gave the room a cool feeling. Bright white light filled the chamber from a southern exposure. It was a perfect place to read or study.

"Tell me, my son"—he actually called me "son"—"what is it we can do for you."

"It's like I said on the phone, Father. I've been searching for my grandfather's records for nearly three years now. At first, I wanted to get his birth certificate in order to apply for an Italian passport—just in case I ever wanted to work in the European Union. I've searched everywhere. I can find no record of his birth. Anywhere."

The priest nodded and looked amused as I went on without a breath.

"But now I don't really care about a passport. That's not of much importance anymore. What is important, what's become like a cause—*una causa*—for me is to find this man. I *know* he existed. My father is his son. I am my father's son. I know he was Italian. I have records of marriage. But I can find no proof of his birth in Italy, no matter where I search. This cathedral is my last hope—"

The rehearsed words poured out of me at an incredible speed and in an Italian without regard for grammar or tense. It felt like going to confession.

Don Doneti grinned broadly as I spewed on. Finally, he interrupted my ranting with an extended hand. He gently patted my forearm.

"*Ragazzo, stai tranquillo. Calmi,*" he said—the Italian equivalent of telling me to chill out.

"If there are records to be found, *li troveremo*—we will find them."

I surrendered to his sense of serenity.

"Now tell me," he continued, "are you positive you have found the correct province for your grandfather's birth?"

"Yes, absolutely, Father. Here, let me show you."

I opened up the crammed notebook I had carried to our meeting. It was filled with notes, correspondence, and genealogy tables; every shred of evidence I had pointing to Matera as Francesco's place of birth. I showed him the names and dates I had compiled and my grandparents' marriage certificate.

"And when did your grandfather go to America?" he asked.

"Probably sometime around 1908. He returned to Italy to marry my grandmother. He came back at least once, probably twice, after the wedding, since my grandmother had two of her five children in nearby Miglionico. The entire family moved to New York City in 1911. My aunt Mamie says her father was already in America and waiting for them."

"He went to America alone?"

"No, he had two brothers and a sister. That's all of the children I know about from his generation. All of them went to America. The sister married and lived in Brooklyn. All three brothers worked together. They started a newspaper recycling business in New York. Francesco was a teamster, in charge of the horses and driving the wagon.

"All three brothers were dead within ten years. One died in a wagon accident in New York. Another died in the flu epidemic after the First World War. My grandfather was the last to die, in a mill accident near Pittsburgh in 1922."

Don Doneti's gentle smile disappeared. He removed his glasses and massaged two bright red spots on either side of the bridge of his nose with his thumb and forefinger. He quietly listened to my rapid-fire, abbreviated family history. He was undoubtedly used to hearing all sorts of stories from his many years as a confessor.

"Those poor people," he said, when I had finished. He replaced the old lopsided frames on his nose and around his ears. "All the heartbreak, the suffering they went through."

"Yes, it was very difficult for their children."

"I was thinking more so about the parents. The children, after all, had a future. But the future for your great grandparents was their children. Imagine, to send three boys off to America and lose them all so quickly and forever."

I had never thought of the story in that way before. I had never even considered my *great*-grandparents or their feelings. Don Doneti was right. The sorrow and anguish they must have known. If they had survived to a normal age—and longevity, like poverty, was the norm for Southern Italy—they would have still been alive when their boys met with early deaths. Letters had undoubtedly arrived. Someone had come and read the terrible news from America. *Three times.*

Had they survived to hear all three? So much unknown, so much lost. Why had I never thought about this? My mother had a favorite saying about children passed down from her grandmother:

> *When they're little,*
> *they trample your toes.*
> *When they're big,*
> *they trample your heart.*

290

How the hearts of those who remained in the Old Country must have ached. How badly trampled. It is all but impossible to imagine from a late-twentieth-century perspective. How many parents in America have watched their children leave forever to live and die in distant lands?

The old priest shook his head sadly. "Unfortunately, your family's story is not an uncommon one for this part of Italy. It is all too common. Thank God, He has helped us find our way into better times." He hiked his glasses higher on his nose, apparently oblivious to the broken lens. "Now, let's see what we can find."

He picked up a pad and pen and began taking notes. "You are looking for Francesco Paolo, who was born, when do you think?"

"It had to have been in either 1882 or '83. The birth certificate for his first child, my uncle Bill, lists him as twenty-eight. But he's listed as the same age a year and a half later when my aunt Mamie was born. So, if you subtract twenty-eight from those two dates, he has to be somewhere in there, certainly in the first five years of that decade."

Don Doneti made several notes and copied spellings and dates. His smile returned. "Let me see what I can retrieve," he said, rising from his creaky, old swivel chair. "I am going to the archives."

He was gone for what seemed like hours.

I had quit smoking some years before, but if I had seen something—anything—to smoke during that wait, I would have lit up without hesitation.

I anxiously paced by the French doors. I went outside and walked around the bright, hot patio overlooking the ancient Paleolithic graves and the site of the original cathedral dating back to the start of Christianity in this region. At least forty thousand years of continuous living in this very spot. The frontier of classical Greece. A major Roman route. A place I'd never even heard of until my self-imposed research project came into my life.

I paced restlessly about in the increasing heat of the day. It had come down to this, my final weekend in Italy. I had learned so much, yet any definitive proof of my grandfather's family and birth still eluded me.

How many thousands—*millions*—of lives had passed here over forty-plus centuries? And I was looking for one man in all of that history, all of that humanity, just to prove his existence. Just to prove . . .

Through the reflection from the sun glinting off the windowed wall, I spotted Don Doneti's stained white cassock. He shuffled back into the room carrying a huge, leather-bound book under his arm.

I returned indoors and joined him at the table. The old man sat. I stood next to his chair and tried to read the volume over his shoulder.

The priest had retrieved a list of baptisms from the years 1870 to 1895. Only the Italians could have organized that particular grouping—why not 1875 to 1900? But I was using my American sensibility again in a useless pursuit of what I believed was logic.

The priest went through the pages carefully. The aging, yellowing paper appeared brittle. All of the entries were made in elegant, beautifully scripted Latin. Don Doneti scanned each name and listing with a steady, bony forefinger.

"Go to 1881," I said.

I hardly recognized my own voice. I was as surprised by the

force of my statement as the old priest. Something was at work inside me, a sense or feeling I'd only had maybe once or twice before in my entire life, but *something* was speaking to me.

Don Doneti looked up with a puzzled expression. "But you said it must be no earlier than 1882." He must have seen an expression on my face, or read my eyes, for without words he returned to the book and leafed to the year 1881.

"Il ventinove septembre," I said. "Go to September twenty-ninth."

"The twenty-ninth?"

"The twenty-ninth," I said quickly.

I *knew* it was the correct date, but didn't know *how* I knew. The priest glanced up again, smiled, and in the spirit of the moment found the page for September in the year 1881. His old finger scanned the neatly written lines. I spotted a name in the middle of the left-hand side of the page. My finger went to it.

There he was.

Francesco Paolo Paolicelli.

Born at eight o'clock on the evening of September 29, 1881.

It was easy to see how a quick check of this record would have missed the name. The entire page was written as a flowing narrative, there was no clear marking between each separate record. Our family name had been hyphenated so a finger scan would have shown the name "Paoli"; the hyphen could have easily been overlooked.

I studied the carefully written script and copied down the exact words in Latin. Don Doneti translated into Italian.

The same day, I, parish priest Gaetano Pomarici, a priest of this Diocese have baptized a baby born on the 29th of Sep-

tember around eight p.m. from the parents Emmanuele Paolicelli son of Antonio and Filomena Pizzilli, from our Parish,
whom they have named Francesco Paolo, attended by the mid-
wife Maria Giuseppa Capece.

The old priest shook his head and grinned as I pored over
every word. He seemed to be enjoying my elation at finding
this old, forgotten passage. I couldn't have been happier if I'd
found the Dead Sea Scrolls.

"You see," he said, as he typed up an official copy, "I told
you we'd find them, though you seemed to have known where
they were all along."

"I can't explain that, Father. I really can't explain that."

Don Doneti pulled the finished document from the type-
writer, signed it, and stamped it with the official chancellery
seal. He handed the paper to me with a broad smile and slight
bow. "Now you have your certificate," he said. "May God help
you do good work with it."

The *Municipio* had closed just before I arrived. The sign on
the wall painfully reminded me the office was open only for a
half day on Saturdays. I stood by the locked door and knocked
on the glass, hoping to find someone still inside who might
help.

A woman walked up to the door where I stood. She unmistakably carried a ring of keys—Italian keys are huge, at least
two to three times larger than American ones, and easy to spot.
She was an off-duty municipal employee who had come by to
retrieve some forgotten item from her office. Her children
waited in the car.

She asked what business I needed to have done.

I showed her the document from Don Doneti. "This is my last day in Italy. For nearly three years I've been trying to find this baptism certificate before I can get the official document from you, from the state office. I forgot you close early on Saturdays. Can't some exception be made?"

She looked over the paper. "What is it you want?"

"An official, state-issued birth certificate."

"Is that all?"

"That's all."

"This is no problem," she responded cheerfully. "Please, come in. It is cooler inside."

I offered a silent prayer of thanks for the kindness of strangers.

I reached my father by telephone that same afternoon. I called Pittsburgh from a pay phone overlooking the beach near Metaponto. I scanned the shore as the call was connected.

"Dad, you'll never guess the date of your father's birthday."

"You've found the records."

"I found his baptism certificate, which enabled me to get a birth certificate, which will make everything else possible."

It was late in the hot, early-summer afternoon. Only a few determined beachgoers lay apathetically on their *lettini*—or cots—as they browned in the sun. Heat visibly rose in waves off the bright sand and wafted skyward. The Ionian Sea lay sluggish on the horizon.

"It was September twenty-ninth."

"What was?"

"Your father's, my grandfather's birthday."

"But that's—"

"I know. That's my birthday, too."

Our intercontinental connection remained silent for several seconds.

"You know, Dad, I've been thinking. If your father had lived until I was born, we'd have probably had a very special relationship, particularly since we shared names and birthdays. It's such a shame we never got the chance to meet."

"Isn't that something?" My father shared my sense of wonder. "Isn't that something?" he repeated at least three times.

It wasn't until I had hung up the phone that it hit me—hit me harder and faster than anything I had ever known.

I am Francesco Paolo's special grandchild.

We do have a special relationship.

I do know him, and know him in a meaningful and significant way.

. . .

Maybe I had company on the path I had chosen? I ruled nothing out on this day of coincidence.

Now I knew their stories—that beautiful word in Italian, *la storia*—which means both story and history; now I knew both.

I knew where my grandparents—all of them—had been born. I had seen the towns and read the records. I knew why some of them couldn't read—those born in Matera and raised in the Region of Basilicata of pre–World War One Italy.

I traveled the roads my ancestors had traveled, though under far more comfortable circumstances, and walked about the countryside they had seen in youth. I had visited the churches where they had been baptized and prayed; where their parents, their parents' parents, and untold generations before had worshiped, been married, confirmed, and been given the final requiem.

I saw the mountains they had scaled, both literally and fig-
uratively, and I had a good sense of the sizes and dimensions
in their lives, the sheer scope of their lives.

I had an understanding that would have been impossible for
a grandparent to hand down to a grandchild in normal circumstance.

And Francesco, in a way, might have wished for me to go
through this struggle. After all, had I found the records on my
first visit, I'd have never been forced to ask so many questions,
make so many visits, learn either intentionally or inadvertently
the facts of his country at the time he was born. I might not
have even been interested in either the region or the local lore.
Maybe this was as it was supposed to be.

Was it coincidence we shared a name and a birthday?

When I had first come to Italy, I wasn't sure of my direction,
only that I had been given the extraordinary gift of time and
resources to make an extended stay in a beautiful land.

And as the search for the past became more difficult, I became more determined. It was in the search, what had seemed
like casual questions at first, where I learned about the real
people my families had been; the Italy they had been born to;
how it had changed, how both my grandparents and Italy had
overcome the problems they had encountered.

Now I knew the horrible tales of World War II that had
been resting in the mountains of Abruzzo for all these years.
The stories Pietro didn't want to tell. And now I felt I knew
why he chose to stay silent. Part of his silence had to have been
to try and protect us from such awful truth—now still awful,
but once removed from passion in the cooling of many years.

Had my footsteps been guided?

I thought about the tawdry, dingy cemetery where Francesco

was buried. It sat opposite a huge slag dump near the U.S. Steel coke works—the same plant where he had been killed.

I remembered as a young boy my father and I visiting my grandfather's grave. His name—our name—misspelled on the headstone. An aging photograph of a mustachioed man was glass-encased in the stone's center, one of only two photographs I had ever seen of him.

I wasn't very interested in the grave during these visits. Like any youngster, I was completely fascinated by the trams on the opposite hill carrying their red-hot loads. The small trains chugged across the top of the gray heap and, one by one, dumped glowing red rivers of flaming slag down the length of the mountain of hardened ashes.

It was an unforgettable and Dickensian view from that cemetery—the industrial age in all its shabbiness. The air had a smell like no place else I'd ever known or have ever known since.

Though he never said so, I know my father thought his father deserved better.

And what had Francesco's life, which ended tragically and was marked by such bleak circumstances, including his grave, been about? Other than struggle and sacrifice and early death?

Now, standing in a very different place by the Ionian Sea in the late afternoon of a bright warm late spring day and embraced by a sweet-smelling sea breeze, I felt a closeness with Francesco I knew would always be there.

And respect for a man I never knew in life.

It was sacrifice, after all, that made all of our American lives so much the better. It was Francesco's sacrifice and ambition, Pietro DePasquale's self-assuredness and determination, it was *all* of them having the desire, the youth, the sheer guts to get up and go; to *find* America and to define it for us. To forge a home there, despite their lack of language skill or formal education. To be willing to leave their parents and families and to establish new ones across an ocean.

And I had learned so much about this modern land, this beautiful place called Italy, which had so terribly failed so many of its sons and daughters in the last century and forced them to live elsewhere. I had come to know the survivors of those terrible times, the people of this modern place, as kind, considerate, funny, articulate, and very much alive.

One day, nearly two years before, I'd received a letter from my father, who was now using Italian phrases in person and in correspondence from time to time—something we'd never done when I was young.

He signed his letter *"Ti volgio bene,* Dad."

I understood the words, but not the meaning. Naturally, I took it to Luigi.

Luigi explained that in Italian the phrase *Ti amo,* "I love you," had been reserved, before Hollywood and the current generation, strictly for romantic situations. Words to be used between lovers and spouses. Family members, and close friends, at least in olden Italy, my grandfather's Italy, would have said, *"Ti volgio bene*—I wish you well, I want good things for you."

A saying perhaps as important as professing love, or even more important, for wanting good for one's family means action. Love can be isolated in feeling alone.

"Ti volgio bene." Not for the self. For you.

The phrase helped explain Francesco's dying words, *"Povri*

figli mie'—my poor kids." It wasn't about his death, it was about the hardship his death would mean for his children. It was about his duties and responsibilities to and for his family.

It was about the future.

On that last Saturday in Italy at the beach near Francesco's birthplace, I knew one certain thing: if I could spend one minute with my grandparents, all of my dark-eyed, laughing, robust family again—steal one second out of eternity and rearrange time—I would want to say one single Italian phrase . . .

Grazie, ti volgio bene.

EPILOGUE

May 1999

Shortly after my return from Italy I met a young woman who, within a year, became my wife. When I shared my secrets with Laurie, confessed my sense of frustration and defeat at facing fifty on my next birthday and not having a daughter to serenade me on that epochal event, she stared at me with her common-sense, midwestern, German-Irish curiosity.

"So what's the big deal?" she asked. "Fifty. Sixty. What's a decade?"

This month our daughter, Cara Antoinette, turned three. In her eyes I can see my father's smile. We won't start the piano lessons for at least another year.

SOURCES AND READING MATERIALS

Nonfiction

Alexander, Paul J. *The Ancient World to* A.D. *300* (second edition). New York: Macmillan, 1968.

Barzini, Luigi. *The Europeans*. London: Penguin, 1983.

———. *The Italians*. New York: Atheneum, 1963.

Christ, Karl. *The Romans*. Berkeley and Los Angeles: University of California Press, 1984.

Clark, Martin. *Modern Italy, 1871–1982*. London and New York: Longman, 1984.

di Franco, Philip J. *The Italian Americans* (The Peoples of North America). New York and Philadelphia: Chelsea House, 1988.

Dudley, Donald. *Roman Society*. London: Penguin, 1975.

Durant, Will. *Caesar and Christ*. New York: MJF Books, 1971.

Gilbert, Felix. *The End of the European Era, 1890 to the Present* (third edition). New York: Norton, 1984.

Ginsborg, Paul. *A History of Contemporary Italy, Society, and Politics, 1943–1988.* London: Penguin, 1990.

Gissing, George. *By the Ionian Sea.* Evanston, Ill. Marlboro Press, n.d. (Reprint of the 1920 edition).

Harrison, Barbara Grizzuti. *Italian Days.* New York: Weidenfeld & Nicolson, 1989.

Kane, Robert S. *Italy at Its Best.* Chicago: Passport Books, 1989.

Levi, Carlo. *Christ Stopped at Eboli (Cristo si è fermato a Eboli).* Translated by Frances Frenaye. New York: Farrar, Straus, 1947.

Longo, R. Giura. *Sassi e secoli.* Matera, Italy: BMG, 1986.

Mack Smith, Dennis. *Mussolini.* London: Weidenfeld & Nicolson, 1981.

Manchester, William. *A World Lit Only by Fire.* New York: Little, Brown, 1992.

Mangione, Jerre, and Ben Morreale. *La Storia, Five Centuries of the Italian American Experience.* New York: HarperCollins, 1992.

Masson, Georgina. *A Companion Guide to Rome.* New York: HarperCollins, 1991.

Mayes, Frances. *Under the Tuscan Sun: At Home in Italy.* New York: Broadway Books, 1996.

Murray, William. *The Last Italian.* New York: Simon & Schuster, 1991.

Robb, Peter. *Midnight in Sicily.* New York: Vintage Books, 1998.

Scarre, Chris. *Chronicle of the Roman Emperors: The Reign-by-Reign Record of the Rulers of Imperial Rome.* London: Thames and Hudson, 1995.

Schoener, Allon. *Gli italo americani.* Rizzoli Libri, 1988.

Sciulli, Aniceto. *Gamberale, il comune più alto della provincia di Chieti.* Pro Loco di Gamberale, 1986.

Stille, Alexander. *Benevolence and Betrayal: Five Italian Jewish Families Under Fascism.* New York: Summit Books, 1991.

Talese, Gay. *Unto the Sons.* New York: Alfred A. Knopf, 1992.

Toscano, Giorgio, and Pina Basile. *La storia di Oriolo.* Rome: Tip. Olimpica di C. Sterpi, 1985.

Fiction

Binchy, Maeve. *Evening Class.* New York: Delacorte Press, 1996.

Eco, Umberto. *The Name of the Rose (Il nome della rosa).* Translated by William Weaver. New York: Harcourt Brace Jovanovich, 1983.

Helprin, Mark. *A Soldier of the Great War.* New York: Harcourt Brace Jovanovich, 1991.

Lampedusa, Giuseppe di. *The Leopard (Il gattopardo).* Translated by Archibald Colquhuon. New York: Pantheon, 1960.

Manzoni, Alessandro. *The Betrothed (I promessi sposi).* Translated by Bruce Penman. New York: Penguin, 1984.

McCullough, Colleen. *The First Man in Rome.* New York: William Morrow, 1990.

———. *The Grass Crown.* New York: William Morrow, 1991.

———. *Fortune's Favorites.* London: Random House UK, 1993.

———. *Caesar's Women.* New York: William Morrow, 1996.

———. *Caesar.* New York: William Morrow, 1997.